THE DEAF HISTORY READER

THE DEAF
HISTORY READER

John Vickrey Van Cleve,
EDITOR

GALLAUDET UNIVERSITY PRESS
Washington, DC

WITHDRAWN
UTSA LIBRARIES

Gallaudet University Press
Washington, D.C. 20002
http://gupress.gallaudet.edu

© 2007 by Gallaudet University.

Published in 2007
Printed in the United States of America
Front cover photograph courtesy of the Gallaudet University Archives

Library of Congress Cataloging-in-Publication Data

The deaf history reader
  John Vickrey Van Cleve, editor.
     p. cm.
     Includes bibliographical references and index.
     ISBN-13: 978-1-56368-359-6 (alk. paper)
     1. Deaf—United States—History. 2. Deaf—Education—
        United States—History. I. Van Cleve, John V.
HV2530.D43   2007
305.9'08209730903—dc22

                                              2007014161

⊖The paper used in this publication meets the minimum requirements of
American National Standard for Information Sciences—Permanence of
Paper for Printed Library Materials, ANSI Z39.48-1984.

CONTENTS

PREFACE

The essays in this volume enrich our understanding of the history of the American deaf community in a variety of ways. Some articles focus on the traditional subject of deaf education; yet each of these takes us beyond issues of pedagogy to address matters of wide social and historical importance to deaf people and to the societies of which they have been members. Others look at specific deaf lives situated in particular places and times. These illuminate questions about deaf agency, oppression, and constructions of deaf identity in American history. One contribution examines closely the famous—and famously disliked by many deaf Americans—Alexander Graham Bell and places him in a new relation to the deaf community. Finally, two of the essays use intensive examinations of local deaf organizations, informed by documents scholars have not examined previously, to challenge traditional interpretations of American deaf history. They argue forcefully that historians need to broaden their research agendas and pay greater attention to what deaf people were doing at the local level. Together, these articles provide evidence, interpretations, and arguments about deaf history that encourage a reexamination of assumptions about deaf experiences in American History.

Acknowledgments

All scholars have debts, intellectual, professional, and personal. I have been fortunate in thirty years of teaching, studying, and writing about deaf history to have received many kinds of support from an extraordinarily broad range of people, from faculty and staff colleagues to deaf community historians, from various friends inside of and outside of the American deaf community, and from supportive family members. I cannot begin to acknowledge what I owe each of them, but I want to mention two individuals in particular: Paul Kelly, the Vice President for Administration and Finance at Gallaudet University, a lawyer and accountant by training, whose commitment to scholarship and the academic enterprise is unsurpassed; and Deborah Ellen Van Cleve, an accomplished and busy administrator in her own right, and my companion and wife of many years.

One remarkable fact about this particular book, however, is that three of the contributors have been my students. My largest debt is to them and to all the students at Gallaudet University whom I have been privileged to teach. Their interest in deaf history has spurred mine and somehow made worthwhile all the time and effort historical scholarship requires.

1

Genesis of a Community:
The American Deaf Experience in the Seventeenth and Eighteenth Centuries

Harry G. Lang

Editor's Introduction

Most histories of the American deaf community start with the immediate events leading to the founding of the American School for the Deaf in 1817, but deaf biographer and historian Harry Lang goes farther back into history. In this essay, Lang identifies deaf children, deaf adults, and deaf couples in the seventeenth and eighteenth centuries, and he uses textual evidence to evaluate their lives and their communication methods. He concludes that sign communication was recognized long before Laurent Clerc introduced French Sign Language to the United States, and his evidence suggests that many deaf people lived fully and autonomously in colonial America. Lang also argues, however, that other deaf colonists suffered from oppression because of their deafness.

The learned . . . are not unapprized, that for two hundred years past there have appeared . . . Deaf . . . persons more or less instructed; which was then regarded as a species of miracle; but the rest of mankind did not imagine that this attempt had ever been made, and much less that it had been made with success.

Abbé Charles-Michel de l'Epée[1]

In *American Colonies*, Allan Taylor wrote that "the traditional story of American uplift excludes too many people."[2] He described a narrow cast

that showcased male English colonists in the East and seldom satisfac-
torily covered the interplay of colonial and native people or the regional
explorations and "human places" of other cultures, even those of other
Europeans. Though Taylor did not say so, the "human place" of deaf people in the American colonies and post-Revolutionary War period is also
relatively unexplored. This paper attempts to begin to fill that gap, to enhance our understanding of both the complex attitudes played out in the
lives of deaf people and their methods of self-empowerment during
America's formative years.

Seeds versus Roots

The biography of a community, as with biographies of people, should include tracing its life to the seeds of its existence. In the case of an individual, we usually study parental heritage. In the case of a community, we
search for the seeds from which key elements or characteristics have
evolved. For the deaf community in America, this heritage includes the
seeds of American Sign Language and the creation of a new definition of
normality within a group that typically has been segregated and mis-
treated because of its differences.[3] From this new identity grow sociological, economic, and distinctly cultural features.

Other writers have recognized that the "roots" of the American deaf
community took hold in the nineteenth century. Harlan Lane and his
colleagues have described three New England deaf communities at
Henniker, New Hampshire; Martha's Vineyard, Massachusetts; and
Sandy River, Maine, from which they examined genetic patterning, language, and marriage practices.[4] The subsequent founding of residential
schools and the gradual empowerment of deaf people as they took increasing control over their own destiny in the nineteenth century have resulted in not only a deaf community today but also a rich cultural tradi-
tion. The American Deaf culture we now experience is the flowering plant
that has grown from the seeds and roots of past generations.

In contrast with roots, seeds, in their gestational state, manifest fewer
obvious outward signs of life. Their germination may be influenced by
both internal and external factors, and subsequent growth may be affected by cultivation and tolerance. It is in such isolated episodes of cultivation and tolerance that we find the earliest evidence of germinating
seeds, or the genesis, of the American deaf community. Isolated clusters of
deaf people, particularly deaf marriages and deaf families, were the seeds
of small communities in themselves.

A second indication of genesis may be the cultivation and tolerance of visual and gestural communication in a world dominated by spoken communication. As this paper will show, since the early 1600s there have been numerous reports of sign language varieties, gestures, and even tactile communication (for deaf-blind persons) in the American colonies.

Third, genesis may be evidenced by examples of deaf people experiencing life in varied contexts, sometimes seemingly oppressed, other times apparently enjoying a full life despite their differences from the majority. Deaf people owned land, married, conducted business, and joined religious organizations during the seventeenth and eighteenth centuries. The search for the deaf experience in the American colonies provides substantial evidence of the genesis of the deaf community.

The Seventeenth Century

From the earliest documented times in American history, there were reports of deafness among the indigenous Indians. In 1618, the Jesuits in America wrote to church officials inquiring whether a "deaf-mute Indian" could be admitted to the church.[5] In seeking clarification of the church's stance on the ability of a deaf person to learn and to demonstrate acceptance of the word of God, the pioneer Jesuits must have believed there was such potential. Two decades later, Roger Williams, a church leader and founder of the colony of Rhode Island, noted that among the Wampanoag Native children, "some are born deaf and so dumb."[6]

Faith in the spiritual capability of deaf persons is also found in the story of Andrew Brown, who had embarked for America in 1636. Brown was involved in a reformation movement in Larne, county Antrim, Ireland. Having attended the monthly meetings led by George Dunbar, a minister of the Irish Presbyterian church at the parish of Larne, the "deaf and dumb" man had been administered communion. According to an American writing in the nineteenth century, it was a "singular, and almost solitary, case of a mute professing spiritual religion, previous to the recent successful efforts of giving them instruction" in Spain.[7] Brown was described as "deeply affected, and had given satisfactory evidence, by signs connected with a godly life, of having been truly converted."[8] On September 9, 1636, Brown set sail on the 150-ton vessel *Eagle Wing* with 140 emigrants seeking freedom to practice their Protestant faith. The *Eagle Wing* weathered terrible storms near Lough Ryan and after almost foundering off Newfoundland with a master joist broken by fierce wind, the ship returned to Ulster, never having landed in New England.[9]

Although Brown did not land in New England, the story of an educated, signing, deaf man attempting to emigrate to the colonies in the
early 1600s suggests that other deaf people did successfully emigrate
from various countries at this time. Both deaf and hearing emigrants may
also have carried deafness genetically from their homelands. Historian
Nora Groce has speculated that the occurrence of hereditary deafness
among many people who lived on Martha's Vineyard can be traced to
about 200 inhabitants of the Weald in the English county of Kent, who followed Jonathan Lothrop, another minister, on the *Hercules* and *Griffin* in
1634. The first known deaf man on the Vineyard was born on Cape Cod in
1657 and moved to the island in 1692. Family records from the seventeenth century reveal that, in other colonies, there were various cases of
children also born deaf.[10]

Attitudes toward deafness and other physical disabilities varied in the
colonies. Historian Margret Winzer has written that people with deafness,
blindness, and physical disabilities were generally viewed by the colonists as the "natural concerns of the family, the local community, or the
church rather than the state."[11] In 1641, Massachusetts adopted a code of
laws protecting people who should be "exempted by any naturall or per-
sonall impediment, as by want of yeares, greatness of age, defect of minde,
fayling of sences, or impotencie of Lymbes."[12] By the mid-seventeenth
century, the generally mixed views about people who likely had mental
disabilities were evident in the fact that those who might become a
burden were expelled from some towns, even with public whippings,
whereas in other areas there was public support. In 1676, for example, the
Pennsylvania colony provided for the assistance of a mentally disabled
individual.[13]

The Puritans' theological beliefs shaped thinking about disability in
seventeenth-century New England. In 1679, for example, Philip Nelson of
Rowley, Massachusetts, already having "difficulties" in the church, was
questioned by a council of ministers for "pretending to cure a deaf and
dumb boy in imitation of our Savior by saying [Ephphatha]." This was a
risky endeavor at this time due to the belief in witchcraft. The deaf person, Isaac Kilbourne, was brought before the church officials. "He was in-
terrogated, but 'there he stood . . . like a deaf and dumb boy as he was.'
They could not make him hear, nor could he speak."[14]

The fact that the Puritans viewed affliction as God's chastisement for
sin did not completely prevent people with "afflictions" from functioning
in society or participating in Church rites and ceremonies. Cotton Mather,
the son of the zealous Puritan clergyman Increase Mather, was himself a
strong clerical figure among early New England Puritans. He was also a

stutterer who associated his speech impediment with the sins of pride and anger. But many Puritans also understood affliction as "God's rod descended in loving concern." Mather saw his own stuttering as something that would guide him to greater holiness, "yea, to make me more happy than other men."[15]

The complexity of attitudes toward deafness in the Massachusetts commonwealth became evident in 1684 when deaf Isaac Kilbourne was permitted to marry Mary Newbury of Cambridge, Massachusetts. In 1685, church records report the baptism of their child, "Deaf lad's [Kilbourne's] daughter Elizabeth." Thus, in a span of only a few years, Isaac Kilbourne appears to have become an accepted member of the church.[16]

A marriage between two deaf people occurred in Weymouth, Massachusetts, even earlier. Matthew Pratt, who was born in Plymouth Colony in 1629 and had been deaf since about the age of twelve, was taught to read and write, and he spoke "scarce intelligibly" and very seldom. In 1661, he married Sarah Hunt, a woman who had been deaf since the age of three, who also did not use speech. They had seven children and owned twenty acres of farmland in east Weymouth as well as eighteen acres on the west side of "Mill River."[17] Cotton Mather mentioned that Sarah "spoke with signs" and that her children learned to speak "sooner with eyes and hands than by their lips." Evidence that an attempt was made to educate Sarah is found in the report that she was not raised a Christian but was later converted with the help of Matthew and several relatives, "who were able to communicate with her easily."[18]

Other deaf people also owned land in the colonies.[19] Among them was Jonathan Lambert, who, in 1694, bought from the Indian Sachem Josias Wampatucke a tract of land on Martha's Vineyard bordering on Great James pond, and "ever since that date the name of Lambert's Cove has been a memorial of his residence in that region."[20] In 1695, Lambert was dispatched to Quebec to bring back prisoners. A contemporary, Samuel Sewell, somewhat humorously referred to him during his visit in 1714 to the Vineyard: "We were ready to be offended that an Englishman . . . in the company spake not a word to us . . . it seems he is deaf and dumb."[21]

Strangely, Jonathan Lambert's life was described as "uneventful as he was a deaf mute, and the records give but little to indicate any public activities."[22] Yet Lambert was master of the brigantine *Tyral*, a slave ship. He had been given a share in Narragansett township for his military service under Sir William Phips in an expedition to Quebec in 1690. The fact that he owned land, raised a family, interacted with visitors to the Vineyard, and was involved in transporting prisoners reveals a man whose life was as eventful as that of many hearing people of his time.

Two of Lambert's children were also deaf, the first known cases of congenital deafness on Martha's Vineyard.[23] The influx to the New World of emigrants carrying a gene for deafness from the Weald in Kent to Scituate, near Plymouth and Cape Cod Bay, has been one of the better documented phenomena of the deaf experience in the American colonies. Many of these emigrants moved to Martha's Vineyard, and over time, a sign language developed on the island, used by both deaf and hearing islanders. As in the colonies, deaf people on Martha's Vineyard married and raised families. But on this island, they also held public office and conducted business in sign language at town meetings.[24]

Numerous stories of those who became deaf in old age also reveal an acceptance of disability in the American colonies during the seventeenth century. Richard Williams, born circa 1606, was descended from a family in Glamorganshire, Wales. In about 1636, he established himself as a tanner in Plymouth Colony. In 1666, he was one of the selectmen and, for many years, a deacon of the church. A friend recalled that "when blind and deaf from age, he was accustomed to attend public worship, saying, 'that although he could neither see nor hear, yet it was consoling to his feelings to know that he was present while the people of God were at their worship.'"[25] He died in 1692.

In contrast, that same year, a deaf woman was executed. Rebecca Nurse, a wife and mother to eight children, was a devout churchgoer, but at the height of the Salem hysteria, she was accused of witchcraft. Nurse's own arguments included mention of her deafness: "And I being something hard of hearing, and full of grief, none informing me how the Court took up my words, and therefore had not opportunity to declare what I intended."[26] However, although the inability to hear was one "affliction" associated with the bewitched, Nurse's deafness had little to do with the witchcraft allegations, according to historian Mary Beth Norton:

> Goody Nurse's conviction constitutes one of the most persuasive pieces of evidence that the Massachusetts authorities in general believed unhesitatingly in the truth of the witchcraft allegations. These men . . . were by midsummer heavily invested in the belief that Satan lay behind the troubles then besetting their colony. . . . Unable to defeat Satan in the forests and garrisons of the northeastern frontier, they could nevertheless attempt to do so in the Salem courtroom.[27]

The governor attempted to give her a reprieve, but this effort was voided by the church. Rebecca Nurse was hung at the age of 70, on July 19, 1692.

The Eighteenth Century

Since the early 1730s, when monthly news periodicals such as *Gentleman's Magazine* and *London Magazine* made their debut, readers in England followed the events in the colonies, studying maps of the French and Indian War, enjoying the musings of Benjamin Franklin, and examining a variety of items of interest, including reports on the education of deaf children. In 1747, *Gentleman's Magazine* reported on the work of Jacobo Pereire in teaching young children, deaf from birth, to speak articulately.[28] In 1750, another report summarized how, after two years of instruction, a twenty-one-year-old man, deaf from birth, was presented to the king of France, "giving answers very properly and distinctly, he also pronounced several lines from a book, which he had not before seen. His master discourses with him by a manual alphabet, almost as expeditious as speech; but this is not uncommon."[29]

Educated American colonists kept in touch with Europe through these magazines as well as through the *American Magazine and Historical Chronicle*, which boldly reprinted much of the content of its British counterparts. American periodicals also included tidbits about deafness and deaf people. In 1740, for example, in his *Poor Richard's Almanac*, Benjamin Franklin included the grim report that "[w]e hear from Macanja in Bucks County [Pennsylvania], that last Week two Brothers, the youngest about 10 Years of Age, and the eldest about 18, both of them deaf and dumb, went out into the Woods together, where the eldest cut the Throat of the youngest."[30]

Other records provide evidence that deaf people headed families, conducted businesses, and participated in religious activity. James Anderson's hearing son, James Anderson, Jr., was summoned in November 1768 for "not supporting his children in a Christianlike manner."[31] In the records of the Scotch-Irish settlement west of the Blue Ridge Mountains in Virginia, known as Augusta, the father is noted familiarly as "Deaf James." In Virginia about 1784, the Reverend Lee, a Methodist itinerant preacher, recorded his observations after one visit to a family, describing the religious potential of the deaf head of the household and making reference to his signs:

> . . . preached at John Randall's, who is deaf and dumb, yet can pronounce the name of his wife and the name of his brother; but I could not learn that he ever uttered any other words. He is esteemed a pious man, and by signs will give a good experience of his conviction, conversion, and progress in the service of the Lord, and of his pleasing hope of Heaven when he leaves the world.[32]

Sign language is also mentioned in the family records of Andrew Moore, whose descendents included two deaf brothers in Pennsylvania, Joseph and Jacob Moore, and a deaf relative, Jeremiah Moore. All three deaf men led productive lives. Jacob Moore, the first of Andrew Moore's deaf descendents, was born in Lancaster County in 1781 and was described as an "ingenious mechanic, a man of strong will and indomitable energy."[33] He married Hannah (Sharpless) Neal, a widow, and learned the trade of cabinet making. More details are available about Jacob's deaf brother, Joseph:

> [Joseph Moore] dreamed where to go and find a wife, and going by his dream, found the place and the young woman [Jane Smith] he had seen in the vision; which resulted in a suitable companionship for life. Their children all had their hearing and speech, and in his anxious desire to know if they could hear he would sometimes make a loud noise, and then intently watch if they would notice it. He kept bees, and at one time had some stolen, and early next morning went to one of the neighbors, tapped one of the thieves on the shoulder, and by signs charged him and some others with the theft; which proved to be correct, and all of whom Joseph pointed out.[34]

Joseph Moore moved to Cecil County, Maryland, where he owned a farm and sawmill and was a member of the Society of Friends (Quakers). He attended services whereby he would "gaze intently at the minister, as if he gathered something of what was delivered. Various instances might be mentioned of his finding out circumstances, and of his pointing upward, intimating that he had great faith and confidence in the way of truth and right."[35]

Jeremiah Moore, born in 1775, married Phebe Jones of Columbia, Pennsylvania. Passmore writes that "Jeremiah being a deaf mute, could not be married by [The Society of Friends], so they were married by a magistrate.[36] Jeremiah entered millwrighting as an occupation and kept his own account book, which has been described this way: "It was a model of ingenuity; when he had difficulty spelling a word, as for instance 'Plow,' he would make the drawing or representation of it."[37]

The description of the deaf members of the Moore family reveals that deafness was not necessarily an impediment to a full and rewarding life, even before the educational opportunities of the nineteenth century were available. Here were three deaf men, all married and holding respectable occupations as well as taking care of their own business dealings. Most likely, Joseph's wife was also deaf (his "suitable companion"), particularly because he felt compelled to test their children's hearing through making loud noises. Moreover, the family account that Joseph was "apt in making himself understood by signs, and in understanding others in the same way," indicates that the use of signs was accepted by his neighbors and that they had learned some to communicate with him.[38] There are no details available on the sign language the Moores used, but such records not only of signing but also of marriages and business being conducted with signing neighbors show the beginnings of community in areas other than Martha's Vineyard.

More information about the use of both sign language and gestures in the seventeenth and eighteenth century American colonies may become available through further research, as is suggested by a study of American Indians and sign language:

> That we find no positive evidence [in contemporary historical chronicles] of the existence and use of gesture speech does not necessarily show that there was none, as is shown by the following notable examples. Circumstances forced Lewis and Clarke in their exploration of the then unknown West to spend the winter of 1804–5 with the Mandans, Gros Ventres, and Arickarees in their village on the Missouri, only a short distance below the present site of their camp at Fort Berthold. During the winter the Cheyennes and Sioux visited this village, and there can be no doubt that gesture speech was daily and hourly used by the members of these tribes as it is to-day when they meet, but no mention is made of the fact, and not until these explorers met the Shoshones near the headwaters of the Missouri do we find any note made of signs being used. If these explorers who entered so minutely into the characteristics of the Indians in their writings failed to make a record of this language, I do not think it very surprising that earlier investigators should have, under less favorable auspices, also neglected it.[39]

In addition to this work by William Philo Clark in 1884, detailed accounts and analyses of the use of sign language among Native Americans have been published by other researchers, including Garrick Mallery, who compared the signs of North American Indians with those of deaf people in his 1881 book, *Sign Language Among North American Indians;*[40] and, more recently, in 2006, Jeffrey E. Davis examined the linguistics of Indian signs.[41]

In fact, the gestures and signs used by deaf people in the various American colonies and the French signs brought to America by Thomas Hopkins Gallaudet and Laurent Clerc likely merged with the various existing sign language varieties, especially those brought to the school by the first students. In 1835, Frederick A. P. Barnard referred to such a melting pot in describing his early teaching experience at the American School for the Deaf:

> Each pupil brings with him, on his arrival, the signs of reduction which he has been accustomed to employ among his friends. But he readily lays aside his own signs for those of the community.[42]

Evidence of some exposure to various forms of fingerspelling among the colonists may also be found. In 1776, the *Pennsylvania Magazine* published a manual alphabet referred to as "Dumb Speech" as a means of carrying on a secret conversation. "This invention," the anonymous correspondent explained, "consisteth of a natural alphabet composed on the human hand, and may be learned in the space of an hour, and executed with so much readiness, when often practiced, that you may be able to express our sentiments sooner this way, than the most skilfull artist can write his words at length with pen and ink."[43] The two-handed alphabet illustrated in this publication (and shown here in figure 1) originated in England.

Isolated Attempts at Tutoring in the Eighteenth Century

Because scarce records are available, we can only surmise how many deaf children received some individual tutoring. Nahum Brown, for instance, a deaf descendent of the first Englishman to settle in Concord, Massachusetts, was only four years old when the Declaration of Independence was signed, and there is no record of how he was taught. At seventeen, he moved to Henniker, New Hampshire, with his family, and he became a successful farmer. He had a 100-acre tract of land given to him by his father. He married a hearing woman, who interpreted in sign language for him during business transactions. They had two deaf children, and many of their descendents were deaf.[44]

Probably the first documented attempt at tutoring a deaf child in the American colonies before the Revolutionary War is found in the diary of John Harrower, an indentured servant at the Belvedere plantation on the Rappahannock River in Virginia. Harrower had notable success with his individual instruction of John Edge, the fourteen-year-old deaf son of a neighboring planter, Samuel Edge. On June 21, 1774, Harrower wrote in his diary that "This day M[r]. Samuel Edge Planter came to me and begged me to take a son of his to school who was both deaf and dum, and I consented to try what I cou'd with him."[45]

The Belvedere plantation had been built for Colonel William Daingerfield, and Harrower was the in-house tutor to the Daingerfield

Figure 1. Two-handed manual alphabet published in *The Pennsylvania Magazine*, 1776.

children. It is not known whether Harrower, who had lived in Shetland, Scotland, and left Lerwick in 1774 for America, was familiar with the work of Thomas Braidwood in Edinburgh or with the father of Charles Shirreff, who had approached Braidwood in 1760 about educating his own deaf son. Both Harrower and Shirreff were merchants in nearby towns. In 1771, two years before Harrower left Scotland, Colonel Thomas Bolling of Virginia had sent his deaf son John to the Braidwood school in Edinburgh. Regardless of the possible reasons for Harrower's confidence in John Edge's ability to learn, he appears to have made progress with the deaf adolescent. There are several other entries in his diary, but the most relevant one occurs on December 6, 1774, when he wrote the following:

> I have as yet only ten scollars One of which is both Deaff and Dumb and his Father pays me ten shilling per Quarter for him he has now five [months] with [me] and I have brought him tolerably well and understands it so far, that he can write mostly for anything he wants and understands the value of every figure and can work single addition a little.[46]

Harrower's instruction of John Edge ended, apparently as a result of his father's failure to pay for the tutoring. The last entry was in December, indicating that approximately five months of lessons took place.

One influential parent who sought support for his deaf child in late eighteenth-century America was James Rumsey, one of the inventors of the steamboat. Rumsey bitterly fought Robert Fulton, John Fitch, Oliver Evans, and others over patent rights. On May 15, 1788, before leaving for a patent battle in England, he wrote an emotional letter to his brother-in-law Charles, asking that his deaf son, also named James, be kept

> with the doctor if possible, or some other school. I shall endeavor to have him some clothing got against winter, and if nothing else can be done, send him to Joseph Barnes. I have a train for him to finish his studies, but it will be expensive, and therefore must be the last shift except [if] my circumstances change. . . . Charles, take [care] of my child and all the little business I left with you. I can make no promises, but I think I shall not go to Europe for nothing.[47]

Rumsey died in London, England, in December 1792, leaving his wife and children penniless, but his deaf son apparently did receive some tutoring as a young boy. He was considered "talented, ingenious, ready and dextrous at various mechanical employments" but nevertheless struggled in adulthood to earn but a "scanty subsistence by daily labor."[48] Years after the inventor's death, the United States Senate and House of Representatives passed a resolution to present to the deaf son of James Rumsey a gold medal, "commemorative of his father's services and high agency in giving to the world the benefits of the steamboat."[49] But the attorney for Rumsey's heirs prevented the resolution from passing in the Senate. Edward Rumsey, a cousin of the deaf man and congressman from Kentucky, was also not satisfied with this tribute. He stood in front of the House of Representatives and pleaded for additional support:

> When I have reflected that the only son of this man was toiling for his daily bread, smitten by his God, and neglected by his country—when I have contemplated that and this spectacle, the steamboat and the unfortunate son of its inventor, feelings, emotions, reflections, have crowded upon me of a character which, as a patriot, a philanthropist, and a Christian, I acknowledge it was improper and sinful to entertain. To the support of that stricken one, I have thought his country, abounding in resources . . . might contribute something more substantial than a medal, with extraordinary stretch of liberality.[50]

Rumsey's will provided boarding and clothing for his deaf son for about six years. At the age of 21, he would receive one of four equal shares of his father's estate.

Deaf Experiences during the Revolutionary War

In the late eighteenth century when the Revolutionary War began, encounters between Indians and colonists could be violent and tragic. Several reports of these incidents involve deaf people. In 1777, the grandparents of frontiersman Davy Crockett were killed by Indians in their cabin in the territory that became Tennessee. Two of their sons were at home that day. Joseph suffered a broken arm from a rifle bullet, but his brother, "Deaf and Dumb Jimmy," was kidnapped by the Indians and rescued twenty years later by his older brothers. We are left to wonder whether Jimmy communicated in signs with his captors during the two decades he spent with them. The manner in which he communicated with his family, too, is not known. On his return, he sought unsuccessfully to show his brothers the gold and silver mines he had been taken to blindfolded while a captive.[51]

Similarly, in Salisbury, Vermont, Joshua Graves, who was exempted from military duty because of his deafness, was living in a log house he had built with his son when a clash with Indians occurred. Graves and his son had cleared and planted a few acres of land, the first clearing for agricultural purposes in Salisbury, but in June 1777, he and one of his sons were captured by a party of about 250 Indians. They were taken to Lake Champlain and then by a British vessel to Montreal. The Indians demanded a bounty for the father and son, but the British officers released them because they were not considered "rebel heads." The Indians had captured them while they were engaged "in quiet and peaceable prosecution of their labors as farmers." The prisoners were allowed to find their own way back to their families and finally arrived home after an absence of three weeks. After the Revolutionary War, Graves built the first framed barn in Salisbury. Four of his sons served in the militia in defense of the frontier area north of Rutland.[52]

Deafness from artillery and disease were common during the Revolutionary War. Jonathan Gillett, who was held prisoner in New York by the British in 1776, mentioned observing deafened soldiers:

> After giving you a small sketch of myself and troubles, I will endeavor to faintly lead you into the poor situation the soldiers are in, especially those taken at Long Island when I was. In fact, their cases are deplorable, and they are real objects of pity. They are still confined, and in houses where there is no fire, poor mortals, with little or no clothes, perishing with hunger. . . . Some almost lose their voices, and some their hearing.[53]

Deaf civilians during the American Revolution were also victims, as in the case of Fountain Smith, born in Norwalk, Fairfield County, Connecticut, in 1725. Smith was a deaf cooper married to Hannah Wassan. The British kidnapped him in front of his house on Raymond Street and took him to prison. He died in a British prisoner of war camp on Long Island in 1779.[54]

Formal Education of Deaf Children of American Colonists

Among deaf colonial children, those of influential parents were the first to receive formal private instruction. These privileged children included John, Thomas, and Mary Bolling, the children of Major Thomas Bolling, a descendent of Pocahontas; Charles Green, born in Boston in 1771, the son of Francis Green, a businessman; John Brewster, Jr., born in Hampton, Connecticut, in 1766, the son of a physician; and William Mercer, born in Fredericksburg, Virginia, in 1765, whose father had fought in the Kittanning Expedition and was a close friend of George Washington.

One option for Americans with means was the Braidwood Academy in Edinburgh, Scotland. In 1771, Thomas Bolling of Virginia enrolled his ten-year-old son John in the Braidwood Academy. One report stated that "Mr. John Bolling was deaf and dumb, he was extremely sensible he understood Geography, Arithmetic, Globe—he has a good sense and fine Education from Scotland."[55] Thomas and Mary followed their brother in 1775 and attained similar satisfactory educations. Charles Green likewise attended the Braidwood Academy for six years. After only two years, his father reported that he had acquired a "very perceptible" improvement "in the construction of language, and in writing; he had made a good beginning in arithmetic. . . . I found him capable of not only comparing ideas, and drawing inferences, but expressing his sentiments with judgment."[56]

Other deaf children received private education in the colonies or in the early republic. William Mercer's education, for example, focused on painting, for which he showed great talent. His father, General Hugh Mercer, was stabbed by British bayonets in the Battle of Princeton while assisting George Washington on January 3, 1777. He died on January 12. His brother-in-law, George Weedon, became the Mercer family's guardian, taking responsibility for financial affairs and schooling of the children, including William, whom he sent to study under the distinguished Philadelphia artist Charles Willson Peale in 1783. Peale and his wife considered William an "adopted son" and pledged lifelong love and devotion to him.[57] The American deaf community considers Mercer one of the first known congenitally deaf individuals in the United States to become a distinguished artist. Unfortunately, with the exception of the painting of the Battle of Princeton and an oval miniature on ivory of Edmund Pendleton of Virginia, now held by the Virginia Historical Society of Richmond, Mercer's other works have been lost.[58]

Like Mercer, John Brewster, Jr., received private tutoring in painting, but many more of his works have been located over the years. Joseph Steward, a friend of Brewster's father, taught the deaf boy, who later established himself as a freelance artist in Massachusetts and Maine. On December 13, 1790, the Reverend James Cogswell of Scotland Parish, Windham, wrote, "Doctr Brewster's Son, a Deaf & Dumb young man came in . . . the Evening, he is very Ingenious, has a Genious for painting & can write well, & converse by signs so that he may be understood in many Things, he lodged here."[59]

Brewster produced folk art for decades. Before the turn of the century, he painted a large portrait of his father and stepmother and a pair of portraits of Mr. and Mrs. James Eldredge of Brooklyn, Connecticut. His technique included portraying couples on separate canvasses and with highly decorative backgrounds. He lived for some time in the luxurious Prince mansion in Maine, where he painted James Prince and three of Prince's children. Among his full-length portraits were three of his half-sisters, completed in Hampton, Connecticut, about 1800.[60]

The Role of Scientific Societies

The interest expressed by American scholars, most notably members of scientific societies, in the education of deaf children was significant in laying the foundation on which Gallaudet and Clerc built formal education for deaf children in the United States. In Europe, members of the French Academy of Sciences and the Royal Society of London had a longstanding interest in the education of deaf children. John Wallis, Robert Boyle, William Holder, Kenelm Digby, Georges Buffon, Charles Marie de La Condamine, and Jean-Jacques Rousseau were a few of the scientists and philosophers who explored the potential of deaf children to learn.[61]

Occasionally, deaf scientists distinguished themselves in their associations with these early societies. For example, John Goodricke, who had been a pupil at the Braidwood Academy in the 1770s, received the Copley Medal from the Royal Society for his work in astronomy. He was elected a fellow in 1786. Charles Bonnet, who was tutored privately in the 1740s in Switzerland, became one of the first scientists to study parthenogenesis. He, too, was elected a fellow of the Royal Society of London and was a corresponding member of the French Academy of Sciences. Saboureux de Fontenay, deaf since birth, published a memoir on meteorology, and Guillaume Amontons, deaf since his youth, followed in Kepler's footsteps in the study of barometric pressure and laid the foundation for Fahrenheit's work with the thermometric scale. An active member of the French Academy of Sciences, Amontons was one of the first profoundly deaf persons in history to author a book, *Observations and Physical Experiences on the Construction of a New Clepsydra, on Barometers, Thermometers and Hygrometers*, which was published in 1695.

Before the turn of the century, there were numerous interactions between American scholars and their counterparts in Europe in relation to the issue of educating deaf children. In 1781, Richard Bagley, the Health Officer of the Port of New York, carried a letter to Samuel Mitchill, the New York surgeon general, from Francis Green, who had been visiting the Braidwood Academy every day for six weeks.

"During this time I had the ineffable pleasure of marking the daily progress of improvement in my boy, and in the other pupils. . . . By the means of this interesting art . . . a certain portion of the human species is rescued from uselessness, ignorance and lamentable inferior-

ity and rendered capable of every useful accomplishment, every degree
of erudition, and pleasure of social conversation and enjoyment."[62]

Two years later, Francis Green published *Vox Oculis Subjecta* ("Voice
Made Subject to the Eyes"), a work that received complimentary recognition in the *Boston Magazine* in 1784 and 1785. Despite the death by drown-
ing of his deaf son Charles in 1787, Green frequently visited the school for
the deaf in Paris. He also helped to establish a school for deaf children
in London in 1792. At the turn of the century, living in Medford,
Massachusetts, he published numerous translations of the writings of
Abbé Charles-Michel de l'Epée, the founder of the Paris school, under the
nom de plume "Philocophus." These writings appeared in columns of the
New England Palladium. Green's dedicated efforts laid the foundation for
subsequent work by Samuel Mitchill and others in establishing a school in
New York. Many years later, Alexander Graham Bell wrote that Francis
Green "was the first to collate the literature of this art; the earliest
American writer upon the subject; the first to urge the education of the
deaf in this country; the pioneer-promoter of free schools for the deaf—
both in England and America; the first parent of a deaf child to plead for
the education of all deaf children."[63]

Benjamin Franklin and John Quincy Adams were among the
Americans who were aware of the pioneering educators in Europe during
the eighteenth century. According to Francis Green, Franklin was an observer of the "celebrated Mr. Braidwood of Edinburgh."[64] In 1784, Adams
sent a letter to William Cranch of Cambridge, Massachusetts, describing
"one of the greatest curiosities that Paris affords,—the school of Abbé
Charles-Michel de l'Epée."[65] Adams explained that Epée taught deaf
pupils "not only to converse with each other by signs, but to read and
write, and comprehend the most abstracted metaphysical ideas."[66]

In 1793, The American Philosophical Society published in the
Transactions of the American Philosophical Society William Thornton's treatise on elements of teaching speech and language to deaf children in the
United States. His essay, which earned him a Magellenic Gold Medal, was
titled "On the Mode of Teaching the Deaf, or Surd, and consequently
Dumb, to speak."[67] Thornton was an inventor and architect as well as director of the patent office. He was involved in many social causes, and he
had probably observed the work of the followers of the Braidwoods and
l'Epée during his own studies in Edinburgh and Paris. His perceptions on
deaf education were provocative, covering topics such as the phonological basis for reading; the importance of vocabulary building; and methods
of communicating with deaf people, including speech, fingerspelling, and

signs. On this last topic, Thornton wrote that "a deaf person not perfectly skilled in reading words from the lips, or who should ask anything in the dark would be able to procure common information by putting various questions, and by telling the person that, as he is deaf, he requests answers by signs, which he will direct him to change according to circumstances."[68]

Conclusion

Literature of the seventeenth and eighteenth centuries reveals that deaf life in the American colonies was varied and, for some individuals, fulfilling. Although the evidence does not provide detailed information about a core congregation of deaf people during that time, we have evidence of deaf individuals who achieved spiritual authority, religious participation, and legal rights. We see the planting of educational seeds, which came to fruition in the lives of early artists and in some deaf people who owned land and managed their own business interactions associated with trades. We also see the darker, disturbing elements at work in deaf people's lives, as surely as they appear in mainstream history. At least a few deaf people were involved in superstitious acts, intolerance, the slave trade, and the disenfranchisement of native people. Deaf people cannot and should not be consigned to sainthood or victimhood in the colonial era or during any other period.

Many of the achievements noted in this study of the genesis of the American deaf community were nurtured in the acknowledged presence of a visual language or languages. We can only surmise how married deaf people like the Pratts in the Massachusetts colony or deaf siblings in other families in the seventeenth and eighteenth centuries communicated, but it would not be a stretch of the imagination to assume that they did so by signs. Although the ship that Andrew Brown boarded did not disembark its passengers in New England, his story indicates that signing deaf people from Europe may have emigrated to the colonies before the Vineyard families. Some early use of gestural or tactile communication is also evident, including a case of an emigrant described by John Winthrop in 1637:

> There was an old woman in Ipswich, who came out of England blind and deaf, yet her son could make her understand any thing, and know any man's name, by her sense of feeling. He could write upon her hand some letters of the name and by other such motions would inform her. The governour himself had [trial of] when he was at Ipswich.[69]

In his seminal research on American Sign Language (ASL), William Stokoe questioned the assumption that Gallaudet and Clerc brought the French system of signs to the United States. His skepticism was based on the linguistic phenomenon of the "rapid flourishing of the language and the schools using the method."[70] Later, other scholars also explained that there must have been some influence on French signs from native signs already existing in the United States.[71] The present paper indicates that decades before Clerc accompanied Gallaudet to Hartford to establish the American School for the Deaf, Americans such as John Adams, Francis Green, and William Thornton had visited Epée's school for deaf students in Paris and shared their observations with both scholars and parents back home.

In discussing the history and bases of ASL in a more general context, James Woodward wrote that "it is not unreasonable to assume that whenever there have been deaf people associating with each other, there has been sign language variety. These varieties developed through normal patterns of interaction, not through the invention of hearing people."[72] Woodward provides arguments for possible earlier creolization in ASL based on the analysis of sociolinguistic situations in other locales. The anecdotal accounts in the present paper provide evidence that there were indeed numerous patterns of interaction, including, but not limited to, British signs and fingerspelling (Martha's Vineyard and in other colonial sites), signs used by various Indian tribes, tactile communication with deaf-blind people (early 1600s), and various reports of what were likely home signs. Although it is presently not known whether any of these cases had French origins, the anecdotal reports support the contention that there was likely language contact among the sign language varieties. Additional research on sign language contact and sign language varieties in America in the seventeenth and eighteenth centuries will no doubt shed more light on the history of ASL.

The genesis of community presupposes the broad range of human experience. As the early colonists imagined free and full participation as citizens of a community, despite some notable failures, so, apparently, did their deaf neighbors. And these neighbors moved forward, albeit slowly, to express a distinct culture in the context of that new world.

Notes

1. Extracts from the Institution des Sourds et Muets of Abbé de l'Epée, as translated by Francis Green. Published in the *New England Palladium*, 1803, reprinted in the

American Annals of the Deaf 8 (1861): 9–10. The extracts were taken from the earlier work of the Abbé de l'Epée, writing that he did not incorporate into his first major description of his methods. As summarized in the *Annals*, the extracts appeared as a series in vol. 22 of the *New England Palladium*, a Boston newspaper.

2. Allan Taylor, *American Colonies* (New York: Penguin Putnam, 2001), x.

3. Kathy A. Jankowski, *Deaf Empowerment: Emergence, Struggle, and Rhetoric* (Washington, D.C.: Gallaudet University Press, 1977).

4. See Harlan Lane, Richard C. Pillard, and Mary French. "Origins of the American Deaf-World: Assimilating and Differentiating Societies and Their Relation to Genetic Patterning" *Sign Language Studies* 1 (2000): 17–44.

5. C. G. Braddock, *Notable Deaf Persons* (Washington, D.C.: Gallaudet College Alumni Press, 1975), 58.

6. Duane A. Cline, "Physical Appearances of Wampanoag Natives" in *The Pilgrims and Plymouth Colony*, 1620, http://www.rootsweb.com/~mosmd/appearance.htm.

7. W. H. Foote, *Sketches of North Carolina, Historical and Biographical, Illustrative of the Principles of a Portion of Her Early Settlers* (New York: Robert Carter, 1846), 98.

8. Foote, *Sketches*, 104.

9. J. E. Doan, "The Eagle Wing Expedition (1636) and the Settlement of Londonderry, New Hampshire: Two Episodes in Ulster-Scots/Scotch-Irish History" (written in 1719), *Journal of Scotch-Irish Studies Contents* 1:1–7.

10. Nora. E. Groce, *Everyone Here Spoke Sign Language: Hereditary Deafness at Martha's Vineyard* (Cambridge, Mass.: Harvard University Press, 1985).

11. Margret A. Winzer, *The History of Special Education: From Isolation to Integration* (Washington, D.C.: Gallaudet University Press, 1993), 85.

12. C. Eliot, ed., *American Historical Documents: 1000–1904* (New York: Collier, 1910), 71.

13. T. G. Morton, *The History of Pennsylvania Hospital 1751–1895* (Philadelphia: Times Printing House, 1897).

14. T. Gage, *The history of Rowley, anciently including Bradford, Boxford, and Georgetown, from the year 1639 to the present time* (Boston: Ferdinand Andrews, 1840), 72.

15. K. Silverman, *The Life and Times of Cotton Mather* (New York: Harper & Row, 1970), 34.

16. Alexander Graham Bell, "Historical Notes Concerning the Teaching of Speech to the Deaf," *Association Review* 2 (1900): 35.

17. James Savage, A Genealogical Dictionary of the First Settlers of New England, Showing Three Generations of Those Who Came before May, 1692, on the Basis of Farmer's Register (Boston, 1860–1862). Corrected electronic version copyright Robert Kraft, July 1994, http://puritanism.online.fr/puritanism/Savage/savage.html.

18. Cotton Mather, *Magnalia Christi Americana*, vol. 2, (New York: Russell and Russell, 1967), 495.

19. Examples can also be found in the eighteenth century. In 1772, for example, Luke Hart (born in 1744), a "deaf and dumb man" from Rensselaer, New York, bought property with his two hearing brothers in Dartmouth. They sold the land in 1810. *Bristol LR* 91:554.

20. Charles E. Banks, *The History of Martha's Vineyard, Dukes County, Massachusetts*, vol. 2, (Boston: George H. Dean, 1911), 53.

21. Samuel Sewell, *Diary of Samuel Sewell*, 1674–1729, vol. 2 (New York: Arno Press, 1972), 432.

22. Banks, *History of Martha's Vineyard*, 53

23. Ibid.

24. By the nineteenth century, in some areas of the island, deafness (from intermarriage) was occurring at an extremely higher rate compared with the national average.

25. D. H. Hurd, *History of Bristol County Massachusetts with biographical sketches of many of its pioneers and prominent men* (Philadelphia: J. W. Lewis & Co., 1883), 33.

26. Robert Calef, "More Wonders of the Invisible World, 1700," excerpted in George L. Burr, ed., *Narratives of the New England Witchcraft Cases* (New York: Scribner's, 2002), 359.

27. Mary Beth Norton, *In the Devil's Snare: The Salem Witchcraft Crisis of 1692* (New York: Knopf, 2002), 226.

28. Anonymous, "A remarkable Account of two Children who were deaf and dumb from the Birth, being brought to speak articulately. From the Register of the Academy at Caen in Normandy," *The Gentleman's Magazine* 17 (December 1747): 610.

29. Anonymous, Extract of a Letter from Paris. *The Gentleman's Magazine* 20 (January 1750): 5.

30. Benjamin Franklin, Extract from the Gazette, 1739. *Poor Richard's Almanac,* October 18, 1740, 240–41.

31. Lyman Chalkley, *Chronicles of the Scotch-Irish Settlement in Virginia.* (Baltimore: Genealogical Publishing Company, 1965), 52.

32. John Lednum, *A History of the Rise of Methodism in America Containing Sketches of Methodist Itinerant Preachers From 1736 to 1785* (Philadelphia: John Lednum, 1859), 397.

33. John M. Passmore, *Ancestors and Descendents of Andrew Moore, 1612–1897* (Lancaster, Penn.: Wickersham, 1897), 75.

34. Ibid, 74.

35. Ibid, 74.

36. Ibid, 63.

37. Ibid, 63–64.

38. Ibid, 74.

39. William P. Clarke, *The Indian Sign Language* (Lincoln: University of Nebraska, 1982), 11.

40. Garrick Mallery, "Sign Language among North American Indians Compared with that among Other Peoples and Deaf-Mutes." First Annual Report of the Bureau of Ethnology to the Secretary of the Smithsonian Institution, 1879–1880 (Washington, D.C.: Government Printing Office, 1881), 263–552. Reprinted as Garrick Mallery, *Sign Language among North American Indians.* (Mineola, N.Y.: Dover, 2001).

41. Jeffrey E. Davis, "A Historical Linguistic Account of Sign Language among North American Indians," in Ceil Lucas, ed., *Multilingualism and Sign Languages: From the Great Plains to Australia* (Washington, D.C.: Gallaudet University Press, 2006), 3–35.

42. H. G. Lang and W. C. Stokoe, "A Treatise on Signed and Spoken Language in Early 19th Century Education in America," *Journal of Deaf Studies and Deaf Education* 5:204.

43. Anonymous, To the Publisher of the Pennsylvania Magazine (letter). *The Pennsylvania Magazine* 2 (1776): 73–76.

44. Harlan Lane, Richard C. Pillard, and Mary French. *Origins of the American Deaf-World, Sign Language Studies* 1 (2000): 17–44.

45. "The Diary of John Harrower, 1773–1776," *The American Historical Review* 6:88.

46. Ibid.

47. R. John Brockmann, "Feeling 'The Old' on Main Street in Warwick," Historical Society of Cecil County (Web site). http://cchistory.org/warwick1.htm.

48. Ella May Turner, *James Rumsey: Pioneer in Steam Navigation* (Scottdale, Penn.: Mennonite Publishing House, 1930), 204.

49. Ibid, 205.

50. Ibid, 204.

51. James A. Shackford, *David Crockett: The Man and the Legend* (Chapel Hill, N.C.: University of North Carolina Press, 1956).

52. John M. Weeks, *History of Salisbury, Vermont* (Middlebury, Vt.: A.H. Copeland, 1860), 236.

53. "A Revolutionary Reminiscense," *Anamosa Eureka* 3 (May 20, 1859): 1. [Letter submitted by J. B. Loomis and was written by his grandfather in 1776.]

54. http://www.three-systems.com/gen/hoyt/d0024/g0002415.html

55. Alexander Graham Bell, "Historical Notes Concerning the Teaching of Speech to the Deaf," *Association Review* 2 (1900): 270.

56. Alexander Graham Bell, "Historical Notes Concerning the Teaching of Speech to the Deaf," *Association Review* 2 (1900): 43.

57. Harry G. Lang and Bonnie Meath-Lang, *Deaf Persons in the Arts and Sciences: A Biographical Dictionary* (Westport, Conn.: Greenwood Press, 1995).

58. Lang and Meath-Lang, *Deaf Persons in the Arts and Sciences*. Another early deaf artist was George Ropes (born in 1788), who became a pupil of the early American marine artist Michele Felice Corne. He was a "deaf and dumb painter" of Salem, Massachusetts. In 1804, he made a copy of an old portrait of Salem's first church, and this copy is preserved in the museum of the American Antiquarian Society at Worcester, Massachusetts. He died in January 1819.

59. "Nina Fletcher Little and John Brewster, Jr," in J. Lipman and T. Armstrong, eds., *American Folk Painters of Three Centuries* (New York: Hudson Hill, 1980), 18. Cogswell was the grandfather of Alice Cogswell, whose deafness led Thomas Hopkins Gallaudet and Laurent Clerc to found the American School for the Deaf. She was born fifteen years after this encounter with young Brewster.

60. Lang and Meath-Lang, *Deaf Persons in the Arts and Sciences*.

61. For detail, see Harry G. Lang, *Silence of the Spheres: The Deaf Experience in the History of Science* (Westport, Conn.: Bergin and Garvey Press, 1994).

62. Francis Green, "On Teaching the Deaf to Understand Language and the Dumb to Speak," *Medical Repository* 2 (1804): 73–75.

63. Alexander Graham Bell, "Historical Notes Concerning the Teaching of Speech to the Deaf," *Association Review* 2 (1900): 61–62. In 1803, Francis Green published in a Boston newspaper a request to the clergy in Massachusetts to obtain information on the number of deaf children residing in the state. It was his intention to determine whether the number warranted the establishment of a special school. In the following year, the Reverend John Stanford found several deaf children in an almshouse in New York City and began to teach them.

64. Francis Green, *Vox Oculis Subjecta*, 12.

65. John Quincy Adams to William Cranch, December 14, 1784. Reprinted in the *American Annals of the Deaf and Dumb* 8 (1856): 248.

66. Ibid.

67. The article appeared as an appendix to a work with the lengthy title "CADMUS, or a Treatise on the Elements of written language, illustrating, by a Philosophical Division of Speech, the Power of each character, thereby mutually fixing the Orthography and Orhoepy."

68. William Thornton, "On Teaching the Surd, or Deaf, and Consequently Dumb, to Speak," *Association Review* 5: 414.

69. John Winthrop, *History of New England* (Boston: Little, Brown & Company, 1853), 281. In the same year (1637) that Winthrop reported this case, colonists in Virginia also petitioned to England for payment for the guardianship of an individual with an "intellectual disability."

70. William Stokoe, Sign Language Structure: An Outline of the Visual Communication of the American Deaf, *Studies in Linguistics*, Occasional Papers 8, (Silver Spring, Md.: Linstok Press 1960), 13.

71. Susan Fischer, Influences on Word Order Change in American Sign Language. In C. N. Li (Ed.), Word Order and Word Order Change. (Austin, TX: University of Texas Press, 1975) and James Woodward, Historical Bases of American Sign Language. In P. Siple (Ed.), *Understanding Language Through Sign Language Research*, pp. 333-348. (New York: Academic Press 1978).

72. James Woodward, "Historical Bases," 345.

2

Hearing with the Eye: The Rise of Deaf Education in the United States

Barry A. Crouch and Brian H. Greenwald

Editor's Introduction

Historians Barry A. Crouch and Brian H. Greenwald ask why the first organized school for deaf children in the United States, Cobbs School, founded in rural Virginia in 1815, failed in 1816, whereas the American School for the Deaf, established in Hartford, Connecticut, in 1817, succeeded spectacularly. They argue that profound cultural and economic differences between the Northern and Southern states, the inherent limitations of oralism, and the personal characteristics of the founders of the two schools resolve this mystery. Their article is notable for its heavy use of primary sources and its situating of deaf history within the broad sweep of American social history.

T wo schools for educating deaf people emerged in the United States between 1815 and 1817. The first began in Virginia as a private endeavor in 1815, financed by a Southern slaveholder named William Bolling. The second opened its doors in Hartford, Connecticut, in 1817, under the patronage of a prominent Northern eye doctor, Mason Fitch Cogswell, and became the first permanent school for educating deaf children in the United

Barry Crouch and I collaborated on this article before his death in 2002. Although we did not finish the manuscript together, I am indebted to Barry for taking the initiative on this research. I also thank John Van Cleve and Gallaudet University Press for their editorial work. Special thanks to Elizabeth Fenn for her incisive comments on the manuscript.

States. The two schools contrasted sharply in their founders' intentions, teaching methods, and longevity, despite being the first institutions established for this purpose and despite being founded at nearly the same time. The story of these two efforts demonstrates how individuals in the North and South envisioned deaf education and maintained their schools.

Much historical debate has focused on whether the North and the South were vastly different in their social, economic, and political development in the nineteenth century. Most certainly, the primary subject of the dispute often is their respective labor and political systems. But it may have been in the educational sphere that the two sections varied the most. When it came to deaf and other disadvantaged individuals, the question at hand was what to do about their status in society, and the two entities approached this "problem" with contrasting philosophies. Northerners believed state cooperation was a necessity; Southerners, until much later, believed in individual undertakings. In the South, education was not a governmental prerogative.[1]

From perhaps the sixteenth century onward, a war of methods raged among those interested in educating deaf children over how those deaf children should be taught. One approach advocated the use of sign language, a method known as "manualism," which created a unique deaf community. The other approach, known as "oralism," called for teaching deaf children skills that facilitated social integration and impaired the creation of a distinct deaf culture. This debate raged across Europe before it took center stage in the United States about 1890. Germany and England largely cultivated oralism whereas Spain and France advocated manualism. Although oralism made an appearance in America, it was manualism that soon stole the show, becoming the established method for instructing deaf students in the first half of the nineteenth century.[2]

The Southern Endeavor

In the eighteenth century, Martha's Vineyard contained a small deaf community. But neither schools nor teachers for deaf children existed in the English mainland colonies during the colonial and revolutionary eras. The only option for families with deaf offspring was to send their children to Europe. A New Englander, Francis Green, a loyalist banished to Great Britain with the advent of war, was the first to follow this path. But the Bollings of Virginia were the most prominent colonials to dispatch their nonhearing youngsters overseas to become literate. In the colonies, Thomas Bolling (1735–1804), and his wife and first cousin, Elizabeth Gay, had three deaf children: John (1761–1783), Mary (1765–1826), and Thomas

Jr. (1766–1836). They were sent to Scotland to be educated at the Braidwood Academy.[3]

The Bollings

John Bolling, the second child of Thomas and Elizabeth, was the first to be sent abroad when he became old enough (the age of ten years). Among prominent and wealthy Americans with deaf children, the Braidwood Academy in Edinburgh, Scotland, which emphasized the oral method, was the best known institution. Established in 1760 by Thomas Braidwood (1715–1806), the school was known as the "Academy for the Deaf and Dumb." It was private, expensive, and secretive.[4] The school kept pedagogical methodology a tightly held secret among few people.

Arriving in Scotland in 1771, John advanced rapidly. Writing to his mother from St. Leonards in November, he stated he was "very well and very happy, because I can speak and read. My Uncle and Aunt are very kind to me, they give me many fine things." With the prospect of his brother and sister joining him, a letter from his mother made him "very happy, as [he] had got none for a long time." Informed that Mary (Polly) had seriously injured her leg and might not retain its use, John hoped for a quick recovery so she could "come over here with my dear brother Tom." Should they be sent to Scotland, he promised to do them "all the service" he could. John had been "long expecting to see them," and would "be glad how soon they come."[5]

With their large coterie of friends, the Bollings made sure that John, and later Thomas and Mary, were well looked after. Thomas Bolling, the father, had a surrogate in Edinburgh named John Hyndman, who supervised affairs for him, monitored John's progress, and arranged for payment of the children's educational bills. Individuals visited them in Scotland and reported back to the family. John, for example, was "obliged" to a Mr. McKenzie "for his good report of me." Miss Dean had sewn and hemmed some pretty ruffles for him. Nevertheless, family remained important to the deeply homesick boy. "I often think with pleasure of the happiness I shall enjoy with you all when I come home," he wrote in 1771.[6]

In late 1773, Samuel A. Johnson, one of the most well-known writers at the time, visited the Braidwood School in Edinburgh during John's tenure. Johnson viewed the school as a "philosophical curiosity" that "no other city has to shew; a college of the deaf and dumb, who are taught to speak, to read, to write, and to practice arithmetick." The approximately twelve pupils, he explained, were instructed "according to their several degrees of proficiency." "How far any former teachers have succeeded,"

Johnson could not ascertain. Nevertheless, he judged the improvement of Braidwood's pupils "wonderful": They "speak, write, and understand what is written." If a speaker looked at them, modified "his organs by distinct and full utterance," they knew "so well" what was spoken. They heard "with the eye."[7]

Whether any "attained the power" of "feeling sounds, by laying a hand on the speaker's mouth," Johnson did not know, but he did suggest that a short sentence might "possibly be so distinguished." It will readily "be supposed," Johnson noted, that for those who considered the subject, Braidwood's pupils spelled accurately. "Orthography," however, was vitiated among those who learned first "to speak, and then to write, by imperfect notions of the relation between letters and vocal utterance; but to those students every character is of equal importance; for letters are to them not symbols of names, but of things; when they write they do not represent a sound, but delineate a form."[8]

By 1775, John had become a rather accomplished letter writer, considering the method of instruction and the knowledge surrounding deafness during the eighteenth century. He had to endure separation from his parents for twelve years, with the war making transatlantic travel unsafe for civilians and combatants alike. John was learning to draw, and his "Master," John Braidwood, the grandfather of the Englishman who later came to America and taught John's nephew, William Albert Bolling, commended his progress.[9]

When the first Bolling child went to Scotland in 1771, America was still under English rule. But when John, Mary, and Thomas Jr. returned home on July 7, 1783, after a ten-week voyage and settled at the family manor in Cobbs, Virginia, the thirteen colonies had been transformed into a new nation. All three children became ill soon after arriving home. John, who contracted "bilious fever" on August 29, struggled, wrote his father Thomas, "with as much patience as ever a poor Soul did," but died on October 11. Because of his early demise, it is impossible to gauge the extent of John's progress or to determine the effectiveness of the ten years of oral instruction he received.[10] Both Mary and Thomas Jr. survived their illnesses, however, and lived at least four decades, supported by their family. Although neither married nor established a professional career, their experience provides some evidence of the success of their education in Scotland.

Comments about Thomas are particularly easy to find. One family member noted that he was "a miracle of accomplishments." His oral articulation was good and he could be understood "in conversation and reading aloud." On his death, the Richmond *Enquirer* observed that "he composed and wrote in a peculiar, clear and graphic style and attained an artificial faculty of speech almost equal to natural. His grace of manner, vivacity and power of imitation made him the wonder and admiration of strangers and the delight of friends and relatives." Although people probably did not make such distinctions, it has been contended that Thomas Bolling was the first formally educated deaf individual in America.[11]

However beneficial the education the Bolling children received in Scotland, the balance due for their tuition remained to be settled between Thomas Bolling and Thomas Braidwood for many years. The Bollings appreciated Braidwood's care and attention to their "Dear Children" in both education and morals because they now appeared to answer the parents' "most sanguine expectation," but Bolling felt the ravages of the Revolutionary War. A large tobacco house, containing the crop for two years, a "good deal of corn," and "many other things" had been burned. He intended to pay Braidwood whenever he had the resources. For fourteen years, from 1783 until 1797, Bolling's debt to Braidwood remained unpaid. This issue had to be settled in court when Braidwood brought suit from England.[12]

The court papers were filed in Richmond, with Philip Richard Fendall serving as Braidwood's attorney. Bolling agreed that he stood "justly indebted" to Braidwood for 999 pounds sterling, four shillings, and four pence. In addition, legal interest would be computed from the date of April 12, 1794.[13]

The settlement was predicated on the fact that Bolling had sustained losses during the war, so instead of charging Bolling 100 pounds for each child per annum, Braidwood eventually agreed to a sum of forty pounds a year for John, and sixty each for Thomas and Mary. The fee included board, lodging, washing, and instruction as well as additional charges such as school necessities, assistants and servants, pocket money, and "incidental expenses." Bolling had kept abreast of the costs until the spring of 1777, when revolutionary affairs became critical. Fees then outstripped his yearly payments. Braidwood even charged Bolling two pounds and five pence for transporting the children to the boat at Port Glasgow for their trip home.[14]

The suit is important in two respects. First, it reveals how expensive it was to educate a deaf child in the latter part of the eighteenth century. Second, it provides a seminal portrait of the nature, care, and instruction of the three Bolling children in Scotland. Added to the drama was the fact that the case continued for three years and that Braidwood received his pay, ironically, through the sale of forty-one slaves.[15]

The next generation of hearing Bollings, who also produced deaf children, desired that those children be educated in the United States. William Bolling (1777–1845) was the final offspring of Thomas and Elizabeth. Born at Cobbs in Chesterfield County, Virginia, (where the first deaf school was later established), he was the only hearing son to live to maturity. Following his father's pattern, William also married his first cousin, Mary Randolph of Curles Neck, Henrico County, Virginia, which allowed the expression of a shared recessive gene for deafness. The couple moved to Bolling Hall, in Goochland County, where Bolling became a prominent planter, Episcopalian church official, and justice of the court.[16]

During the course of their marriage, Mary bore five children, two of whom were deaf. The first, William Albert, was born in 1798. He became a catalyst for his father's desire to establish an American school to educate deaf children. Committed to oralism, like his father had been, William Bolling's motives were sincere. His experience with his two brothers, John and Thomas, and with his sister Mary had taught him much.[17] Families were disrupted when children were sent to England or Scotland to receive schooling. Bolling was determined to avoid separation from his own deaf son if at all possible. The 1812 arrival in America of John Braidwood, the grandson of Thomas Braidwood, seemed providential.

John Braidwood

John Braidwood had decided to follow in the footsteps of his predecessors and thus had received the secrets of the Braidwood method. He received his first opportunity to lead an educational institution in 1810, when the city of Edinburgh established a school for deaf children to replace the Braidwood Academy, which had moved to Hackney, outside of London. Funds were raised, and Braidwood, who had assisted his mother at the Hackney school, was hired for the position. He received a liberal salary, was allowed to charge those who could afford to pay a "price he thought reasonable," and at the same time to limit the number who would be taught "gratuitously." Walter Geikie, an early student, paid nine guineas, or $38, a quarter in fees. This, claimed Geikie's brother, was an "extravagant charge." For two years, John Braidwood headed the Edinburgh Institute, but he left abruptly in 1812, causing the institution to collapse.[18]

Arriving in America in 1812, Braidwood consulted with Secretary of State James Monroe, with whom he had become acquainted while Monroe had served as the guardian of John Randolph's deaf nephew, St. George Tucker, who attended the Braidwood school. Monroe had even visited London in that capacity. Braidwood desired to establish an

"Institution for the Education for the Deaf and Dumb under the sanction of the President and Congress of the United States." He "obtained every assurance," Braidwood later wrote, from President James Madison. Soon thereafter, he contacted James Pleasants, a Virginia representative and friend of William Bolling's, with whom Braidwood later associated.[19]

In March, Braidwood wrote to William Bolling explaining that he planned to establish an American institution "for the Instruction of the Deaf and Dumb, and the Removal of Impediments in Speech." His goal was to give deaf children "every facility of education which their peculiar situation so strongly demands, without subjecting the parents to a long and painful separation." Knowing that Bolling had deaf children, Braidwood felt no "small repugnance" at writing on "so delicate a subject." He intended to exercise his "professional abilities," even while aware that Bolling's knowledge of his family had "great claims upon" him.[20]

Braidwood's presence and intentions received favorable notice in the nation's capital from the *National Intelligencer*. The editor announced to the public "with great pleasure that the Englishman had arrived in this country with an idea which would benefit those who could not hear." Braidwood was "a relative of the gentlemen of that name who have acquired so much celebrity by their academy for the instruction of the deaf and dumb, originally established at Edinburgh, but now at London." The purpose of the foreigner's visit was to "effect the institution of a similar academy in this country; and every patriot and philanthropist must second so useful and honorable an undertaking."[21]

Deaf children, the editor continued, who would be "benefitted by such an institution, are peculiarly deserving of commiseration; and though we may justly boast that the hard offspring of our countrymen are less defective in their organization than the natives of more luxurious nations, in spite of the flimsy aspersions of Buffon [Georges Louis Le Clerc, a famous French naturalist], yet nature even in America has deprived many human beings of the two important faculties of receiving and communicating knowledge." Braidwood's method was "calculated to restore" these faculties. *Nile's Weekly Register* also commented on Braidwood's presence and hoped the Englishman would favor all those interested with the "general outlines of his plan of education, and his views of residence among us."[22]

When Bolling learned of Braidwood's arrival, the Virginian sought to contact him because his two brothers and sister had all been taught by the Braidwood family. Bolling had tried to contact Braidwood previously and seized the opportunity when he learned that Braidwood was actually in the English colonies. Representative Pleasants served as an intermediary for Bolling. "The unfortunate situation of my Son," Bolling wrote

Braidwood, caused "much anxious solicitude and many disagreeable re-flections" in his mind. The want of a friend "with whom he had been in the habit of associating and who would feel disposed to go with him to a foreign country, added to the meek and affectionate disposition" of the boy, and deterred the father "from a separation which would have been so distressing to all parties."[23]

Bolling invited the Englishman to his Virginia home so they could com-municate more fully "on an affair which is to me of so much importance." In fact, Bolling suggested that it might be wise for Braidwood to spend some time with a private family "previous to the necessary arrangements you will have to make for a permanent establishment, toward the accom-plishment of which the deep interest I feel on the subject will ensure to you every aid in my power." Bolling knew nothing of the controversial as-pects of Braidwood's background or character and failed to fully realize the instability of the Englishman. Generally a shrewd man, Bolling's desire to aid his son and others in his situation blinded him to the facts.[24]

Bolling noted that Thomas and Mary were living with his mother at Cobbs, fifty miles from Bolling Hall. They were in good health and would "no doubt be overjoyed at the possibility of seeing" Braidwood. Bolling told Representative Pleasants that he "pressed Braidwood to visit Virginia" because of his "anxious solicitude" about the fate of his son. Pleasants was an excellent individual through whom Bolling could ex-press ideas and from whom he learned of others who shared his son William Albert's absence of hearing.[25]

Braidwood accepted Bolling's invitation to meet with him in Virginia and reiterated that his mission in coming to America was to settle in a "permanent situation" and "open a seminary similar to our Institution in England." Philadelphia, as a central urban location with "more advan-tages" than any other city for a deaf school, had been strongly recom-mended to Braidwood. As yet, a site was still undetermined. But, what-ever Braidwood decided, he hoped the arrangements would meet with Bolling's approval and might "materially lessen the repugnance which you have hitherto felt at the idea of parting with your Son." Braidwood made it as far south as Norfolk, Virginia, where he became ill. He finally reached the Bolling residence in the latter part of April.[26]

Northerners also took note of Braidwood's mission. Mason Fitch Cogswell, a Connecticut resident, attempted to contact the English edu-cator after seeing the notice in the *National Intelligencer* and becoming curious about Braidwood's future plans. Cogswell's interest arose from the situation of his daughter Alice, "who belongs to the class of unfortu-nate beings" who claimed Braidwood's "solicitude and attention," as did five children of prominent Hartford physician and attorney, Sylvester Gilbert.[27]

Cogswell's idea for a school had been germinating for some time. His intention was to apply to the Connecticut state legislature for financial support and to obtain an appropriation from an already established state school fund. The money would be used to hire an instructor "until the Institution would support itself." The doctor entertained no doubts that in a "few Years" a "competent" teacher would be amply rewarded "for whatever pains he might bestow on a plan of such extensive benediction and utility." Cogswell queried Braidwood to find out whether he had already settled on a site for a school or whether he intended to visit various places before reaching a final decision.[28]

Cogswell also inquired "whether an Institution of this kind [could] be as eligibly established in the large cities as in the small ones?" Cogswell believed that an urban area, where a school could be financed by the state, would have more drawing power than a privately funded rural version, such as Bolling seemed to be pursuing. Although Cogswell was not especially concerned with what method would be used to teach deaf children, his ideas about how to financially support and maintain a deaf school were superior to those of Bolling.[29]

It was Braidwood and Bolling, however, who first attempted to create a system of education for deaf children in the United States, albeit a system that was private and geared toward the wealthy. Both men were intimately connected with deaf people but in different ways and for different reasons. Certainly, Bolling's motivation's were clear. His father, Thomas Bolling, had two deaf sons and a deaf daughter—all of whom had been sent to Edinburgh to study with Thomas Braidwood—and William was himself the father of a deaf son and daughter. In contrast, Braidwood's motivations were primarily pecuniary.

Although the Braidwoods had attempted to keep their teaching techniques under wraps, they were not as well guarded as one might assume.[30] Historians know a little about the pedagogical strategies they used. To aid in speech teaching, for example, Thomas Braidwood used a small silver rod, "about the size of a tobacco-pipe," flat on one end with a bulb at the other. He used this instrument to place the tongue "in the right positions." This effort was indeed a laborious task and generally had mixed results. Because of the time required to instruct students with such a method, enrollments remained low, and tuition costs were high. Generally, only wealthy parents could afford to have their deaf children participate. Thomas's grandson, John Braidwood, marketed the family secrets for his own personal financial benefit, hoping to profit from the fact that, in the early nineteenth century, there was no other school in the United States that educated deaf children.

In between his travels, Braidwood ran an advertisement in the Richmond Enquirer in early June 1812 that indicated the Englishman's grandiose intentions. Because of "repeated applications" from persons of the "highest respectability," several of whom had visited the Edinburgh Institution, Braidwood proposed forming a similar school in Baltimore on July 1, 1812. (Why Philadelphia was abandoned as a possible site is unknown.) The Baltimore school would be "calculated to restore to society an unfortunate class of our fellow-creatures, who from being deprived of the Education they are so capable of receiving, are excluded from the knowledge of everything except the immediate objects of sense."[31] Children admitted to the school would be "taught to speak and read distinctly" and "to write and understand accurately the principles of Language." They would also receive instruction in arithmetic, geography, and "every branch of education that may be necessary to qualify them for any situation in life."[32]

Bolling thought Braidwood should establish an institution within the vicinity of Richmond. Whether Bolling intended to lure Braidwood to Virginia as a private tutor is not known, but his major concern was making sure William Albert received instruction without being sent to Europe. The sequence of events that led to Braidwood's residence at Bolling Hall, and later at Cobbs, surely created uneasiness in Bolling's mind, but his overweening concern for his son would override his normally keen acumen and cloud his judgment.

The Cobbs School

After Braidwood visited the Bolling family in April 1812, William advanced him $600 on the fees that would be due for William Albert's instruction in Braidwood's school. After Braidwood enjoyed the hospitality of the Bollings, he left to travel north. Thereafter, Bolling heard nothing from the Englishman for several months. Pleasants wrote Bolling that Braidwood had been in Washington for a short time and had mentioned that he wished to write to the Virginian, but Pleasants had nothing to forward.[33]

After seeing Braidwood's advertisement in the Virginia Argus in late June, and assuming that Braidwood was going ahead with this project, Bolling made "all necessary arrangements" to send William Albert to Baltimore as soon as the school opened. It did not open, however. By the middle of August, Braidwood was in New York City, in trouble and in dire straits, pleading to Bolling for assistance.[34] Braidwood claimed to have written Bolling from Baltimore in July and from Philadelphia in August, although Bolling never received the letters. Braidwood said that when he heard nothing in response, his anxiety mounted. His discomfort was further aggravated by what the Englishman described as his "many painful and unpleasant occurrences." Because of the "unhappy situation" and "increasing turbulence" of Baltimore, Braidwood proposed giving up the idea of establishing an institution and offered his services to the Bolling family "alone as a private tutor." He allegedly repeated the same proposition in the Philadelphia letter.[35]

There was good reason for the hiatus of nearly four months in communication between John Braidwood and William Bolling. When Braidwood finally contacted Bolling, he assumed that Bolling had "perused" the "horrible scene" in the newspapers. Braidwood did not state specifically what had occurred in Baltimore, but he did say that nothing could induce him to reside in that city and that the "fears of every parent would be excited in the idea of a further repetition of similar events." The Englishman's Baltimore difficulties did not end the trouble in which he found himself. Other circumstances, "almost too painful to relate," urged Braidwood to "seek in the retired bosom" of Bolling's family "an asylum."[36]

The historical record does not reveal exactly what happened. Braidwood told Bolling that he had met a fellow countryman in Norfolk named Harrison who accompanied him to Baltimore. Harrison hired a carriage to convey them to Washington, but on the way an accident occurred. Neither man was "materially injured." Braidwood would have remained in Baltimore, but "various inflammatory rumors" led him to expect "further disturbances" and trouble. Harrison was also involved in another accident with a vehicle, which destroyed the carriage and injured him.[37]

Braidwood left Baltimore and traveled to New York, supposedly to search for deaf children willing to relocate to Richmond. While in the city, to Braidwood's "astonishment," he was thrown into jail for Harrison's debt. The situation, aggravated by the Englishman's "folly" and his "miserable and distracted mind," forced him to turn to Bolling to find "that friendship at your hands which will relieve me from my present distress." The debt was five to six hundred dollars. Until the obligation was satisfied, Braidwood would remain "confined in a loathsome Jail," forced to "mingle" with the many poor ragged unfortunates in a "receptacle of despair."[38]

Bolling advised Braidwood to write immediately to the creditor to whom Harrison owed the debt for which Braidwood had been jailed. Braidwood should state that Bolling would meet this person at any time in Richmond to discharge the amount owed. If the man doubted Bolling's responsibility, "let him refer me to any correspondent he may have." Bolling, through this agent, would "give him every necessary assurance." Surely, his reputation would suffice. To Bolling, this plan was the only feasible one for Braidwood's relief and release from custody. Certainly, Bolling would not remit the money to a jail.[39]

Undoubtedly, however, Bolling was now in a financial bind. He had earlier advanced Braidwood $600 for tuition. Now he would have to borrow the necessary cash because his crops were sold, and he would have to resolve the situation without traveling to New York because his plantation duties precluded his leaving. Additionally, his mother, whom he had been visiting at Cobbs, had been "dangerously ill" but now seemed to be recovering. When Bolling arrived home from that visit, he found his wife in "great distress" on account of Braidwood's plight. Bolling promised to send a duplicate of his letter in case it should "miscarry" and to await Braidwood's reply, "in the hope that the arrangement I have suggested may meet the approbation of all the parties concerned." For all of Braidwood's difficulties, Bolling refused to disassociate himself from the Englishman.[40]

A grateful Braidwood arrived at Bolling Hall in late 1812, as war began between the United States and Great Britain. As a private tutor, Braidwood supervised the education of thirteen-year-old William Albert, three-year-old Mary (Polly), and their hearing brother and sister, Thomas and Anne Meade. As an English citizen, however, Braidwood was in an awkward position with the outbreak of war. In March 1813, while yet to be called for military duty, Bolling reported the Englishman's residence to the marshals of Maryland and Virginia as the law required. He asserted that Braidwood was "personally acquainted" with James Monroe (when he was Ambassador to Great Britain). In addition, from President James Madison, Braidwood received "every assurance of safety" in remaining in the United States.[41]

Bolling argued that Madison and Monroe surely considered Braidwood's teaching of "the utmost importance to many unfortunate beings who otherwise would be doomed to a life of ignorance, idleness, and misery." Bolling trusted that no occasion would arise "for removing [Braidwood] from my house where my unfortunate son is making a rapid progress in his education." Braidwood was a "gentleman of liberal education and sentiments and not in the smallest degree inclined" to interfere in the events of the time. If Bolling thought there was any "possibility of his being an injury in any respect to my Country now engaged in a just and necessary conflict with his, no private considerations could prevent my saying so." He assumed "no objection" would arise over Braidwood staying

with him.[42] Bolling's pleadings proved effective, and Braidwood was allowed to continue as a tutor.

   After Braidwood had tutored for one year, Samuel Branch, who had
several friends with deaf offspring, visited Braidwood and inquired
whether he planned to form a school. Branch and his friends were ready
to place their youngsters, six in all, under Braidwood's care "at any
moment and imposed to meet any terms [he] might suggest with liberality." Branch urged him to "extend to such claimants benefits which
[Braidwood] was called upon to give to as many as lay in [his] power."[43]

   Braidwood "candidly stated" his obligations to Bolling in his response
to Branch. He viewed their engagement as "conditionally binding."
Changing his situation without Bolling's "absolute and free concurrence"
was not Braidwood's intention, he wrote. Bound to Bolling by "feelings
honorable and friendly [and] strengthened by sincere regard," Braidwood
said he would meet the Virginian's "every claim." Braidwood believed
that on Bolling's return from the war (Bolling was a captain, later a colonel, in the Goochland County militia), they could converse freely on the
subject, and if any arrangements could be made "compatible" with
Bolling's wishes without "marring" their comfort, he would inform
Branch.[44]

   Braidwood felt that the good intentions demonstrated by his decision
to reside in Bolling's "immediate neighborhood for some years" would
aid his sullied reputation. He already intended to speak with Bolling
about a school, but the conflict with England and Braidwood's proclivity
for drink had intervened. The germination for the idea of locating the first
American school for deaf children at Cobbs had been planted.[45] The relationship between Braidwood and Bolling remained amicable while
Bolling was active in the war. The Englishman kept the Virginian apprised
of events at home, and Bolling dispensed advice and inquired about the
Englishman's health, apparently a veiled reference to his drinking.

   Braidwood's teaching method was relatively guarded. Although
Braidwood believed that deaf children were often physically ill, which retarded their educational progress, he was optimistic about the progress of
the children he taught at Cobbs. William Albert had retained "all he
learnt," previous to his illness. Braidwood then turned critical and as-
sessed the price of oralism and its effects on teachers. The "drudgery of
my profession," he wrote, "which in the instruction of many of the sounds
to be obtained, is great: I happily (I must say unexpectedly) escape."[46]

   Braidwood also called oralism the "most laborious profession perhaps
at this time known." His description of the time required to produce tan-
gible results as "drudgery" summarized the enormous challenge facing

instructors of the deaf who relied on the oral method. Certainly, Braidwood's situation with the Bolling family was almost ideal for the task and its time requirements. America was virgin land when it came to what method should be used in instructing the deaf; there had been no previous schools, which was probably the major reason Braidwood emigrated to the United States. By attaching himself to a prominent Virginia family (especially after his encounters with the law), his shaky reputation was briefly rejuvenated.[47]

Once Braidwood became ensconced at Bolling Hall, word of his special "skill" spread to other areas of Virginia and, indeed, beyond. For example, John McNutt of Fairfield, in Rockbridge County, Virginia, heard about the "foreigner" in Bolling's family from a mutual acquaintance. The Englishman, McNutt had learned, was a "master of the art of teaching the deaf and dumb to read and write." McNutt's inquiry arose from his concern for a sister whose "unfortunate situation" was his excuse for "intruding" on Bolling's notice. In this case, McNutt was unacquainted with Bolling personally, but obviously Bolling's family situation was well known to many. McNutt wondered whether it would be "practical" for Bolling to admit his sister into his school for the "purpose of receiving some instruction from Braidwood," who had "with success taught some to read and write that were deprived of the sense of hearing."[48]

Although little is known about the Cobbs School, which Braidwood eventually opened in Virginia, the routine and pedagogical approach were similar to those developed by his family in Scotland and England. In March 1815, Braidwood began his school at Cobbs with an enrollment of five students: William Albert Bolling, Marcus Flournoy, John M. Scott, John Hancock, and George Lee Tuberville. Also in attendance was Thomas Bolling, Jr., William Albert's deaf uncle. Precisely what type of schedule Braidwood maintained for the pupils is unknown, but surely he emphasized the "drudgery" of articulation and enunciation.

The Demise of the Cobbs School

The isolation of Cobbs and the lack of continuous contact with other adults probably distressed Braidwood and may have contributed to his dissipation and apparent struggle with alcoholism because, in 1816, he left the school. The school's collapse may also have been related to Bolling's lack of financial resources to continue it, even with a few students' parents paying tuition.[49] Cobbs closed in the fall of 1816.

Virginia was now without an institution for deaf students. Braidwood's departure left the Cobbs school's students and their guardians without educational options. Thomas Jefferson had been approached

about moving Cobbs to the University of Virginia, but the former president would have no part of the scheme. He believed the "objects of the
two institutions are fundamentally different." One school emphasized
"science; the other, mere charity." Jefferson compared the proposed at-
tachment of a deaf school to the University of Virginia with "gratuitously
taking a boat in tow, which may impede, but cannot aid the motion of the
principal institution."[50]

One individual who was distressed by the situation was William
Maffit, whose stepson, George L. Tuberville, was a Braidwood pupil.
Maffit arranged for a "respectable man to conduct" George home and pay
Bolling for any money spent. "I now know not what to do with my unfortunate boy," he wrote. Maffit was "truly distressed at the account" Bolling
rendered concerning Braidwood's "conduct" and his "fate." Disturbed by
Braidwood's actions, Maffit thought "his circumstances might be re-
trieved if his habits were correct." Earlier, Braidwood had received the
"required advance" of a six-month payment for board and instruction
that totaled "about $400."[51]

In 1817, Bolling, desperate for some way to educate his deaf children,
rescued Braidwood once more and teamed him with a minister, John
Kirkpatrick, who conducted a school in Manchester, Virginia, near
Richmond. The intention was that the Englishman would instruct the
deaf pupils and train Kirkpatrick in the oral method. By mid-1818,
though, Braidwood's dissipatory habits forced Kirkpatrick to remove
him, thus ending the second attempt to establish a Southern institution
for the deaf. Braidwood, true to form, became a bartender in a Manchester
tavern and died in 1820.[52]

The Northern Endeavor: The American School for the Deaf

As the attempt to found a school for deaf children unraveled in
Virginia, Mason Fitch Cogswell approached the task differently in the
North. After failing to interest Braidwood in locating his school in a major
city, Cogswell, through his well-connected friends who had deaf children,
convinced ministers throughout New England to conduct a census to
identify all who were deaf. They enumerated eighty-four, enough potential students to warrant the establishment of a school. Soliciting funds
from his social and political network, Cogswell accumulated enough
money to send Thomas Hopkins Gallaudet, who had worked with
Cogswell's deaf daughter, Alice, to the British Isles to study and learn
methods for teaching deaf students. Gallaudet would then return to the
United States and implement them.[53]

Supplemental Instruction

Tomás **Rivera** Center

CRJ 3013.902
With Dr. Tillyer

S I of Things

W T H S I

Study groups make it easy to fill in the blanks!!

Questions?
Contact me on blackboard!

S.I. AMANDA

<u>Sessions</u>
Mon. 3:30-4:20pm
Weds. 1:00-1:50pm
Fri. 12:00-12:50pm

<u>Office Hour</u>
Mon. 12:30-1:30pm

<u>Locations</u>
All sessions and office hour
will be held in the TRC
DB 2.114

In 1815, while Braidwood was still at Cobbs, Gallaudet sailed to England. There he encountered the entrenched Braidwood system, steeped in secrecy and focused on profit. The administrators at the Braidwood school wanted Gallaudet to sign a contract, remain several years to learn how to teach oralism, and agree not to pass on to others the tenets of teaching articulation. Gallaudet refused and by happenstance attended an exhibition outside London by some deaf French pupils, led by Abbé Sicard, who impressed the audience with their "lectures" through sign language. Sicard was the head of the Royal Institution for the Deaf in Paris in 1815. Gallaudet knew about the French school of Abbé Sicard from information given to him by Cogswell. Sicard invited Gallaudet to Paris to study at the French school. Gallaudet readily accepted.[54]

At the Paris Institution, Gallaudet convinced Laurent Clerc, formerly a star pupil at the Paris school and now an instructor there, to accompany him back to the states and teach in Connecticut at the planned school. Clerc, who did not speak, taught Gallaudet French Sign Language and fingerspelling on the voyage home, and Gallaudet helped Clerc to learn to read and write English. They arrived in New York in late summer 1816 and immediately began a tour of New England to raise money and public support for the projected academy. Meanwhile, Cogswell and his supporters convinced the Connecticut state legislature to incorporate the school and appropriate $5,000 for its benefit. Although Gallaudet has been accused of being a "benevolent paternalist," in 1817, he, Cogswell, and Clerc, succeeded in launching the Connecticut Asylum for the Education and Instruction of Deaf and Dumb Persons, which became the American School for the Deaf. It is still in existence today.[55]

George Tuberville, one of the former pupils of the Cobbs school, eventually attended the American School, despite his stepfather's concerns about sign language. His stepfather, Maffit, favored articulation but did not know whether George could acquire that skill because he was now in his early teens. He believed that the method was "practicable in infancy when the organs are pliable" but that it had "never been accomplished after they have attained the rigidity of Manhood" and asserted that Braidwood's method of instruction was "much preferable to that of the French" (meaning sign language). Maffit studied Abbé Sicard's system and was "persuaded that he can succeed only with scholars of uncommon genius." This misguided opinion was confirmed by individuals who had "witnessed [Sicard's] success." Nevertheless, on May 1, 1818, George Tuberville enrolled at Hartford's American School for the Deaf.[56]

Maffit's discussion of this decision reflects on Braidwood, his conduct at Cobbs, and the contrast between the Virginia and Connecticut schools.

Maffit wrote that his stepson had acquired bad traits from the Englishman, "very expensive habits." Tuberville's estate, although large, claimed
Maffit, "would hardly have been competent to his support" if these habits
persisted. After obtaining information from Hartford, Maffit decided to
place George "among a plain and economical people." From a member of
Congress, he learned that the "family of the Deaf and Dumb" at Hartford
(the American School for the Deaf) was the "most interesting that he had
ever seen."[57] Thomas Hopkins Gallaudet and Laurent Clerc, the two major teachers at the American School, were described as "prodigies of genius and humanity." The asylum had three instructors, was preparing a
fourth, and had thirty pupils. With this ratio, each instructor could "exclusively" devote himself to "only" ten students. Maffit hoped, however,
that the system of instruction might be improved through "combining the
advantage of the English with those of the French."[58]

Radically Different Fates of Two Schools

The contrasting personalities between Braidwood and Bolling, on the
one hand, and Gallaudet and Clerc, on the other, do not adequately explain the radically different fates of the first two schools for deaf children
in North America. The wider context is also important. The North and the
South diverged significantly in social, political, and economic matters.
The Southern economy was essentially agrarian, and the Bolling family
was among hundreds of successful slaveholding families in Virginia on
which the plantation lifestyle was dependent. Indeed, they used part of
the proceeds from the sale of forty-one slaves to finance debt incurred for
Braidwood's tuition charges in Scotland. The New England economy, in
contrast, was based on merchant trade with England. Thriving seaports in
Boston, New York, Baltimore, and Philadelphia, helped ensure that economy's success.

Religious revivals swept both North and South by the early nineteenth
century, but it was the ministers in the North who successfully converted
these powerful sentiments—as if they were chosen by God—to usher deaf
children to schools to learn how to communicate with God. Thomas
Hopkins Gallaudet was one of the ministers affected by the revivals. He
believed that God, as the supreme being, could understand infinite languages, and the quickest way for a deaf person to learn a language, and
therefore have an opportunity for salvation, was through signs. Reaching
the souls of deaf children would not be delayed with signs, unlike with
the oral approach, which Braidwood once termed "laborious." Once deaf

children mastered sign language, they could immediately "communicate" with God through their hands.

Braidwood's insatiable thirst for financial comfort led him to one of Virginia's premier families, the Bollings, who needed to hire a private tutor to provide an education for their deaf offspring. Braidwood had discovered a family who would readily provide funds without significant objection. However, the personal contractual arrangements did not provide a solid foundation on which to build a school nor did it lead to having additional teachers to relieve the "drudgery" of teaching. In contrast, Cogswell had surveyed the need for a deaf school by identifying deaf children in the region and had cultivated support from the state government while Gallaudet had seen fit from the beginning to prepare teachers.

Furthermore, the physical and geographical locations of the two schools are worthy of consideration. The Connecticut school was in a more populated area where students had easier transportation access. The Cobbs School was distant, isolated, and rural: the school was surrounded by acres of plantation land with slaves working the soil. The agrarian economy of Virginia was bolstered by cash crops made possible through slave labor.

At the Hartford school, which was far more cosmopolitan than its Cobbs counterpart, Cogswell could tap into Hartford's philanthropy to assist the school. If this resource was limited, Cogswell did not have to look far. Boston's wealthy merchants and businessmen provided another potential source of donation revenue. In contrast, although there were wealthy Virginia planters in the vicinity of the Cobb School, the vast majority of the state's white men were yeoman farmers with few, if any, slaves. The planters did not have the luxury of having an extended network that one might find in the more populated and urban areas.

As the private Southern oral schools at Cobbs and Manchester, Virginia, collapsed, the public institution in the North thrived and became a model for all other state institutions for deaf education. When the Connecticut Asylum opened its doors on April 15, 1817, it enrolled thirty-one students, mostly older than age fifteen, and the majority were prelingually deaf. The Cobbs School, in contrast, had only seven pupils. Maffit's decision to place his stepson "among a plain and economical people" in Hartford after the Braidwood disaster tells us much about the enrollment policies of the American School as opposed to those practiced by Bolling. But Maffit's perspective was wide of the mark when he wrote that the English system (articulation) was much preferable to the French approach because the latter method could "succeed only with scholars of uncommon genius." In fact, the reverse was true. Larger numbers could be truly educated through manualism than through oralism.

Aside from the differences between the way the Cobbs School and the American School approached the instruction of deaf children, the schools' foundations rested on contrasting philosophies and financial models. Bolling believed such undertakings should be private endeavors without state interference or support. Moreover, he believed that by adopting the oral method, the deafened children of the planter class would become more "normal." Cogswell, however, understood that a permanent school could be maintained only through consistent financial support from the state, augmented by donations from wealthy benefactors. Unlike Bolling, Cogswell also realized that deaf people already practiced sign language and would do so naturally and inevitably. The American School gained the imprimatur of the Connecticut legislation, enhanced the development of a standardized form of visual language, which is now known as American Sign Language, and became a magnet for deaf individuals throughout New England.

The American School model spread throughout the nation and remained the standard until it came under assault by Alexander Graham Bell and others starting in the 1870s. Although this oralist movement would control residential schools and the teaching of deaf people until the 1960s, it has once again been superseded by instruction in American Sign Language. The Deaf President Now student revolution at Gallaudet University in 1988 confirmed the benefits of American Sign Language, the value of the American School for the Deaf, and the reemergence of the American Deaf community as a force.

Notes

1. For a sampling of the North-South difference or similarity theses, see Edward Pessen, "How Different from Each Other Were the Antebellum North and South?," *American Historical Review* 86 (1980): 1119–49; James M. McPherson, "Antebellum Southern Exceptionalism: A New Look at an Old Question," *Civil War History* 29 (September 1983): 230–44 (also in *Drawn With the Sword: Reflections on the American Civil War* [New York: Oxford University Press, 1996], 3–23); Marc Egnal, *Divergent Paths: How Culture and Institutions Shaped North American Growth* (New York: Oxford University Press, 1996); Peter A. Coclanis, "Tracking the Economic Divergence of the North and South," *Southern Cultures* 6 (Winter 2000): 82–103.

2. Harlan Lane, *When the Mind Hears: A History of the Deaf* (New York: Random House, 1984), 3–154. Also see the relevant essays in Renate Fischer and Harlan Lane, eds., *Looking Back: A Reader on the History of Deaf Communities and Their Sign Languages* (Hamburg: Signum Press, 1993); John Vickrey Van Cleve, ed., *Deaf History Unveiled: Interpretations from the New Scholarship* (Washington, D.C.: Gallaudet University Press,

1993); Susan Plann, *A Silent Minority: Deaf Education in Spain, 1550–1835* (Berkeley: University of California Press, 1997); Anne T. Quartararo, "The Perils of Assimilation in Modern France: The Deaf Community, Social Status, and Educational Opportunity, 1815–1870," *Journal of Social History*, 29 (Fall 1995): 5–23; Susan Burch, "Transcending Revolutions: The Tsars, the Soviets, and Deaf Culture," *Journal of Social History*, 34 (Winter 2000): 393–401; Douglas C. Baynton, *Forbidden Signs: American Culture and the Campaign against Sign Language* (Chicago: University of Chicago Press, 1996); Barry A. Crouch, "The People of the Eye," *Reviews in American History* 26 (June 1998): 402–7.

3. Nora Groce, *Everyone Here Spoke Sign Language: Hereditary Deafness on Martha's Vineyard* (Cambridge, Mass.: Harvard University Press, 1985); Barry A. Crouch, "A Deaf Utopia?: Martha's Vineyard, 1700–1900," *Sign Language Studies* 53 (Winter 1986): 381–87; Francis Green, *Vox Oculis Subjecta: A Dissertation on the Most Curious and Important Art of Imparting Speech, and the Knowledge of Language to the Naturally Deaf* (London: Benjamin White, 1783); John Vickrey Van Cleve and Barry A. Crouch, *A Place of Their Own: Creating the Deaf Community in America* (Washington, D.C.: Gallaudet University Press, 1989), 21.

4. James S. Patton, "John Bolling, 1761–83," Biographical File, TheValentine Richmond History Center Richmond; "William Bolling," Biographical File, Gallaudet University Archives, Washington, D.C.; Peter W. Jackson, *Britain's Deaf Heritage* (Edinburgh: Pentland Press, 1990), 21, 40. See also *The Scots Magazine* (Edinburgh), for January 1766, August 1767, and July 1769, for additional information on Braidwood's school. Also, see Jan Branson and Don Miller, *Damned for Their Difference: The Cultural Construction of Deaf People as Disabled* (Washington, D.C.: Gallaudet University Press, 2002), 100–104.

5. John Bolling to "My dear Mama," November 26, 1771, and March 2, 1775, both in the *National Deaf Mute Gazette*, 1 (November 1867), 14. Apparently, the originals of these letters no longer exist.

6. Ibid.

7. Samuel A. Johnson, *A Journey to the Western Islands of Scotland* (London: W. Strahan and T. Cadell, 1775), 254–55.

8. Ibid. Sir Walter Scott also discusses the Braidwood Academy in his novel *The Heart of Midlothian* (Boston: DeWolfe, Fiske, & Co., 1830), which was part of the Waverly Novel series. Branson and Miller contend in *Damned for Their Difference* that Thomas Bolling signed. It is not clear whether Thomas Bolling used "home signs" from his Virginia farm or whether he learned British Sign Language at the Braidwood Academy. The distinction, however, is the incorporation of signs in instruction. Simply because Thomas Bolling knew signs does not necessarily indicate that Braidwood actually used sign language in educating Bolling.

9. Job Turner, "A Notice of Thomas Bolling, the First Educated Mute in America," *The Silent World* (Washington, D.C.) 3 (July 15, 1873): 3–4.

10. Thomas Bolling to Thomas Braidwood, October 1783, in *Braidwood vs. Bolling*, 1797, Federal Circuit Court, Ended Cases (unrestored), B-C, Box 39, The Valentine Richmond History Center.

11. Mrs. Amos G. Draper to Percival Hall (President, Gallaudet College), October 28, 1915, Amos G. Draper Papers, Gallaudet University Archives, Washington, D.C.; Turner, "A Notice of Thomas Bolling," 3–4.

12. Thomas Bolling to Thomas Braidwood, October 1783, in *Braidwood vs. Bolling*, 1797, Federal Circuit Court, Box 39, The Valentine Richmond History Center.

13. *Braidwood vs. Bolling*, Judgment, January 26, July 18, July 22, September 9, October 23, December 11, 1797, Federal Circuit Court, Box 39, The Valentine Richmond History Center. Interest was computed at five percent from September 9, 1797, until the

full amount was paid. Braidwood may have asked for the amount based on the higher tuition rate to pressure Bolling into a final and definite settlement. It is obvious there were several judgments against the Virginian, and he effectively postponed payment for a period of four years. Whether it was straightened circumstances on Bolling's part or a suspicion that Braidwood's demands were somewhat exorbitant are possible considerations with respect to the final settlement.

14. Braidwood vs. Bolling, Judgment, January 26, July 18, July 22, September 9, October 23, December 11, 1797, Federal Circuit Court, Box 39, The Valentine Richmond History Center.

15. Ibid.

16. Barry A. Crouch, "William Bolling," in *Dictionary of Virginia Biography* (Richmond: Library of Virginia, 2001), 2:72–73.

17. Draper to Hall, October 28, 1915, Draper Papers, Gallaudet University Archives.

18. "Braidwood's Advertisement of His Proposed Baltimore School, 'Institution for the Deaf and Dumb and For Removing Impediments in Speech,'" *The Maryland Bulletin* 61 (December 1940): 38; Archibald Geikie, "Brief Sketch of the Life of Water Geikie, Esq., R.A.S., Edinburgh, Scotland," *American Annals of the Deaf and Dumb* 7 (July 1855): 232; Jackson, *Britain's Deaf Heritage*, 40–42.

19. John Braidwood draft, June 1817; James Pleasants to William Bolling, March 5, 1812, William Bolling Papers, Manuscript Department, William R. Perkins Library, Duke University, Durham, North Carolina; John Randolph to John S. G. Randolph, July 3, 1806, James H. Whitty Papers, Manuscript Department, William R. Perkins Library, Duke University; Laurent Clerc, "Notice of the Late St. George Randolph,—With Other Reminiscences," *American Annals of the Deaf and Dumb* (January 1858): 51–54; Betty Miller Unterberger, "The First Attempt to Establish an Oral School for the Deaf and Dumb in the United States," *Journal of Southern History* 13 (November 1947): 557, n. 3; *Biographical Directory of the American Congress, 1774–1971* (Washington, D.C.: Government Printing Office, 1971), 550.

20. John Braidwood to William Bolling, March 5, 1812, Bolling Papers, Duke University.

21. *National Intelligencer* (Washington, D.C.), March 14, 1812, p. 2; *The Weekly Register* (Baltimore), 2 (March 21, 1812): 53–54; Mason Fitch Cogswell (Hartford) to John Braidwood, April 20, 1812, in *Father and Daughter: A Collection of Cogswell Family Letters and Diaries (1772–1830)*, ed. Grace Cogswell Root (West Hartford, Conn.: American School for the Deaf, 1924), 66–67.

22. *National Intelligencer*, March 14, 1812, p. 2; *The Weekly Register*, 2 (March 21, 1812): 53–54.

23. William Bolling to John Braidwood, March 17, 181[2], Bolling Letterbook, Valentine Museum; also reprinted in *The Maryland Bulletin*, 61 (December 1940): 37.

24. Ibid.

25. William Bolling to John Braidwood, March 17, 181[2] and William Bolling to James Pleasants, March 17, 1812, both in Bolling Letterbook, The Valentine Richmond History Center.

26. John Braidwood to William Bolling, April 1, April 23 (Norfolk), and August 15 (New York), 1812, Bolling Papers, Duke University.

27. Mason Fitch Cogswell to John Braidwood (Washington, D.C.), April 20, 1812, in *Father and Daughter*, 66–67. Alice became deafened by meningitis when she was two, but "after she had begun to talk."

28. Ibid.

29. Ibid.

30. Branson and Miller, *Damned for Their Difference,* 101. They argue that Braidwood was "far from oralist in method or orientation" (123). See also "Thomas Braidwood," in *Dictionary of National Biography* (London: Oxford University Press, 1921), 2:1107–8.

31. *Enquirer* (Richmond), June 2, 1812, p. 1.

32. Ibid.

33. William Bolling to John Braidwood, August 9, 1812, Bolling Letterbook, The Valentine Richmond History Center.

34. John Braidwood to William Bolling, April 1, April 23 (Norfolk), and August 15 (New York), 1812, Bolling Papers, Duke University; William Bolling to James Pleasants Jr., March 17, 1812, Bolling Letterbook, The Valentine Richmond History Center.

35. John Braidwood to William Bolling, August 15, 1812 (New York), Bolling Papers, Duke University.

36. Ibid.

37. Ibid.

38. Ibid.

39. William Bolling to John Braidwood, August 22, 1812, Bolling Letterbook, The Valentine Richmond History Center.

40. Ibid.

41. Ibid; William Bolling to Andrew Moore (Marshall of Virginia), March 21, 1813, Bolling Letterbook, The Valentine Richmond History Center.

42. William Bolling to Andrew Moore, March 21, 1813, The Valentine Richmond History Center.

43. John Braidwood to William Bolling, August 28, 1813, Bolling Papers, Duke University.

44. Ibid.

45. Ibid.

46. John Braidwood to William Bolling, September 12, 1813, and draft of letter by John Braidwood, [June 1817], both in Bolling Papers, Duke University.

47. Ibid.

48. John McNutt to William Bolling, May 18, 1814, Bolling Papers Duke University.

49. "William Albert Bolling Manuscript School Book," Volta Bureau (Washington, D.C.); Richmond *Enquirer,* (February 15, 1815, p. 1.)

50. Thomas Jefferson to Joseph C. Cabell, January 24, 1816, in *Early History of the University of Virginia, as Contained in the Letters of Thomas Jefferson and Joseph C. Cabell* (Richmond: J. W. Randolph, 1856), 49.

51. William Maffit to William Bolling, October 8, 1816, Bolling Papers, Duke University. Braidwood had the audacity to write Maffit "stating the circumstances of his failure, and begging" him to "suspend his opinion as to its cause until I should again hear from him."

52. *Enquirer* (Richmond), June 27, 1817, p. 4; Van Cleve and Crouch, *A Place of Their Own,* 27; O'Dell, *Chesterfield County* 302.

53. See the Mason Fitch Cogswell Papers and the Laurent Clerc Papers, Beineke Memorial Library (Yale University); see also Thomas Hopkins and Edward Miner Gallaudet Papers, Manuscript Division, Library of Congress.

54. Ibid. For a marvelous essay on Gallaudet, his religious philosophy, and his promotion of "Natural Language," see Jill Lepore, *A Is for American: Letters and Other Characters in the Newly United States* (New York: Alfred A. Knopf, 2002), 91–110.

55. Archives of the American Asylum, American School for the Deaf, Hartford; James John Fernandes, "The Gate to Heaven: T. H. Gallaudet and the Rhetoric of the Deaf Education Movement" (Ph.D. diss., University of Michigan, 1980); Phyllis

Valentine, "Thomas Hopkins Gallaudet: Benevolent Paternalism and the Origins of the American Asylum," in *Deaf History Unveiled*, 53–73. For more detail, see Van Cleve and Crouch, *A Place of Their Own*, 30–45.

56. Maffit to William Bolling, December 5, 1817, and May 10, 1818, Bolling Papers, Duke University. By this time, the Hartford institution had been open for eight months. See *Reports for the American Asylum for the Deaf and Dumb*, vol. 1, *1817–1838*. See the *Third Report of the Directors of the Connecticut Asylum, May 15, 1819* (Hartford: Hudson and Co. Printers, 1819), 11; See also the *Tenth Report of the Directors of the Connecticut Asylum for the Deaf and Dumb, May 13, 1826* (Hartford, Conn.: W. Hudson and L. Skinner, Printers,1826), 8.

57. Maffit to William Bolling, May 10, 1818, Bolling Papers, Duke University.

58. Ibid.

3

Origins of the American Deaf-World: Assimilating and Differentiating Societies and Their Relation to Genetic Patterning

Harlan Lane, Richard C. Pillard, and Mary French

Editor's Introduction

Harlan Lane and his collaborators have used the intensive study of a few deaf families in New England to trace the rise of "class consciousness," or the awareness deaf people have of themselves as a group apart from others in society, in the middle of the nineteenth century. They argue that genetically dominant deafness leads to class consciousness, as exemplified by the Brown-Swett families of New Hampshire, whereas recessive deafness, which characterized Martha's Vineyard, does not produce the same class aware-ness. Apart from this central thesis, the authors' meticulously recon-structed narratives of particular deaf lives are remarkably rich, and they of-fer insightful views of the ways of American deaf people as they began to coalesce into a recognizable group.

T he Deaf-World in the United States has major roots in a triangle of New England Deaf communities that flourished early in the nineteenth century: Henniker, New Hampshire; Martha's Vineyard, Massachusetts;

In this article, the authors use capital *D* in *Deaf* throughout because they are writing about people who are culturally Deaf. "*Deaf-World*" is an English gloss on the ASL name that culture uses to refer to itself.

This revised chapter was originally published as "Origins of the American Deaf-World: Assimilating and Differentiating Societies and Their Relation to Genetic Patterning," *Sign Language Studies* 1(1): 17–44.

and Sandy River Valley, Maine. The social fabric of these communities differed, a reflection of language and marriage practices that were underpinned, we hypothesize, by differences in genetic patterning. To evaluate that hypothesis, the authors of this article use local records and newspapers, genealogies, the silent press, Edward Fay's census of Deaf marriages,[1] and Alexander Graham Bell's notebooks to illuminate the Henniker Deaf community for the first time and to build on prior work concerning the Vineyard community.[2]

Henniker, New Hampshire

The first great American Deaf leader was Thomas Brown (1804–1886), who was born in Henniker, New Hampshire, thirteen years before the American Asylum for the Deaf and Dumb opened in Hartford, Connecticut, and who died in Henniker six years after the Congress of Milan. We begin with his story.

Thomas Brown's grandfather, also named Thomas, lived in Stow, Massachusetts, with his wife, eight daughters, and a son, Nahum—the first, as far as anyone knew, Deaf-Mute in the family (see figure 1). The senior Thomas Brown was the grandson of Jabez Brown (see figure 1), who emigrated from England and settled in Concord, Massachusetts. Jabez's son, Joseph, moved to Stow, where his son, Thomas, was born and raised, took up the trade of blacksmith, and in 1763 married Persis Gibson.

In 1785, fearing debtor's prison, senior Thomas Brown set out by himself for Henniker, a virtual wilderness some hundred miles away where his wife's family, former residents of Stow, had moved. Thomas had contracted a hard currency debt that he was unable to pay because of the rapidly depreciating value of colonial currency. His troubles stemmed from an abundance of "fiat money," money printed by the colonies during the American Revolution that was not backed by coin. Because too much of this money was printed, Thomas's money lost its value. According to his son, Nahum, he once took a bushel of fiat money and dumped it into a grain bin in the attic.[3] Increasingly, lenders wanted repayment in British gold, pounds, or other hard currency. Thomas, not being able to repay his debt, fled to Henniker.

On arriving, Thomas made a clearing and built a log cabin that stood for nearly a century and came to be known as the Brown House. Then, according to one account, he sent word to Nahum, his thirteen-year-old Deaf son, to hitch two yoke of oxen to a sled, load the furniture and food, bundle his mother and sisters atop the load, and, armed with a goad, prod

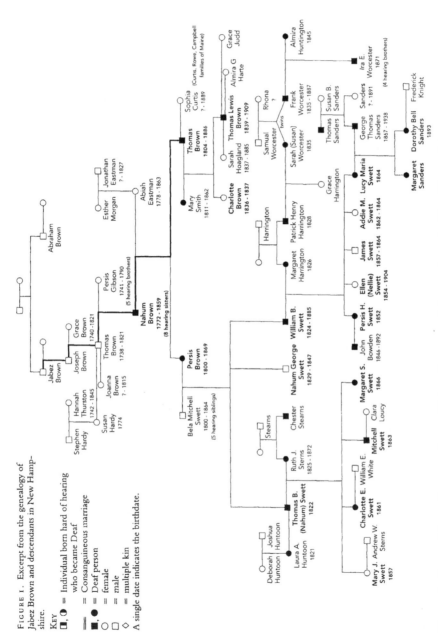

FIGURE 1. Excerpt from the genealogy of Jabez Brown and descendants in New Hampshire.

KEY
■, ● = Individual born hard of hearing who became Deaf
= Consanguineous marriage
■ = Deaf person
○ = female
□ = male
◇ = multiple kin
A single date indicates the birthdate.

Figure 1. Excerpt from the genealogy of Jabez Brown and descendants in New Hampshire.

the oxen 100 miles through the snow to Henniker (it is not clear how he would have told Nahum to do this challenging task).[4] According to another account, Nahum preceded his father to Henniker and was living with his uncle; it was his father, Thomas, who brought the family.[5]

The contemporaries of Thomas Brown Sr. described him as smart, energetic, and fond of books; in later years, he held minor elected posts. His eight daughters—tall, blue-eyed, and good-looking—were said to be brilliant, witty, and well educated; most became teachers. Neighbors and relatives had a harder time judging Nahum's intellect because he was Deaf; he was called plucky, skillful as an axeman and hunter, a model farmer, and a first-rate teamster of oxen and horses. Of course, no one thought of his becoming a teacher or even of his going to school.

Curiously, the first deed of land to the Browns that is recorded was 100 acres to Nahum, who was only seventeen at the time. Perhaps his father could not afford to buy land some four years after moving to Henniker, and it was Nahum's mother's family that bought the land and gave it as a gift to Nahum, endeavoring to provide for their Deaf grandchild. The elder Thomas Brown died when he was eighty-two—old enough to outlive two of his three wives; to attend the marriage of his son Nahum to Abiah Eastman, a hearing woman of the town; to witness the birth of their daughter, Persis, in 1800, and their son, Thomas, in 1804, both Deaf; and to hear of the opening of the first school for Deaf students—in Hartford in 1817. His grandson Thomas would enroll there five years later.

As a young man in Henniker, Nahum did not wear shoes; to chop wood, he stood on warm planks in the doorway of his family cabin. The many chores he performed as the sole male child with eight sisters prepared him for a life of responsibility and hard labor. According to his son Thomas, he worked hard from dawn to dusk and was known as a good parent and neighbor.[6] He never learned to read or write, however, and communicated in pantomime or "natural sign." His wife served as his interpreter and aided him in activities such as buying and selling cattle.

Like his father, Nahum had a long life, dying at age eighty-seven. He raised his two Deaf children, Persis and Thomas and saw them marry and raise his five grandchildren, three of them Deaf. The following generation brought nine great-grandchildren, five of them Deaf. In an era when being born Deaf was most often attributed to maternal fright,[7] Nahum and his family must surely have been puzzled.[8]

Nahum saw his son Thomas become educated, among the first Deaf-Mutes in the nation to do so, and emerge as a preeminent Deaf leader, beginning at mid-century. Five years before Nahum's death, a group of Thomas's friends gathered in the Brown household to draft a constitution for the first enduring Deaf organization in the United States, the New England Gallaudet Association of Deaf Mutes. Nahum's sight had begun to fail. He suffered severe headaches and became blind first in one eye and then the other. "During his helpless and blind situation," son Thomas related, "he would sign for [us] to come and see what he wanted. With his arms moving slowly, he understood the movement of our hands."[9] Just before his death, he signaled for his wife to come near; with her hands on him, he passed peacefully away.

When Thomas Brown was eighteen—a slender, powerful man with a large head, gray eyes, and a facial tic from a childhood encounter with an ox—he enrolled at the American Asylum. The town of Henniker annually voted funds to assist Thomas in paying his educational expenses until the state legislature undertook to pay for Deaf-Mute pupils from New Hampshire.[10] Thomas—"shrewd, wild but not vicious"—and his sister Persis, four years older, were both considered bright and both could no doubt have attended the school, but Persis was bound by a marriage contract to a hearing carpenter from Henniker, Bela Mitchell Swett, and was not free to go.[11]

Thomas studied under the founders of American Deaf education, the Deaf Frenchman, Laurent Clerc, and hearing American, Thomas Gallaudet, and under a hearing intellectual leader of the profession, Harvey Peet, who would later direct the New York School for the Deaf.[12] Thomas, we are told, was an excellent student; at the completion of his five-year course, he agreed to stay on for two years as monitor and carpentry instructor. However, at the end of that period, now twenty-five years old, he declined an offer from the Ohio School for the Deaf to become a teacher and returned instead to Henniker to help his parents work their 123 acres. (After the death of his father and a protracted family wrangle over the settlement of Thomas Sr.'s estate which he had left to his third wife, Nahum had sold his house and land in what later became the center of town and had moved to a farm in West Henniker in 1825 while his son Thomas was away at school in Hartford.)

In view of Thomas's tireless efforts in later years to organize Deaf people, to honor their leaders past and present, and to promote their interests, one wonders to what extent and in what ways his years at the American Asylum developed his early consciousness of Deaf people as a distinct social group. The Central Society of the Deaf in Paris, with its annual banquets honoring Deaf language, history, and leaders, began shortly after Thomas left school, so he could not have learned about it while he was a pupil of Clerc's, although no doubt he learned of it subsequently because it was clear to American educators of Deaf students that their methods derived from the French, and transatlantic visits were made in both directions.

Perhaps the sense of Deaf people as a distinct group was part of the milieu at the American Asylum in the 1820s. After all, a single language was emerging that connected Deaf people despite wide differences among them in region, family circumstances, isolation, and former methods of communication; with it, a sense of we-who-use-this-language might naturally have emerged. Indeed, the first initiative for creating a Deaf state was organized by a group of seniors at the American Asylum just two years after Thomas left.[13] It was, however, short lived.

Chilmark, Massachusetts

One of the scattered enclaves of Deaf people that were gathered and to some extent amalgamated by the schooling of their number at the American Asylum was the Deaf community of Martha's Vineyard; it was indeed the largest single source of pupils at the asylum for several years. While at school, Thomas met Mary Smith, whose family came from the Vineyard, where Deaf people—especially in some remote communities "up island" such as Tisbury and Chilmark—were quite common. Three years after his return to his father's farm in Henniker, Thomas made the journey to the coast, where he took a boat to the Vineyard, six miles off the Massachusetts shore, and then traveled a day on horseback to arrive at the village of Chilmark, where he and Mary were married (April 1, 1832) in the presence of her many Deaf and hearing relatives and friends.

Mary Smith's mother, Sally Cottle, was hearing; she was the daughter of Silas Cottle (hearing) and Jerusha Tilton (Deaf). Jerusha's mother and father (Mary's great-grandparents) were cousins and descendants of Governor Thomas Mayhew, who bought Martha's Vineyard in 1640 from the two patentees under royal charter then disputing ownership of the island. Jerusha's father, a Tilton, also traced his island ancestry back to one Samuel Tilton, who had come to the Vineyard in 1673. Because the Tiltons early intermarried with the Skiffes, Mary was also descended from James Skiffe, who in 1699 purchased land on the Vineyard, settled in Tisbury, and sold the remaining tracts there to friends. Jerusha's maternal great-grandmother was James Skiffe's daughter (see figure 2 for Mary's maternal ancestry).

Mary's father, Mayhew Smith, was hearing, but her paternal grandfather, Elijah Smith, was Deaf and married a hearing woman; he was descended from the island's first Smith, John Smith, who arrived in 1653 (see figure 3 for Mary's paternal family tree). Mary had eight hearing siblings

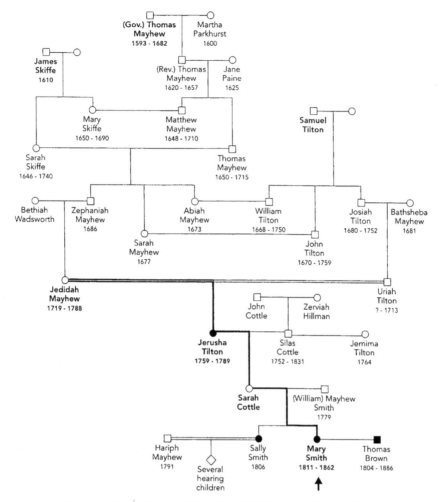

FIGURE 2. Excerpt from the Mayhew-Tilton-Skiffe-Lambert pedigrees as they relate to Mary Brown's maternal ascendants on Martha's Vineyard. Mary Smith, the wife of Thomas Brown, is marked by an arrow.

KEY

◨, ◐	=	Individual born hard of hearing who became Deaf
═══	=	Consanguineous marriage
■, ●	=	Deaf person
○	=	female
□	=	male
◇	=	multiple kin

A single date indicates the birthdate.

Figure 2. Excerpt from the Mayhew-Tilton-Skiffe-Lambert pedigrees as they relate to Mary Brown's maternal ascendants on Martha's Vineyard. Mary Smith, the wife of Thomas Brown, is marked by an arrow.

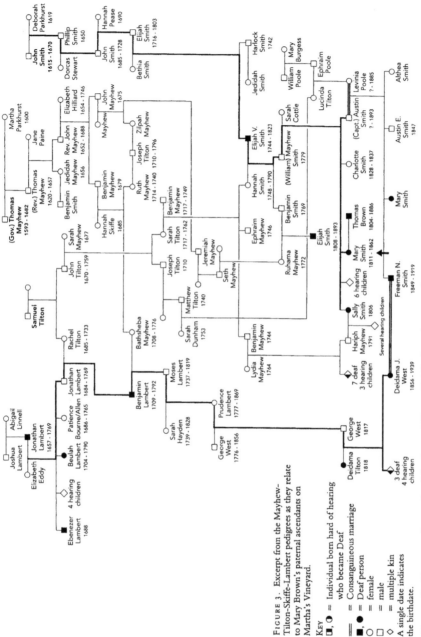

FIGURE 3. Excerpt from the Mayhew-Tilton-Skiffe-Lambert pedigrees as they relate to Mary Brown's paternal ascendants on Martha's Vineyard.

KEY

■, ● = Individual born hard of hearing who became Deaf

= Consanguineous marriage

●, ■ = Deaf person

○ = female

□ = male

◇ = multiple kin

A single date indicates the birthdate.

Figure 3. Excerpt from the Mayhew-Tilton-Skiffe-Lambert pedigrees as they relate to Mary Brown's paternal ascendants on Martha's Vineyard.

and one older Deaf sister, Sally, who also attended the American Asylum. Sally married a hearing cousin, Hariph Mayhew, who had seven Deaf and three hearing siblings. Mary's brother, Capt. Austin Smith, married Levinia Poole (she was hearing and also descended from Samuel Tilton); they had four children, two hearing and two Deaf. One of their Deaf children, Freeman, married a Deaf cousin, Deidama West. (There is no record of the other three children marrying.) Deidama had three Deaf siblings and four who were hearing. Deidama's parents (mother, Deaf; father, hearing) were distant cousins, both descended from Gov. Thomas Mayhew, and her father was descended from the first recorded Deaf person on the island, Jonathan Lambert, a carpenter who arrived from Barnstable in 1694.

In her work on the Vineyard Deaf population, Groce identified seventy-two Deaf individuals, of whom sixty-three could trace their ancestry to James Skiffe, thirty-two to Samuel Tilton, and nine to Jonathan Lambert.[14] Most of the Deaf people on the island had all three of these colonists in their pedigrees. Remarkably, Groce found that all three families were linked before they arrived on the Vineyard. In 1634, a minister named Lothrop and some 200 members of his congregation and their servants, all from parishes in an area in the English county of Kent known as the Weald, arrived in Boston harbor. They made their way to Scituate, where half the population was from the Weald, and then to Barnstable on Cape Cod. In 1670, several of these families moved to the Vineyard when James Skiffe, who was from Kent, sold land in Tisbury. In the ensuing decades, more of these families—Tiltons, Lamberts, and others—moved across Vineyard Sound, settling in the Chilmark area.[15] Because of the very early appearance of Deaf people on the island and because not all the known Deaf Vineyarders can be traced to a common Vineyard ancestor, Groce concludes that the island's Deaf heritage, and thus Mary Smith's, originated in the Weald and arrived on the island with the colonizing families.

The colonizers were drawn to the Vineyard by availability of farmland, the long growing season, the surrounding sea that abounded in lobster and fish, and the numerous ponds, where game birds were to be found, along with fish and shellfish of vast variety. The sandy soil was adapted to raising sheep. The Indians were friendly and taught the islanders how to catch whales—nearly every family on the Vineyard had a member aboard a whaler by the time of Thomas's wedding there.[16] In 1700, 400 people lived on the Vineyard; the population stopped growing about 1800 at some 3,000. Not surprisingly for this relatively isolated community whose ancestors were from the same parishes, most people married someone to whom they were already related and who was from their own village on the island.[17] A symptom of this practice was the proliferation of the same family names: An 1850 census counted 132 Mayhews and eighty-seven Tiltons in Tisbury and Chilmark.[18] In 1807, thirty-two names composed three-fourths of the island population![19]

Mary Smith's marriage to a man from off-island was thus an anomaly, one brought about by the opening of the American Asylum and the desire of families on the Vineyard to see their Deaf children educated. The number of Deaf people gradually rose, peaking at forty-five close to the time of Thomas's marriage. Groce estimates that, later in the nineteenth century, one in every 155 people on the Vineyard was born Deaf (0.7 percent), almost twenty times the estimate for the nation at large (one in 2,730, or 0.04 percent).[20] An 1830 census found twelve Deaf people in Chilmark; no doubt Mary Smith was one of them. The town's population was 694; hence, 1.7 percent of the town was Deaf whereas only 0.01 percent of the population in the neighboring islands was Deaf—a ratio of more than 100 to one.[21]

The marriage of Thomas Brown and Mary Smith was anomalous in a second sense: Unlike the practice on the mainland, most Deaf people on the island married hearing people. On the mainland, only about 20 percent of Deaf people's marriages were to hearing people; on the Vineyard it was closer to 65 percent, and it was even higher before the opening of the American Asylum.[22] The high rate of mixed marriages on the Vineyard was probably a reflection of, and contributor to, a broader feature of life on the island—the blending of Deaf and hearing lives.

Like Mary Smith (and her Deaf grandmother, Jerusha), most children born Deaf on the Vineyard had two hearing parents as well as many hearing siblings, the more so because birth rates were high on the island.[23] Another reflection of, and contributor to, this blending was the widespread use of a sign language among both Deaf and hearing people (no doubt with varying degrees of fluency).[24] The language may have originally been British Sign Language brought over by the colonizers: When Martha's Vineyard signs that had been elicited from elderly hearing residents in 1977 were presented to a British Deaf signer, he identified 40 percent of the signs as British Sign Language cognates. (An ASL informant found 22 percent overlap.)[25] Twelve generations have passed since Jonathan Lambert settled on the Vineyard, so Martha's Vineyard sign language has had lots of time to diverge from its origins, the more so because most Deaf children, like Mary Smith, were sent to the American Asylum where they encountered other sign language practices, and most, unlike Mary, returned to the island.

Bahan and Poole-Nash maintain that Deaf people on the Vineyard were thoroughly assimilated, and similar to Deaf people in the Mayan community studied by Johnson,[26] they valued their village more than they valued the company of other Deaf people: "Being Deaf itself is irrelevant, as Deaf people have access to everyone in the village."[27] In accord with this "village-first" value in assimilative societies, the Mayan villagers, according to Johnson, tended to identify first with their family, then with the village, and then with Mayan society. When Johnson gave a party for all the Deaf people in the village and their families, he learned that it was the first event in the village that singled out Deaf people. Similarly, Groce relates that, on the Vineyard, "[a]ll these [Deaf] people were included in all aspects of daily life from their earliest childhood. . . . One of the most striking aspects of this research is the fact that rather than being remembered as a group, every one of the Deaf islanders who is remembered is remembered as a unique individual."[28]

Mary Smith would find her life quite changed when she took up residence on the mainland in the intensely Deaf Brown family, far from her hearing family, numerous relatives, and friends on the island. She decided to take with her some remembrances of her island home—a whalebone, some big beautiful seashells, and shark teeth with scrimshaw sailor carvings on them.[29] And then Mary and Thomas began the trek to Henniker. Their descendants would have the combined Deaf heritage of the Vineyard, some six generations deep, and that of the Henniker Deaf enclave, merely a generation old at that time.

Henniker, New Hampshire

Thomas and Mary settled on his parents' farm; his father was sixty, his mother sixty-six, and strong hands were sorely needed. More than that, Thomas brought to the task many natural gifts. He was a good horseman. He drove his own oxen and won prizes at the county fairs in Concord, New Hampshire, for drawing a load with a large boulder, weighing more than a ton, the allotted distance. He won awards for his plowing and for his colts, and Mary drew a premium of $2 for a nice lot of cheese she had prepared.[30] Thomas raised cattle and poultry and he grew fruit, wheat, and hay. He divided the large farm into lots of pasturage, tillage, orchard, woodland, and so on, and each lot had a name. The names that have come down to us were figures in Deaf education such as Gallaudet, Clerc, and Peet.[31] Thomas kept his accounts carefully and was frugal, practical, and methodical.[32] Some years were very hard: At times, early and severe frosts killed the crops; sometimes, seasons were extremely dry, and then small fruit withered and fell from the trees and clouds of grasshoppers settled on the fields, devouring everything.[33]

The close-knit family and Deaf community made the hard times bearable, even rewarding. In addition to his Deaf father, Nahum, and his Deaf sister, Persis, the family included Persis and Bela's two Deaf sons, Thomas B. Swett (called Nahum in honor of his grandfather), born the year Thomas went off to school, and William B. Swett, two years older. In 1837, Thomas B. Swett went to the American Asylum, and Mary gave birth to a hearing daughter, Charlotte, but illness took the infant's life within a year. Then, two years later, William Swett went off to school, and Mary gave birth to a Deaf son, Thomas Lewis Brown. On return from Hartford, the Swett boys took Deaf wives. William married Margaret Harrington, a Deaf woman from Ireland, whose Deaf brother had also married into a large Deaf family. Before he settled down, however, William had a colorful career as an explorer, showman, mechanic, writer, and artist. William and Margaret had three hearing children, two of whom died quite young, and two Deaf daughters, both of whom married Deaf men. William's brother Thomas Swett and Thomas's wife Ruth Stearns had four children—three Deaf and one hearing.

Joseph Livingstone, a Deaf carpenter who owned the blind and sash company where William worked, lived with the Swetts. Sometimes Deaf workmen would live on the Brown farm (for instance, Joel Lovejoy, one of the Deaf Lovejoys from Concord, New Hampshire, and Josiah Smith, who had Deaf relatives in Hillsboro). In addition, a nearby Deaf couple—the Goves—were close friends. (Abigail Clark Gove was from two towns away, New Boston, home of the Deaf Smith clan, who were good friends of the Browns.) So it was quite a little community that worked, celebrated, and prayed together at the interpreted services in the Congregational Church.[34] However, the Deaf community extended beyond Henniker and into contiguous towns. Thomas Brown socialized with Thomas Head and his family in Hooksett and with George Kent and others in Amherst (both two towns away from Henniker); Mrs. Head was from a large Deaf family in nearby Francestown, one town away from Henniker.[35] In his notebooks devoted to genealogical studies of Deaf people, Alexander Graham Bell lists all the Deaf people in New Hampshire according to the Seventh Census of the Deaf and Dumb, conducted in 1880.[36] Thirteen Deaf residents lived in towns that were contiguous to Henniker or that were one removed, and, including Henniker itself, the total came to twenty-seven.

A different gauge of the size of the Deaf community in and around Henniker may be discerned from the 1887 publication of cumulative enrollments at the American Asylum since its opening in 1817. Six children from Henniker enrolled, as did an additional thirty-eight from townships contiguous or one removed, for a total of forty-four. Both the census and enrollment measures are, in one respect, underestimates of the Henniker Deaf enclave because participants could certainly live more than two towns away and, indeed, with the coming of the railroads, could live a considerable distance away. Presumably, however, not all Deaf people within easy reach of Henniker chose to participate in its social life.

As mid-century approached, an idea germinated in Thomas Brown's mind that would prove epochal: bring together the largest gathering of Deaf people to be assembled anywhere, any time in history. Brown proposed that the mutes of the United States should gather to show their gratitude to Thomas Gallaudet (who had retired from the American Asylum in 1830) and Laurent Clerc (who, at sixty-five, was still teaching). Later events would reveal that Brown likely had a political agenda that went beyond gratitude and sought to counteract the inherent diaspora of Deaf people by gatherings that could also serve as a basis for improving their lot. When Brown, no doubt leveraging his standing in the New Hampshire Deaf community, suggested a tribute to Gallaudet and Clerc and asked for contributions, "the flame of love ran like a prairie fire through the hearts of the whole Deaf-Mute band, scattered though they were through various parts of the country" and $600 was soon raised.[37]

Two hundred Deaf people—some from as far away as Virginia—and 200 pupils of the American Asylum gathered in Hartford for the ceremony in which beautifully engraved silver pitchers were presented to the founders of American Deaf education. Significantly, the engraving was rich in symbolism from Deaf history. On one side of the pitcher, Gallaudet and Clerc are shown leaving France; the ship is at hand, and beyond the waves, their future school is visible. On the other side is a schoolroom with Deaf pupils. On the front is a bust of Clerc's teacher, Abbé Sicard, and around the neck are the arms of the New England states.[38] For the presentation, a procession made its way to Hartford's Center Church, in the presence of the Governor of Connecticut, and then Brown, towering above the celebrants, his red beard streaked with gray, gave the welcoming address, the first of several orations in sign. In their replies, Gallaudet and Clerc reviewed the progress of Deaf education from France to the United States. At an evening gathering, there were toasts, addresses, and resolutions, and many Deaf participants stayed on through the weekend to enjoy a religious service interpreted into sign language.

As it turned out, the 1850 tribute in Hartford was the forerunner of conventions and associations of Deaf people in the United States. The following year Thomas Gallaudet died; at his funeral, Clerc announced that Thomas Brown and others would form a society of Deaf people and frame a constitution; the society would raise funds for a Gallaudet monument. In 1853, a convention was held for that purpose in Montpelier, Vermont, with Deaf participants from that state as well as from Massachusetts and New Hampshire; many used free passes provided by the railroads. Brown reported on successful fund-raising for the monument and urged the formation of a permanent society "for the intellectual, social and moral improvement of Deaf-Mutes."[39] A committee under Thomas Brown was appointed to organize such a society.

Accordingly, less than a year later, on January 4, 1854, Deaf representatives from each of the New England states gathered at the Brown household in Henniker for a week to frame a constitution for the New England Gallaudet Association. From the resolutions of thanks for hospitality, it appears that some representatives were lodged in the Brown home, others at the Swetts, and still others at the Goves. The constitution that the representatives drafted envisioned the publication of a newspaper by and for Deaf-Mutes, the *Gallaudet Guide and Deaf Mutes' Companion.* Thomas Brown was chosen president of the new organization, which was scheduled to convene at the same time as the Gallaudet monument unveiling in Hartford in September of that year.

In the fall, Deaf-Mutes from "all parts of the union" gathered at Hartford for the unveiling of the Gallaudet monument. Deaf artist Albert Newsam had designed the monument, and Deaf sculptor John Carlin had created the panels. Indeed, "the whole monument was to be the exclusive product of Deaf-Mute enterprise."[40] Among other Deaf orators, whose sign was interpreted for hearing members of the audience, Thomas Brown gave a speech reviewing the history of Deaf education. As planned, the "Henniker Constitution" was read and adopted, and officers were elected, with Thomas Brown president. Thus was the first formal organization of and for Deaf people created in the United States.[41]

The second biennial meeting of the New England Gallaudet Association took place in Concord, New Hampshire, in 1856.[42] A listing of the members that appeared shortly thereafter showed forty-four from Massachusetts (including four Mayhews and three Tiltons from Chilmark), thirty-four from New Hampshire (mostly from towns close to Henniker), thirty from Connecticut, nineteen from Vermont, eleven from Maine, seven from Rhode Island, one from Illinois, and one from Louisiana. At this meeting, the eminent Deaf minister and teacher, Job Turner, dubbed Thomas Brown "the mute Cincinnatus of Americans" because he was so ready to drop his plough and come to the aid of his fellow mutes. The honorific, Mute Cincinnatus, stuck.

The construction of Deaf people as a distinct class had clearly emerged. It was not too great a step to imagine an enclave of Deaf people much larger than that to be found in the vicinity of Henniker or, for that matter, at the American Asylum. The idea of a Deaf commonwealth, debated at length at the 1858 meeting of the New England Gallaudet Association, responded to the yearnings of many.[43] The next convention was held in 1860 at the American Asylum, with some 300 attending.[44] Brown gave the presidential oration, and Laurent Clerc took the assembly to historic sites in Deaf history, such as the house in which he met the little Deaf girl Alice Cogswell, who had inspired efforts to found American Deaf education. In the evening, the conventional Deaf banquet was held with its toasts, orations, and resolutions.

In 1860, Thomas's friend and collaborator, William Chamberlain, began the association's publication, the *Gallaudet Guide and Deaf Mutes' Companion,* one of the earliest periodicals in the United States printed exclusively for Deaf readers. The publication contained news of Deaf meetings, marriages, illnesses, and deaths as well as discussions of Deaf issues such as education and considerations of broader social issues such as slavery and religion. (Before this publication, the proceedings of the Gallaudet Association's conventions and the organization's communications were judged sufficiently important to be carried in the *American Annals of the Deaf and Dumb,* and all members of the association received a subscription to the *Annals* on joining).

Just at the time when his network of Deaf friends and associates was the strongest yet, Thomas, age fifty-six, suffered a series of personal losses. The year before, he had lost his father, Nahum, age eighty-seven, who had gradually become blind and helpless. Then, two years later, Thomas's wife Mary died at the age of sixty-one, after an excruciating, year-long illness. Some months later, death took his mother, Abiah, age eighty-five. Then Bela Swett and Bela's grandchildren, Addie and James, died. Bela's son, William B. Swett, Thomas's nephew, deeply depressed at the loss of his children to diphtheria, left to pursue the life of an adventurer and guide in the White Mountains. Thomas's son, Thomas Lewis Brown, age twenty, graduated from the American Asylum and accepted a position as a teacher in the Deaf and Dumb Asylum at Flint, Michigan.

It was not uncommon in that era for a widower to remarry. Thomas's thoughts turned to the scion of one of the large Deaf families in Southern Maine, Sophia Curtis.

Sandy River Valley, Maine

In the period after the American Revolution, several of the families on Martha's Vineyard—among them, Tiltons, Smiths, Mayhews, and Wests —decided to migrate to southeastern Maine. They had had enough of the despotic rule of Governor Thomas Mayhew. Then, too, with the growing population, the extensive land required for sheep raising was becoming scarce. The war had crippled the whaling industry, which was increasingly centered in the South Pacific. And Massachusetts offered free land in the province of Maine.[45]

The first settlers from the Vineyard went to the Sandy River Valley, abundantly forested with all sorts of game and streams that teemed with fish such as trout and salmon. Other Vineyarders soon followed, creating the towns of New Vineyard, New Sharon, New Gloucester, and twenty-seven others. Intermarriage among the Vineyard families continued on the mainland, although some of the settlers gave up and returned to the island and still others married into unrelated Deaf families on the mainland. Between the opening of the American Asylum and 1887, twenty-seven of the Deaf pupils who enrolled gave one of these thirty towns as their residence. This body of students includes those from large Deaf families such as the Rowes and Campbells in New Gloucester, Maine, and the Lovejoys in Sidney.

However, significant numbers of Deaf people lived also in nearby townships—for example, the Sebec branch of the Lovejoys; the Jacks and Jellisons in Monroe; the Browns, Jellisons, and Staples in Belfast; and the Berrys in Chesterville. The Lovejoy-Jellison-Berry family of southeastern Maine has the distinction of being one of only two early American Deaf families in the Northeast with three or more consecutive generations of Deaf people (with the first born before 1800); the Brown-Swett-Sanders family of central New Hampshire was the other.[46] Sophia Curtis's family was apparently from Leeds, Maine (two townships away from New Sharon, three from Sidney), but moved to New Gloucester; she and her parents were hearing. Sophia had five hearing siblings and four Deaf; all of the Deaf siblings married Deaf Rowes and Campbells. Perhaps Thomas met Sophia through her brother George, who overlapped with him at the American Asylum. The wedding notice in the *National Deaf-Mute Gazette* (successor to the *Guide*) reveals both Brown's stature and the need to explain his mixed marriage: "Mr. Brown is too well known to need any notice at our hands. His wife is a hearing lady whose relationship to and constant intercourse with mutes enables her to use their language."[47]

Thomas and Sophia were married in Yarmouth, Maine, in November 1864 and then took up residence in Henniker.

Henniker, New Hampshire

Thomas continued his life as a farmer—and Deaf leader. In 1866, the New England Gallaudet Association met in Hartford to coincide with the fiftieth anniversary celebration of the American Asylum. Some 500 people heard Brown give the presidential address, in which he announced that, after twelve years of service, he would resign in favor of his vice-president.[48] Two years later the *Deaf-Mute's Friend* (successor to the *Gazette*) published a letter from Thomas Brown, proposing a national convention of Deaf-Mutes. According to an eminent Deaf teacher and journalist who endorsed the suggestion in the following issue, Brown had first made this proposal "to the convention in Syracuse in 1865"—no doubt the meeting of the Empire State Association of Deaf-Mutes.[49]

In the same year, 1869, Thomas's sister, Persis, died, as did Laurent Clerc.[50] Still vibrant himself, Thomas, age sixty-five, won awards at the state fair and cattle show. His son, Thomas Lewis, came home from Michigan to host a large birthday party for his father. Just as the *Gazette* reassured its readers that Brown's new wife knew sign language, so the *Friend* explained to its readers that one of the storytellers at the birthday party "although a hearing man is a very good sign-maker."[51] In 1874, Brown took on the presidency of the Clerc Monument Association,[52] and four years later, he founded the Granite State Deaf-Mute Mission and was elected president.[53]

William B. Swett followed in his uncle's footsteps in promoting Deaf welfare. He published (with William Chamberlain) the *Deaf-Mute's Friend*, was a director of the Deaf-Mute Library Association, and was business manager of the Boston Deaf-Mute Mission. In addition, he founded a school of industrial arts for Deaf adults, which shortly thereafter added an educational program for Deaf children; it continues today as the Beverly School for the Deaf.[54]

Thomas Brown was a trustee of his nephew's school in its early years.[55] In 1880, the first national convention of Deaf people in the United States was convened just as Brown had proposed—except for the venue: It was held in Cincinnati, not Hartford, and Brown, seventy-six years old, could not attend. He did, however, attend the meeting in New York in 1884 and then traveled to the Vineyard with his son Thomas Lewis to visit the friends of his late wife.[56] Thomas Brown died March 23, 1886.

Assimilative and Differentiating Societies

The story of Thomas Brown and the emergence of the first American organizations of and for Deaf people that he led can be seen as the story
of emerging class consciousness, which surfaced clearly in the mid-
nineteenth century. The formation of the numerous societies of Deaf
people over which he presided; the explicit goals of the first enduring organization, the New England Gallaudet Association, which he founded
("We, Deaf-Mutes, desirous of forming a society in order to promote the
intellectual, social, moral, temporal and spiritual welfare of *our mute community*" [italics added]); the ritual-like rehearsal at meetings of the great
events in Deaf history; the raising of monuments to important figures—all
these testify that Brown and his associates saw the Deaf community as a
distinct group with a language and way of life that should be fostered.
"That these conventions tend to keep alive the feelings of brotherhood
and friendship among the mutes at large cannot be disputed," wrote
William Chamberlain, supporting the gatherings of "the children of silence."[57] In the silent press, Brown was referred to as the "patriarch of the
silent tribe,"[58] and his eulogist stated that Brown was always ready to do
his share "for any plan which promised to promote the welfare of his
class."[59] ("Class" here clearly refers to the "tribe," namely, the Deaf-
World, and in this article we use the term in this sense.)

In stark contrast, the accounts available to us of the lives led by Deaf
and hearing people in Tisbury and Chilmark during the same era are
marked by an apparent absence of events and structures that would set
Deaf people apart from hearing people. These accounts do not reveal any
leader, any organization, any gathering place, any banquet or other ceremony, any monuments—indeed anything at all that suggests that Deaf
people on the Vineyard had class consciousness. Now that we have made
this bald claim, something contradictory may well come to light, but it
seems unlikely that the difference in degree will be eliminated by future
discoveries.

The pedigrees that we have constructed (of which excerpts appear in
figures 1–3), though incomplete, have led us to the hypothesis that a difference in the genetic basis of the Deaf societies in the two locations is responsible for the difference in the emergence of class consciousness. Other
possible explanations come to mind, notably the differences between the
two locations in language and marriage practices. After presenting the genetic hypothesis, we will argue that those differences are, like class consciousness, heavily influenced by the genetic difference.

The hereditary difference between hearing and Deaf people can be traced to any of numerous genes, most often acting singly. As a result, the occurrence of Deaf and hearing people in the family tends to follow the "laws of heredity" first spelled out by Austrian botanist Gregor Mendel in the mid-nineteenth century (but not widely recognized until the end of the century). Mendel identified two main patterns of genetic transmission, called dominant and recessive.

The Brown family of Henniker exemplifies the dominant pattern of inheritance (or transmission). To the best of our knowledge, none of the twenty-three ascendants of Nahum Brown whom we found was Deaf. But Nahum and some of his descendants in every generation were Deaf, indicating that the genetic difference in this family began with Nahum. If the pattern of genetic transmission was dominant in Nahum's family, then on average, half of his children would inherit that genetic difference and be born Deaf whereas the other half would be born hearing. Within a small margin of statistical sampling, this pattern is just what happened. Slightly more than half (nearly 57 percent) of Nahum's descendants were Deaf: twelve out of twenty-one. All Deaf members of the family had a Deaf parent (except Nahum, of course), and all Deaf members who married had at least one Deaf child.

The Mayhew, Tilton, Lambert, and Skiffe families of Martha's Vineyard (figures 2 and 3), who intermarried extensively both before and after arriving on the island, exemplify the recessive pattern of inheritance. In this pattern, many people in the family will possess the critical gene and yet not be Deaf themselves (hence the term *recessive*). If both parents have that gene, then one-quarter of their children will be Deaf, but if only one parent has it, then none of their children will be Deaf, unlike dominant transmission. Many Deaf children will not have Deaf parents (because their parents, though undoubtedly carrying the gene, will not be Deaf themselves). The odds of both parents having exactly the same recessive gene are much greater if they are related to one another. Intermarriage among relatives is most likely in a community that is isolated—and Martha's Vineyard is a prime example. Many Deaf children on the Vineyard had no Deaf parents, and many Deaf parents, provided they married hearing people, had no Deaf children (compare figures 2 and 3). Consequently, far fewer than half the descendants of any progenitor are Deaf; the families of Deaf people have many more hearing people.

In dominant transmission such as we believe occurred in Henniker then, every generation is likely to have Deaf children: Each Deaf person receives a Deaf heritage and may pass it along; each generation of his or her parents and grandparents, children and grandchildren will likely contain Deaf individuals. Marriage between relatives is not necessary for such generational depth to occur. However, in recessive transmission such as we believe occurred on the Vineyard, a Deaf person may have cousins, uncles, aunts, grandparents, or more distant relatives who are Deaf, but that Deaf person is less likely to have Deaf members among the immediate family compared with examples of dominant transmission. In fact, that Deaf person may readily have hearing parents or hearing children, or both; generational depth is less likely, and marriage among relatives is characteristically required to produce any Deaf family members at all.[60] In such a setting, the Deaf person may feel a part of a rather extended family that includes hearing people because he or she is related to so many people in the community. But that Deaf person may not feel like a crucial link in the chain of Deaf heritage.

A clear result of the difference in genetic patterning in the two communities is that the Henniker community necessarily had many fewer hearing people as an integral part of the family structure compared with the Chilmark community. The numerous hearing children of Deaf parents (called CODAs, or children of deaf adults) in Chilmark would be likely to acquire sign language as a native language; they and their Deaf siblings would thus form a critical mass within the family for sign language use. The Deaf children of hearing parents would learn the language from their parents, if they knew it, or, if not, from Deaf peers, elders, and codas, and they would seek to use it with their own parents and hearing siblings. Numerous hearing relatives in the community might also be motivated to master the sign language in use, at least to some extent, to communicate with their Deaf relatives. Thus the difference between Henniker and Chilmark in the spread of sign language into the hearing environment may be traceable, in part, to the difference between them in genetic patterning.

The incidence of mixed hearing and Deaf marriages on the Vineyard seems to have been more than triple that on the mainland, as cited earlier. This difference may be attributable, at least in part, to the more widespread use of sign language among hearing people because a common language greatly facilitates meeting one's life partner in the first place and then developing a deep interest in and affection for that person.

Finally, we hypothesize that the differences in language use and marriage practice, which are underpinned in part by the differences in genetic patterning, mediate in turn differences in class consciousness. What we are suggesting is that it takes a "them" for an "us" to develop, and the blending of hearing and Deaf lives on the Vineyard, because of shared family life and language (underpinned by genetics), discouraged the construction of hearing people as "them." Conversely, many members of the Henniker Deaf enclave had Deaf parents, Deaf grandparents, and Deaf great-grandparents, and the boundary with the surrounding hearing community was relatively sharply demarcated. That said, other factors may also have fostered Chilmark blending of Deaf and hearing lives, such as a sense of isolation on a remote island and an awareness of shared ancestry.

Recent findings concerning Deaf people and hearing residents of a village in Bali help to evaluate the notion that Deaf genetic patterning, marriage and language practices, and class consciousness are related. Of the 2,185 people in this village, 2.2 percent are Deaf.[61] Following Branson, Miller, and Marsaja,[62] we refer to the village as Desa Kolok ("Deaf Village"—not its official name). The genetic patterning in Desa Kolok is recessive as on the Vineyard, and, as on the Vineyard, marriages between hearing and Deaf people are completely acceptable. There are sixteen families in Desa Kolok with two hearing parents and at least one Deaf child, so it is clear that there is more blending of hearing and Deaf lives in the nuclear family than in Henniker, which had no families with hearing parents and Deaf children. However, the blending of hearing and Deaf lives in Desa Kolok may not have been as great as on the Vineyard because, in Desa Kolok, three fourths of the children in the twenty families with a Deaf parent (or two) were Deaf.

Beyond the blending of hearing and Deaf lives within the nuclear family in Desa Kolok, cultural and social forces ensure widespread contact between Deaf and hearing people. Of particular note, Balinese villages are kin based, and Deaf people grow up in house yards shared with their hearing relatives. Thus, with respect to the mixing of hearing and Deaf lives, the extended family of the Desa Kolok house yard may be more like Vineyard families than like Henniker families. Perhaps for this reason, the use of a sign language in Desa Kolok is nearly universal, and Deaf people are integrated in many facets of social life, including groups organized for work and for some religious practices. Moreover, hearing attitudes toward Deaf islanders, many of whom are relatives, are generally positive.[63] Thus, the evidence from Desa Kolok suggests that the mixing of hearing and Deaf people in the family determines their mixing in community life, as we hypothesize was the case on the Vineyard.

It is not clear to us whether Deaf people in Desa Kolok lack class (i.e., group) consciousness, as we hypothesize was the case on the Vineyard. On the one hand, certain activities in Desa Kolok are associated with Deaf villagers who also have specific roles in connection with certain festivals, which might engender such group consciousness. Moreover, being Deaf restricts one's prospects outside the village and limits participation in some skilled labor and in musical events.[64] On the other hand, "the Deaf villagers interact freely and equally with other villagers."[65] Perhaps the mixed evidence for group consciousness is a reflection of an intermediate status for Desa Kolok between Henniker and the Vineyard with respect to the blending of hearing and Deaf lives.

Acknowledgments

We are grateful to the following people for their assistance in preparing this article: Dr. Kathleen Arnos, Genetics Program, Department of Biology, Gallaudet University; Dr. Ben Bahan, Department of Deaf Studies, Gallaudet University; Dr. Jan Branson, National Institute for Deaf Studies and Sign Language Research, La Trobe University; Dr. Nora Groce, School of Public Health, Yale University; Mr. Ulf Hedberg, Gallaudet University Archives; Dr. John Hinnant, Department of Religious Studies, Michigan State University; Ms. Carole Mair, Librarian, Michigan School for the Deaf; New England Genealogical Society; Dr. Don Miller, Department of Anthropology and Sociology, Monash University; Mr. Michael Olsen, Gallaudet University Archives; Dr. Joan Poole-Nash, Newton, Massachusetts; Volta Bureau, Alexander Graham Bell Association.

Notes

1. E. A. Fay, *Marriages of the Deaf in America* (Washington, D.C.: Volta Bureau, 1898).

2. A. G. Bell, Unpublished notebooks [ca 1888], Volta Bureau, Washington, D.C.

3. E. P. Thwing, "White Mountain Memories," *National Deaf Mute Gazette,* April 16, 1868, 8–9.

4. Ibid.

5. G. C. Braddock, *Notable Deaf Persons* (Washington, D.C.: Gallaudet College Alumni Association, 1975); L. W. Cogswell, *History of the Town of Henniker* (1880; repr., Somersworth, N.H.: New Hampshire Publishing Co., 1973).

6. T. Brown, sketch of Nahum Brown, *Gallaudet Guide and Deaf Mutes' Companion* 1, no. 3(1860): 12.

7. N. Groce, "Hereditary Deafness on the Island of Martha's Vineyard: An Ethnohistory of a Genetic Disorder" (Ph.D. diss., Brown University, Providence, R.I., 1983).

8. N. Groce, "Everyone Here Spoke Sign Language," *Natural History* 89:12–15.

9. T. Brown, sketch of Nahum Brown, 12; W. B. Swett, "Obituary of Nahum Brown," *American Annals of the Deaf and Dumb* 11, no. 4 (1859): 237–40.

10. T. L. Brown, *In Memoriam: A Tribute to the Memory of Thomas Brown* (Flint, Mich.: Michigan School for the Deaf, 1888).

11. S. Childs, sketch of Nahum and Thomas Brown, *Gallaudet Guide and Deaf Mutes' Companion* 2, no. 4 (1861): 14–15.

12. H. Lane, *When the Mind Hears: A History of the Deaf* (New York: Random House, 1984).

13. W. M. Chamberlain, "Proceedings of the Third Convention of the New England Gallaudet Association of Deaf-Mutes," *American Annals of the Deaf* 10:205–19.

14. N. Groce, *Everyone Here Spoke Sign Language* (Cambridge, Mass.: Harvard University Press, 1985).

15. C. E. Banks, *The History of Martha's Vineyard, Dukes County, Massachusetts in Three Volumes* (Edgartown, Mass.: Dukes County Historical Society, 1966).

16. J. Freeman, "Dukes County 1807," *Dukes County Intelligencer* 12, no. 4(1976;): 1–51; D. C. Poole, *A New Vineyard* (Edgartown, Mass.: Dukes County Historical Society, 1976); E. R. Mayhew, *Martha's Vineyard: A Short History and Guide* (Edgartown, Mass.: Dukes County Historical Society, 1956).

17. Groce, "Everyone Here Spoke Sign Language" (1980).

18. Groce, *Everyone Here Spoke Sign Language* (1985).

19. N. Groce, "The Island's Hereditary Deaf: A Lesson in Human Understanding," *Dukes County Intelligencer* 22:83–95.

20. Groce, *Everyone Here Spoke Sign Language* (1985).

21. J. R. Burnet, *Tales of the Deaf and Dumb* (Newark, N.J.: Olds, 1835); "Deaf and Dumb of Squibnocket," *Deaf-Mutes' Journal* 24, no. 5(1895): 1.

22. Groce, *Everyone Here Spoke Sign Language* (1985).

23. Groce, "Everyone Here Spoke Sign Language" (1980).

24. B. Bahan and J. Poole-Nash, "The Signing Community on Martha's Vineyard," in *Deaf Studies IV : Visions of the Past—Visions of the Future: Conference Proceedings, April 27–30, 1995, Woburn, Massachusetts* (Washington, D.C.: Gallaudet University, Continuing Education and Outreach, 1996).

25. Ibid.

26. R. E. Johnson, "Sign Language and the Concept of Deafness in a Traditional Yucatec Mayan Village," in *The Deaf Way: Perspectives from the International Conference on Deaf Culture*, ed. C. Erting, R. C. Johnson, D. L. Smith, and B. D. Snider (Washington, D.C.: Gallaudet University Press, 1994), 103–9.

27. Bahan and Poole-Nash, "The Signing Community on Martha's Vineyard," 19.

28. Groce, "Everyone Here Spoke Sign Language," 95.

29. R. E. Colby, "On the Thomas Brown Place" (handwritten ms., Henniker Historical Society, 1961).

30. Anon., article about the annual fair, *Deaf-Mute's Friend* 1, no. 11(1869): 344.

31. W. M. Chamberlain, "Thomas Brown," *American Annals of the Deaf* 31 (1836): 204–10.

32. T. L. Brown, "In Memoriam"; Anon [Sketch of Brown Family History] *Gallaudet Guide and Deaf Mutes' Companion* 2 no. 4(1861): 14.

33. Cogswell, "History of the Town of Henniker."

34. Colby, "On the Thomas Brown Place."

35. Anon., "Letter from New Hampshire," *Deaf-Mute's Friend* 1, no. 1(1869): 26–27; Anon., "A Festival of Deaf-Mutes," *Literary Budget* 1, no. 1(1874): 3; J. Turner, "Biographical Sketch of Thomas Brown," *Deaf-Mutes' Journal* 9, no. 43(1880): 2.

36. Bell, unpublished notebooks.

37. L. Rae, "Presentation of Silver Plate to Messrs. Gallaudet and Clerc," *American Annals of the Deaf* 3 (1851): 41–64, quoted material from p. 42.

38. H. W. Syle, *Biographical Sketch of Thomas Hopkins Gallaudet* (Philadelphia: Cullingworth, 1887).

39. Convention of Deaf Mutes, "Monument to Thomas H. Gallaudet," in *Proceedings 23–24 February 1853* (Montpelier, Vt.: Walton, 1853), 4.

40. L. Rae, "Ceremonies at the Completion of the Gallaudet Monument," *American Annals of the Deaf* 7 (1854), 19–54, quoted material from p. 19.

41. W. M. Chamberlain, "Constitution of the New England Gallaudet Association of Deaf-Mutes," *American Annals of the Deaf* 6 (1854): 64–68.

42. W. M. Chamberlain, "Proceedings of the Convention of the New England Gallaudet Association of Deaf-Mutes," *American Annals of the Deaf* 9 (1857): 65–87.

43. Chamberlain, "Proceedings of the Third Convention of the New England Gallaudet Association of Deaf-Mutes."

44. Anon., "Fourth Convention of the New England Gallaudet Association of Deaf-Mutes," *American Annals of the Deaf and Dumb* 12, no. 4(1860): 236–43; W. M. Chamberlain, "Proceedings of the Fourth Convention of the New England Gallaudet Association of Deaf-Mutes," *Gallaudet Guide and Deaf Mutes' Companion* 1, no. 10(1860): 1–2.

45. Poole, *A New Vineyard.*

46. T. W. Jones, "America's First Multi-Generation Deaf Families (A Genealogical Perspective) *Deaf American Monographs* 46 (1996):49–54.

47. Anon., announcement that T. Brown marries Sophia Sumner née Curtis, *National Deaf-Mute Gazette* 1, no. 1(1867): 6.

48. W. M. Chamberlain, "Celebration of the Fiftieth Anniversary," *National Deaf-Mute Gazette* 1, no. 1(1867): 1–4.

49. T. Brown, "Letter" [signed T. B.]. *Deaf-Mute's Friend* 1, no. 6(1869): 188–90.

50. W. M. Chamberlain, "Obituary of Laurent Clerc," *Deaf-Mute's Friend* 1 (1869): 216–17.

51. W. B. Swett, "A Birth Day Party," *Deaf Mutes' Fiend* 1, no. 4(1869): 123.

52. T. L. Brown, "In Memoriam."

53. J. T. Tillinghast, "Gathering of Mutes at Amherst, New Hampshire," *Michigan Deaf-Mute Mirror,* November 29, 1878, 3.

54. W. B. Swett, *Adventures of a Deaf-Mute* (Boston: Deaf-Mute Mission, 1874).

55. T. L. Brown, "In Memoriam."

56. T. Brown, address by Thomas Brown at his eightieth birthday, *Hillsboro Messenger,* March 6, 1884.

57. W. M. Chamberlain, statements concerning a National Convention, *Deaf-Mute's Friend* 1, no. 8(1869): 241–42.

58. J. O. David, "From New Hampshire: An Interesting Letter from Mr. David," *Michigan Deaf-Mute Mirror,* January 10, 1879, 2.

59. T. L. Brown, "In Memoriam," 14.

60. Recent studies have shown that mutations in the gene GJB2 are very common among people who were born Deaf and as many as one in every forty people in the general population have at least one mutated copy of the gene. If this gene had been widespread on Martha's Vineyard, then marriage among relatives would not necessarily have been required for offspring to be Deaf. See G. Green and others, "Carrier Rates in the Midwestern United States for GJB2 Mutations Causing Inherited Deafness," *Journal of the American Medical Association* 281, no. 23(1999): 2211–16.

61. S. Winata and others, "Congenital Non-Syndromal Autosomal Recessive Deafness in Bengkala, an Isolated Balinese Village," *Journal of Medical Genetics* 32, no. 5(1995): 336–43.

62. J. D. Branson, D. Miller, and G. Marsaja, "Everyone Here Speaks Sign Language, Too: A Deaf Village in Bali, Indonesia," in *Multicultural Aspects of Sociolinguistics in Deaf Communities,* ed. C. Lucas (Washington, D.C.: Gallaudet University Press, 1996), 39–57.

63. J. Hinnant, "Music to Their Eyes. Deaf Life and Performance in a Balinese Village" (address at the National Institutes of Health, Bethesda, Md., October 12, 1998); J. Hinnant, "Adaptation to Deafness in a Balinese Community," in *Hearing Loss and Genetics,* ed. B. Keats and C. Berlin (San Diego: Singular Publishing Group, 2000), Branson, Miller, and Marsaja, "Everyone Here Speaks Sign Language, Too."

64. J. Hinnant, personal communication with H. Lane, 1998.

65. Branson, Miller, and Marsaja, "Everyone Here Speaks Sign Language, Too," 42.

Bibliography

Anon. 1860. Fourth Convention of the New England Gallaudet Association of Deaf-Mutes, *American Annals of the Deaf and Dumb* 12 (4):236–43.

Anon. 1861. (sketch of the Brown family). *Gallaudet Guide and Deaf Mutes' Companion* 2 (4):14.

Anon. 1867. (marriage announcement of T. Brown marries Sophia Sumner née Curtis). *National Deaf-Mute Gazette* 1 (1):6.

Anon. 1869a. (description of the Annual Fair). *Deaf-Mute's Friend* 1 (11):344.

Anon. 1869b. Letter from New Hampshire. *Deaf-Mute's Friend* 1 (1):26–27.

Anon. 1874. A festival of deaf-mutes. *Literary Budget* 1 (1):3.

Bahan, B., and J. Poole-Nash. 1996. The signing community on Martha's Vineyard. Address to the Conference on Deaf Studies IV, Haverhill, Mass. In *Deaf Studies IV: Visions of the Past—Visions of the Future: Conference Proceedings, April 27–30, 1995, Woburn, Massachusetts.* Washington, D.C.: Gallaudet University, Continuing Education and Outreach.

Banks, C. E. 1966. *The history of Martha's Vineyard, Dukes County, Massachusetts in three volumes.* Edgartown, Mass.: Dukes County Historical Society.

Bell, A. G. ca.1888. (unpublished notebooks), Volta Bureau, Washington, D.C.

Braddock, G. C. 1975. *Notable deaf persons.* Washington, D.C.: Gallaudet College Alumni Association.

Branson, J., D. Miller, and G. Marsaja. 1996. Everyone here speaks sign language, too: A deaf village in Bali, Indonesia. In *Multicultural aspects of sociolinguistics in deaf communities,* ed. C. Lucas, 39–57. Washington, D.C.: Gallaudet University Press.

Brown, T. 1860. (sketch of Nahum Brown). *Gallaudet Guide and Deaf Mutes' Companion* 1 (3):12.

———. 1869. Letter (signed T. B.). *Deaf-Mute's Friend* 1 (6):188–90.

———. 1884. (address by Thomas Brown at his eightieth birthday). *Hillsboro Messenger,* March 6.

Brown, T. L. 1888. *In memoriam: A tribute to the memory of Thomas Brown.* Flint, Mich.: Michigan School for the Deaf.

Burnet, J. R. 1835. *Tales of the deaf and dumb.* Newark: Olds.

Chamberlain, W. M. 1854. Constitution of the New England Gallaudet Association of Deaf-Mutes. *American Annals of the Deaf* 6:64–68.

———. 1857. Proceedings of the convention of the New England Gallaudet Association of Deaf-Mutes. *American Annals of the Deaf* 9:65–87.

———. 1858. Proceedings of the third convention of the New England Gallaudet Association of Deaf-Mutes. *American Annals of the Deaf* 10:205–19.

———. 1860. Proceedings of the fourth convention of the New England Gallaudet Association of Deaf-Mutes. *Gallaudet Guide and Deaf Mutes' Companion* 1 (10):1–2.

———. 1867. Celebration of the fiftieth anniversary. *National Deaf-Mute Gazette* 1 (1):1–4.

———. 1869a. (notes concerning a national convention). *Deaf-Mute's Friend* 1 (8):241–42.

———. 1869b. Obituary of Laurent Clerc. *Deaf-Mute's Friend* 1:216–17.

———. 1886. Thomas Brown. *American Annals of the Deaf* 31:204–10.

Childs, S. 1861. (sketch of Nahum and Thomas Brown). *Gallaudet Guide and Deaf Mutes' Companion* 2 (4):14–15.

Cogswell, L. W. 1973. Reprint. *History of the town of Henniker.* Somersworth, N.H.: New Hampshire Publishing Co. Original edition, Concord NH, Republic Press Association, 1880.

Colby, R. E. 1961. On the Thomas Brown place (handwritten ms.), Henniker Historical Society.

Convention of Deaf Mutes. 1853. "Monument to Thomas H. Gallaudet." In *Proceedings, 23–24 February, 1853.* Montpelier, Vt.: Walton.

David, J. O. 1879. From New Hampshire: An interesting letter from Mr. David. *Michigan Deaf-Mute Mirror,* January 10, p. 2.

Deaf and Dumb of Squibnocket. 1895. *Deaf-Mutes' Journal* 24 (5):1.

Fay, E. A. 1898. *Marriages of the deaf in America.* Washington, D.C.: Volta Bureau.

Freeman, J. 1976. Dukes County 1807. *Dukes County Intelligencer* 12 (4):1–51.

Gordon, J. C. 1892. *Education of deaf children: Evidence of E. M. Gallaudet and A. G. Bell presented to the Royal Commission of the United Kingdom on the Condition of the Blind, the Deaf and the Dumb.* Washington, D.C.: Volta Bureau.

Green, G., D. Scott, J. McDonald, G. Woodworth, V. Sheffield, and R. Smith. 1999. Carrier rates in the midwestern United States for GJB2 mutations causing inherited deafness. *Journal of the American Medical Association* 281 (23):2211–16.

Groce, N. 1980. Everyone here spoke sign language. *Natural History* 89:12–15.

———. 1981. The island's hereditary deaf: A lesson in human understanding. *Dukes County Intelligencer* 22:83–95.

———. 1983. Hereditary deafness on the island of Martha's Vineyard: An ethnohistory of a genetic disorder. Ph.D. diss., Brown University, Providence, R.I.

———. 1985. *Everyone here spoke sign language.* Cambridge, Mass.: Harvard University Press.

Hinnant, J. 1998. Music to their eyes: Deaf life and performance in a Balinese Village. Address at the National Institutes of Health, October 12, Bethesda, Md.

———. 1999. Adaptation to deafness in a Balinese community. In *Hearing Loss and Genetics,* ed. B. Keetz and C. Berlin. San Diego: Singular Publishing Group.

Johnson, R. E. 1994. Sign language and the concept of deafness in a traditional Yucatec Mayan village. In *The deaf way: Perspectives from the International Conference on Deaf Culture,* ed. C. Erting, R. C. Johnson, D. L. Smith, and B. D. Snider, 103–9. Washington, D.C.: Gallaudet University Press.

Jones, T. W. 1996. America's first multi-generation deaf families (a genealogical perspective). *Deaf American Monographs* 46:49–54.

Lane, H. 1984. *When the mind hears: A history of the deaf.* New York: Random House.

Mayhew, C. M. 1991. *Vital records of Chilmark, Massachusetts to the year 1850. With additional Chilmark births, marriages and deaths.* Bowie, Md.: Heritage Books.

Mayhew, E. R. 1956. *Martha's Vineyard: A short history and guide.* Edgartown, Mass.: Dukes County Historical Society.

Poole, D. C. 1976. *A new Vineyard.* Edgartown, Mass.: Dukes County Historical Society.

Rae, L. 1851. Presentation of silver plate to Messrs. Gallaudet and Clerc. *American Annals of the Deaf* 3:41–64.

———. 1854. Ceremonies at the completion of the Gallaudet monument. *American Annals of the Deaf* 7:19–54.

Swett, W. B. 1859. Obituary of Nahum Brown. *American Annals of the Deaf and Dumb* 11 (4):237–40.

———. 1869. A birth day party. *Deaf Mutes' Friend* 1 (4):123.

———. 1874. *Adventures of a deaf-mute.* Boston: Deaf-Mute Mission.

Syle, H. W. 1887. *Biographical sketch of Thomas Hopkins Gallaudet.* Philadelphia: Cullingworth.

Thwing, E. P. 1868. White Mountain memories. *National Deaf Mute Gazette,* April 16, 8–9.

Tillinghast, J. T. 1878. Gathering of mutes at Amherst, New Hampshire. *Michigan Deaf-Mute Mirror,* November 29, 3.

Turner, J. 1880. Biographical sketch of Thomas Brown. *Deaf-Mutes' Journal* 9 (43):2.

Winata, S., I. Arhya, S. Moeljopawiro, J. Hinnant, Y. Liang, and T. Friedman. 1995. Congenital non-syndromal autosomal recessive deafness in Bengkala, an isolated Balinese Village. *Journal of Medical Genetics* 32 (5):336–43.

4

Mary Ann Walworth Booth

Jill Hendricks Porco

Editor's Introduction

Most published American deaf history has focused on events and people in New England and the Middle Atlantic states, in part because those areas were the most populous as the deaf community was forming itself. Jill Porco's article below is the first of several in this volume to shift the focus westward. The article also is valuable and unusual in its female subject. Porco argues that Mary Ann Walworth Booth, though isolated on the frontier from a larger community of signers, nevertheless communicated well with diverse people on the frontier. She fulfilled admirably the roles of head of household, mother, and wife to a well-known deaf man, Edmund Booth, who spent five years away from her and their children searching for gold in California.

Little is known about the history of American deaf women, particularly before the twentieth century. Information exists about a few famous deaf women of the nineteenth century, including Agatha Tiegel Hanson, Harriet Martineau, and Laura Redden Searing, but not about many average deaf women of that time.[1] Mary Ann Walworth Booth is a partial ex-

My thanks to Helen Heckenlaible and Wilma Heckenlaible Spice for providing me with the Booth and Walworth family papers used for this article. My gratitude also goes to Ted Ruhstahler, curator of the San Joaquin Pioneer and Historical Society in California, for access to the original correspondence between Edmund Booth and Mary Ann Walworth Booth. Also, thank you to John Vickrey Van Cleve for his help in facilitating this research.

ception to this general statement. She was an American deaf woman who lived in the nineteenth century and left some useful documents for historians, primarily in an obscure book, *Edmund Booth: Forty Niner*, that told part of the story of the lives of Mary Ann and her husband, Edmund Booth.[2] The text includes surviving correspondence between Mary Ann and Edmund during the years he prospected for gold in California, and their letters present a unique opportunity to gain insights into a difficult period in the life of a deaf woman on the American frontier.

Mary Ann and Edmund Booth, both graduates of the American School for the Deaf in Hartford, Connecticut, married and settled in the Iowa Territory in 1840, eventually living in the town of Anamosa, Iowa. They were poor when they married. They had no family inheritance, and they scraped for every penny in an area of the American Midwest that is still poor today.[3]

But these deaf pioneers were a success by nearly every measure. Edmund Booth traveled to California in 1849 at the beginning of the Gold Rush. Mining for gold during the five years he was there, he managed to send a fair amount of money home to his wife.[4] The Booths raised three children to adulthood.[5] They donated land and money for churches, which came, in part, from Edmund Booth's gold rush earnings. They played a major role in local politics, and they literally left their mark: the Anamosa Historical Society building today is located on Booth Street, in an area of the town long identified as the Booth subdivision.[6] Moreover, Edmund was active in deaf politics, served as editor and owner of the local newspaper, the Anamosa *Eureka*, and was well-known to his contemporaries despite his physical isolation.[7]

Mary Ann Walworth Booth

A brief review of Mary Ann's background is necessary before examining what the correspondence between Edmund and Mary Ann tells us about her life. Mary Ann Walworth Booth lived from February 23, 1817, to January 25, 1898, almost eighty-one years. She was the fifth of nine children in her family.[8] Her parents, George Walworth and Philura Jones Walworth, lived in Canaan, New Hampshire, when she was born. Her father served as a selectman, a town official, in Canaan for three terms while her mother stayed at home and raised their family.[9]

Mary Ann was four when she became deaf from scarlet fever. Her parents later sent Mary Ann to the American School for the Deaf, the first permanent school for deaf children in the United States. The American School for the Deaf served the entire New England region for many years, before other states in the area began opening their own residential schools for deaf students.[10]

Mary Ann met her future husband, Edmund Booth, at the American School for the Deaf in 1831 when he was her Classics teacher. She was fourteen then. Edmund also met George Walworth, one of Mary Ann's older brothers, when he dropped her off at the residential school. This meeting was to prove important for Mary Ann's and Edmund's future together.[11]

George Walworth and two of his brothers, Clark and Denison, wanted to move out to the frontier and start their own business. Thus, Mary Ann's brothers went to the Iowa territory in 1839 and constructed a saw and grist mill along the Buffalo forks of the Wapsipinicon River. This location, to-day's Anamosa, was extremely remote, far from the civilization to which they were accustomed. The area, very much a part of the American frontier then, was surrounded by wilderness and lacked a transportation infra-structure such as railroads or government-maintained roads. Indians were still commonly seen. Only about 475 white people lived in and around the Anamosa part of the Iowa Territory by 1840. Dubuque was the nearest market, and it was about fifty miles away. The town of Anamosa did not yet exist, and Iowa would not become a state until 1846. Nevertheless, the rest of the Walworth family decided to follow George, Clark, and Denison to this remote place. Mary Ann, her parents, and her other brothers and sisters, with the exception of one brother, James, moved to Illinois first, then migrated on to Iowa to live near the three brothers already there.[12]

Meanwhile, later in 1839, Edmund Booth quit his teaching job at The American School for the Deaf and moved to Iowa, where he worked for the Walworth brothers at their mills and, of course, was reunited with Mary Ann. They courted, then married in July of 1840.[13] Edmund and Mary Ann settled and farmed in Fairview, a nearby town, before Edmund left in 1849 to prospect for gold in California.[14] The five-year period when Edmund was in California greatly affected their lives, particularly Mary Ann's. Before Edmund left for California, however, he and Mary Ann also started their family. Thomas Eyre Booth, the oldest son, was born in 1842.[15] The next child, Harriet, was born in 1846, but she lived only a year.[16]

Harriet's death was difficult for Mary Ann, as a later letter she sent to Edmund suggests:

> I am tired to have only two children. I wish that I had six or ten children now. You know that I love children more than all gold. You will laugh at me about raising more children but I cannot help it, for I love babies, as little girls love their dolls.[17]

Many nineteenth-century women felt the same way, largely because marriage and motherhood were their key social roles. Unfortunately, it was also typical for babies born in the nineteenth century to die during infancy because frontier life was harsh, and there was no protection against diseases.

Mary Ann and Edmund, however, had another daughter, also named Harriet, in 1848. Their last child, Frank Walworth Booth, was born in 1855, a year after Edmund returned from California.[18] All of the Booth children could hear, unlike their parents, also a typical situation for children of deaf parents then and now.

Much of the information we have about Mary Ann's life is drawn from the correspondence between Edmund and Mary Ann during the period he was in California prospecting for gold from 1849 to 1854. Excerpts from some of the correspondence appear here.[19] Much of their correspondence consists of letters from Mary Ann to Edmund; there are fewer letters from Edmund to Mary Ann. The letters in and of themselves, therefore, do not provide a complete picture of the Booths' lives during this period. Some additional information about Mary Ann, however, comes from Edmund's autobiographical notes; some notes their children, Thomas and Harriet, later added to their father's autobiography; and from some information on the Walworth family that their descendants have made available. Collectively, these sources, though incomplete, give a better understanding of Mary Ann's and Edmund's lives. The Anamosa *Eureka*, the local newspaper, also published Mary Ann's obituary. Little information, however, exists about either Mary Ann's life from the time she became deaf until the time she met Edmund at the American School for the Deaf when she was fourteen or about her life after Edmund came back home from California.

The limited information about Mary Ann points to some research issues. The first is that people simply did not record information about nineteenth-century women the way they did about men of that period. Another issue is that Mary Ann led a life typical of the average nineteenth-century American frontier woman, other than the fact she was deaf. Despite the lack of complete information on Mary Ann from her correspondence, we are able to get a sense of what Mary Ann's life was like, both as a nineteenth-century frontier housewife and as a deaf woman living during that time.

Edmund's absence in California from 1849 to 1854 was a difficult period in Mary Ann's life. Mary Ann and the children moved around a lot and lived in less than ideal conditions during these five years. Edmund originally left them with his brother, Henry Booth, who also lived in

Fairview. Consequently, Mary Ann and the children also had to live with
Julia Booth, Henry's daughter, and with Mary Ann's mother-in-law, the
senior Mrs. Booth. Mary Ann and the children stayed there for slightly
more than a year.[20] Mary Ann found living with Julia difficult. She wrote
to Edmund of her plight:

> I am going to tell you how Julia saucy me. When I read your last letters,
> she laughed at me that I never had a secret letter from you and also
> laughed at me that you could not come back, for you had no money
> enough to come back. I get dreadful mad at her. She thinks herself that
> her father is richer then Ford or you.[21]

In the same letter to Edmund, Mary Ann wrote of problems she was having with Edmund's brother, Henry Booth, with whom she had financial
dealings while Edmund was away.

> Henry is very stingy and selfish as I ever knew, because I use to live and
> see him all time while you are absent. When you were traveling along, I
> tried to borrow fifty cents but he would not, he had ten dollars in gold
> before. I never can like him very well. I wish that we shall live far from
> him and Julia and all our folks. I can not describe what they all done to
> me. I think that they are worse than my own parents done to you when
> we lived with them in Illinois. I often went alone and wept. I wish that I
> can go to Cal. by water. I shall be glad to rid of all our folks.[22]

Then, in the fall of 1850, Henry Booth decided to hire himself out as a
man-of-work for his sister's husband, Gideon Ford. Ford owned a hotel in
Anamosa called the Wapsipinicon House. Henry's decision to work for
Ford meant that everyone had to move into the "Wapsi House," as the hotel was called. Mary Ann and the children were, theoretically, given their
own addition in which to sleep. However, Thomas Booth later recalled
that he actually slept with the Ford boys, and that Mary Ann and Harriet
slept elsewhere in the hotel.[23]

Sometime later, either in November or December of 1850, Mary Ann
and the children lived with some friends in the area. First, they lived with
Lewis Perkins and his wife, a deaf couple, in Fairview for about five
months. This living arrangement also was not ideal for Mary Ann or the
children even though Lewis Perkins was also deaf and she could communicate well with him. Mary Ann wrote to Edmund of her dealings with
the Perkinses:

> Mrs. Perkins is a diabolical woman as I ever saw before, she treated us
> ill almost while I live with her about five months. I can not stay with her

any longer. She uses to make Harriet crying often. Because she does not love any children. No I do not want you to have some present for her. I have paid some her for renting her part of the room which Lewis has not fix any about his house since you went away. I shall certainly move soon. I get rid of them.[24]

They also lived with a Linus Osborn until a flood damaged his house in the spring of 1851, and they had to move out.[25] There is no definitive written information about where they lived between this time and the fall of 1851 when they finally moved into their new house in Anamosa, but evidence suggests they lived with other friends in this period. Also, Mary Ann and the children stayed with her younger sister, Emily Walworth Fifield, and her family in Dubuque during the winter of 1852 and the early part of 1853. Henry Booth looked after their Fairview farm that winter.[26]

A key factor that contributed to the family's difficulties while Edmund was gone was the communication barriers that Mary Ann's deafness created for her and for those around her. She coped with the communication difficulties in a variety of ways. Thomas, as the oldest child, often served as Mary Ann's interpreter when she conducted business in town or went to check on the family farm in Fairview. Mary Ann and Edmund reinforced their dependence on Thomas to interpret for MaryAnn when they encouraged him to develop his English skills. Edmund, for example, sent newspapers home from California and ordered books for Thomas.[27] Also, in a letter to Edmund, Mary Ann referred to another communication strategy she used when she received Edmund's first letter from California proper:

> While I read it, all boarders and children stood around me and watched and felt anxious to know what had become of you, till I finished reading it. I [then] gave it to Durham to read it to them aloud.[28]

Mary Ann probably used other people as interpreters for her, as shown in these examples, because she knew that most people outside her immediate family could not understand her voice.

Mary Ann and her children, however, communicated fluently in sign language, as she often mentioned in her letters to Edmund. For example, she wrote of her daughter, Harriet: "She often asks me if I write to you and I answer yes. She laughs heartily and smiles. She says by signs that you will come back and she will see you [her] father, by and by."[29] In another letter, Mary Ann wrote, "now Harriet just came and saw me writing. She says that I am writing to you and that she wants me to tell you that her uncle George gave her candy and raisins and took her and myself to ride in his Gig, and that he is a good uncle (she says [this] by signs). She can talk by signs with me as well as any mutes."[30]

Mary Ann was forced, out of sheer necessity, to manage the family household and finances during the five years that Edmund was in California. She hired several people, including Lewis Perkins, to work the family farm in Fairview because she could not handle it all herself while also raising two children alone.[31] Frequently, Mary Ann wrote to Edmund of good business deals she had either made or was planning. For example, "I sold my old cow, which is worth twelve dollars, because I wanted money to pay our tax [of] over six dollars,"[32] and "there are fifty bushels of oats in our old field ready for me [to sell]. I shall get somebody to go after my oats here soon. I believe that I shall sell them to the merchants in this town, but I must wait, until one bushel will cost 20 or 25 cents. Now it costs 15 cents."[33] These are two examples of many in the correspondence that show that Mary Ann clearly demonstrated business acumen and knew how to manage money, which was fortunate because Edmund was gone for so long.

Mary Ann scored a real coup in 1851 when she used $90 that Edmund had sent her from California to buy land in Anamosa from a J. H. Fisher. Later, she had a house built on it. Mary Ann wrote to Edmund of this purchase, saying,

> I bought five acres of land at 90 dollars. . . . A man, his name is Handy, heard that I want to build a new house on that land. He came to see me about building a house for me and he said that he would build the very cheapest in this town so I agreed with him. . . . He will finish all [of] my house. He asked for 150 dollars to build and find everything needed for the house, which is very cheap.[34]

Thomas Booth later wrote that his mother "had large visions of the future, and I remember how picturesquely she signed it out, that sometime a man would come and take one thousand dollars out of his pocket— please imagine her oratorical air—and hand it over to us for that five acres!"[35]

Mary Ann was prescient—the acreage she bought eventually became the Anamosa town center, and the Booths later donated some of it to the First Congregational Church in 1861. Main, First, Booth, and South Ford Streets mark the outlines of this property today. The house that Edmund and Mary Ann built was on the corner of Main and Booth Streets, but it burned down in 1881.[36]

Despite Mary Ann's business successes while Edmund was away, she felt keen loneliness and isolation during those five years. Mary Ann did not have any help from Edmund in dealing with her sometimes-difficult in-laws. These troubles were compounded by the communication gaps caused by her deafness. The fact that Mary Ann and the children had to live in different places, often under difficult circumstances, also added to her tribulations. Furthermore, Mary Ann experienced long periods of not knowing of Edmund's welfare; there were gaps of three to five months between letters from Edmund. Mary Ann worried about Edmund, as any wife would have, and repeatedly asked him to come home. The following examples from Mary Ann's letters to Edmund clearly show how lonely she felt.

In August of 1851, Mary Ann wrote,

> If you are not coming back next winter I shall live lonesome in our new house all the gloomy winter. My tears start in my eyes and fall down my cheeks while I am writing, for I think that you will never come back and that you will say that you will stay in Cal. every other year. I did not answer your letters immediately [after] I received them on [the] thirty first of July, because I felt very discouraged that you were not coming home.[37]

In March of 1853, Mary Ann poignantly wrote to Edmund,

> Sometimes my heart is painful. If you do not come back sooner I expect that I will sometimes die suddenly. I do not know what will our children do. I won't let them live with Henry's or Mr. Ford because they are vulgar as I have seen them much while you are absent from home. Pray do come back. Do try to come, come, come along. I hope that God will make your return home in safety and join me again. God bless you.[38]

Several months later, in July, she wrote,

> I quickly sat down to open [your letter] and read it and [al]most cried, for I rejoiced to hear you say that you would be home next winter. I believe that you will certainly be here soon, so I feel much relieved. I wish that you would start for home early in the fall and be home before Christmas or New Year's, so I may make you [a] feast here.[39]

Mary Ann had to practically beg Edmund to come home, which he finally did in March of 1854.[40] Little information exists about Mary Ann after Edward's return, even though she lived more than forty more years. She died in January 1898 at the age of eighty. The *Eureka* obituary of Mary Ann said that she was sick and bedridden much of the year before she died. Edmund was inconsolable and quite lonely after Mary Ann died because he had depended on her during the course of their fifty-seven-plus years of marriage.[41]

Mary Ann Booth lived an ordinary life in many ways as a typical frontier housewife and mother. The rich body of personal correspondence between Mary Ann and Edmund Booth, however, provides us with a unique view of one such pioneer family's life, particularly so because Mary Ann and Edmund were literate deaf individuals. The correspondence further illumines our understanding of the communication challenges deaf people faced in an earlier, more difficult era of American history and shows how well one deaf woman coped with, and even thrived in, unusually adverse circumstances.

Notes

1. For more information about Agatha Tiegel Hanson, the first deaf woman graduate of Gallaudet College, see Edward Miner Gallaudet, *History of the College for the Deaf, 1857–1907*, ed. Lance J. Fischer and David de Lorenzo (Washington, D.C.: Gallaudet College Press, 1983), 166–67. See also Jill Ker Conway, *When Memory Speaks: Exploring the Art of Autobiography* (New York: Vintage Books, Random House, 1998), 88–91, and Harriet Martineau, *Harriet Martineau's Autobiography*, Maria Weston Chapman, ed. (Boston: J. R. Osgood and Co., 1877) for more information about Harriet Martineau and her writings in the Victorian era. For more information about Laura Redden Searing, a deaf American reporter and poet during the nineteenth century, see "Laura Redden Searing 1840–1923" in *A Mighty Change: An Anthology of Deaf American Writing, 1818–1864*, ed. Christopher Krentz (Washington, D.C.: Gallaudet University Press, 2000), 129–30. More in-depth information about Searing can also be found in *Sweet Bells Jangled: Laura Redden Searing a Deaf Poet Restored*, ed. Judy Yaeger Jones and Jane Vallier (Washington, D.C.: Gallaudet University Press, 2003).

2. Edmund Booth, *Edmund Booth (1810–1905), Forty-Niner: The Life Story of a Deaf Pioneer* (Stockton, Calif.: San Joaquin Pioneer and Historical Society, 1953).

3. Booth, *Edmund Booth (1810–1905), Forty-Niner*, 28–29, 30.

4. Booth, *Edmund Booth (1810–1905), Forty-Niner*, 33–34, 56–57.

5. Booth, *Edmund Booth (1810–1905), Forty-Niner*, 33.

6. Booth, *Edmund Booth (1810–1905), Forty-Niner*, 58.

7. Walworth Family Group Record, pp. 1 and 3, given to me for research in May 1997 by Wilma Heckenlaible Spice, great-great-granddaughter of Edmund Booth and Mary Ann Walworth Booth.

8. Walworth Family Group Record, p. 1; "Mary Ann Walworth Booth Obituary," *The Anamosa Eureka* (Thomas E. Booth, Editor), February 3, 1898, 8.

9. Walworth Family Group Record, pp. 1–2.

10. Walworth Family Group Record, p. 3.

11. Booth, *Edmund Booth (1810–1905), Forty-Niner*, 1–3; "Mary Ann Walworth Booth Obituary," *The Anamosa Eureka*, February 3, 1898, 8.

12. Booth, *Edmund Booth (1810–1905), Forty-Niner,* 4–5. Thomas E. Booth, "Thomas Eyre Booth's Remembrances of Father (Edmund Booth)," typescript, Walworth Family Group Record, pp. 6–7.

13. Booth, *Edmund Booth (1810–1905), Forty-Niner,* 4.

14. Booth, *Edmund Booth (1810–1905), Forty-Niner,* 5.

15. "Mary Ann Walworth Booth Descendancy Chart," Walworth Family Group Record; "Mary Ann Walworth Booth Obituary," *The Anamosa Eureka,* February 3,1898, 8.

16. Booth, *Edmund Booth (1810–1905), Forty-Niner,* 5.

17. Mary Ann Walworth Booth to Edmund Booth, March 15, 1852, Edmund Booth Family Papers, San Joaquin Pioneer and Historical Society, Stockton, Calif. Mary Ann wrote strong, effective prose, but with common grammatical and spelling errors. For the purposes of this article, I have corrected some of her errors for greater clarity.

18. Frank Walworth Booth, the youngest child of Edmund Booth and Mary Ann Walworth Booth, was the superintendent of the Nebraska School for the Deaf at Omaha for twenty-five years, from 1911 to 1936, and was an ardent advocate of the use of the oral method in deaf education. "Edmund Booth & Son: 'Eureka' Editor," in *Anamosa 1838–1988 . . . A Reminiscence,* ed. Bertha Finn, Pat Worden Sutton, Jo Ann Mc Roberts Walters, and Mildred Parker Brown (Monticello, Iowa: The Monticello Express), 39. For a good discussion of Frank Booth's advocacy of oralism in deaf education, particularly with respect to the Nebraska Law of 1911, see John Vickrey Van Cleve and Barry Crouch, *A Place of Their Own: Creating the Deaf Community in America* (Washington, D.C.: Gallaudet University Press, 1989), 103–4, 135–8.

19. I decided to leave the excerpts from the correspondence mostly intact in this article, with grammatical errors, to show how Mary Ann wrote and how she thought about the events in her life. I have added words to a few places in the correspondence excerpts to clarify the meaning of Mary Ann's writing, as needed. These explanations are indicated by bracket marks. Despite the formal education Mary Ann received at the American School for the Deaf, her writing reveals the difficulties she had in grasping the fundamentals of English grammar and composition.

20. Thomas E. Booth, "Thomas Eyre Booth's Remembrances of Father," 9.

21. Mary Ann Walworth Booth to Edmund Booth, August 17, 1851, Edmund Booth Family Papers.

22. Mary Ann Walworth Booth to Edmund Booth, August 17, 1851, Edmund Booth Family Papers.

23. Thomas E. Booth, "Thomas Eyre Booth's Remembrances of Father," 19.

24. Mary Ann Walworth Booth to Edmund Booth, April 3, 1851, Edmund Booth Family Papers.

25. Thomas E. Booth, "Thomas Eyre Booth's Remembrances of Father," 19.

26. Mary Ann Walworth Booth to Edmund Booth, November 9, 1852, Edmund Booth Family Papers.

27. Mary Ann Walworth Booth to Edmund Booth, May 2, 1852, and March 19, 1853, Edmund Booth to Mary Ann Walworth Booth, February 2, 1853, and April 16, 1853.

28. Mary Ann Walworth Booth to Edmund Booth, January 3, 1850, Edmund Booth Family Papers.

29. Mary Ann Walworth Booth to Edmund Booth, August 17, 1851, Edmund Booth Family Papers.

30. Mary Ann Walworth Booth to Edmund Booth, October 19, 1851, Edmund Booth Family Papers.

31. Mary Ann Walworth Booth to Edmund Booth, October 19, 1851, Edmund Booth Family Papers.

32. Mary Ann Walworth Booth to Edmund Booth, January 3, 1850, Edmund Booth Family Papers.

33. Mary Ann Walworth Booth to Edmund Booth, March 15, 1852, Edmund Booth Family Papers.

34. Mary Ann Walworth Booth to Edmund Booth, August 17, 1851, Edmund Booth Family Papers.

35. Thomas E. Booth, "Thomas Eyre Booth's Remembrances of Father," 4.

36. Thomas E. Booth, "Thomas Eyre Booth's Remembrances of Father," 4–5.

37. Mary Ann Walworth Booth to Edmund Booth, August 17, 1851, Edmund Booth Family Papers.

38. Mary Ann Walworth Booth to Edmund Booth, March 14, 1853, Edmund Booth Family Papers.

39. Mary Ann Walworth Booth to Edmund Booth, July 22, 1853, Edmund Booth Family Papers.

40. Thomas E. Booth, "Thomas Eyre Booth's Remembrances of Father," 2.

41. "Mary Ann Walworth Booth Obituary," *The Anamosa Eureka*, February 3, 1898, 8.

5

A Tale of Two Schools: The Indiana Institution and the Evansville Day School, 1879–1912

Michael Reis

Editor's Introduction

In this article, Michael Reis uses a detailed study of the histories of the Indiana School for the Deaf and the Evansville Day School for the Deaf to illuminate important issues related to deaf schools, their students, their politics, and their administrators in the late-nineteenth century. A graduate of the Indiana School himself, Reis has spent fifteen years researching on Indiana deaf history–writing articles, a commemorative yearbook and producing various photographic exhibits. He makes several significant arguments about the late-nineteenth-century United States. First, deaf agency during this period was greater than historians have shown before because many more day schools were founded by signing deaf persons than have been generally recognized. Second, schools for the deaf were extremely underfunded, and their impoverishment contrasted sharply with the wealth of some individuals, including some deaf people, of the time. Third, as the nineteenth century drew to a close, the "personalities" of the deaf schools changed, with schools becoming more bureaucratic and less focused on their students. Similarly, partisan politics, rather than educational imperatives, increasingly influenced the governance of deaf schools during the crucial period when schools largely abandoned sign language for oral methods of instruction.

This paper discusses the history of a day school for deaf pupils in the Evansville, Indiana, public school system and its relationship to the state-operated residential school for deaf children in Indianapolis. By the 1880s, when the Evansville day school challenged the Indiana Institution's monopoly of deaf education, the Indianapolis school was powerful and politically well-connected. It had not always been that way. William Willard, a deaf man, founded the Indiana Institution for the Education of the Deaf and Dumb as a small private school in 1843, and it was not until the next year that the state of Indiana took over, ensuring the school's future viability but, at the same time, creating a number of potential problems. The conflict with the Evansville day school brought these problems to light and provides an unusual window into deaf education in the late-nineteenth and early twentieth centuries. It also challenges other interpretations of day schools, sign language, and the role of deaf people in deaf education at the close of the nineteenth century.

The 1844 legislation creating the Indiana Institution gave the governor full authority to appoint the school's board of trustees, who then elected the superintendent. The first superintendent they picked in 1845 was James S. Brown, a hearing man and former teacher in the Ohio Institution for the Deaf. In 1850, the state legislature appropriated funds to acquire seventy acres of land east of Indianapolis to build a campus for the school, which had been functioning from rented rooms. Superintendent Brown resigned shortly after, in 1852, to establish an institution for deaf students in Louisiana. His successor, Thomas MacIntire, served for twenty-seven years. The intertwined account of the Indiana Institution and the Evansville day school starts when MacIntire was removed from his position in 1879, and it continues into the early twentieth century. The linked and contentious history of these two schools demonstrates the influence of politics and personal rivalries in deaf education during a period when the controversies over not only oralism and manualism but also residential institutions and day schools were at their peak.

And the Darkness Fell

MacIntire had some experience in deaf education before being named to succeed Brown. A trained Presbyterian minister, he first taught in the Ohio Institution and had served for several years as superintendent of the Tennessee Institution in Knoxville, where he assisted in the school's early growth by exhibiting educated deaf children all over eastern and central Tennessee. In the nineteenth century, exhibitions were used to inform the general public about the advantages of educating deaf children and to recruit additional pupils. The Indiana Institution hired MacIntire as a teacher in 1852. Brown's resignation took place one month after his arrival, creating an opportunity for MacIntire's promotion.

One possible explanation for MacIntire's long service in the Indiana Institution was that he may have been a close friend of Oliver Morton, a powerful governor of Indiana during the Civil War and then a U.S. senator. There is no specific record of this friendship, but a history of the school hints that a relationship existed.[1]

In 1857, the benevolent institutions, including the Indiana Institution, shortened their academic year as a result of the state government's financial difficulties.[2] This closure affected enrollment at the school for the next few years. During the Civil War, it seemed that the benevolent institutions in Indiana would have to close again. The deaf school did not, however, because Governor Morton intervened, borrowing money from state bonds specifically to keep the deaf institution open.[3]

Morton remained a powerful influence in Indiana as a U. S. senator. He was a Republican, and the Union's victory ensured the Republican Party long control of the state government. The Union army veterans provided strong support to the Republicans. Republican election strategies capitalized on the fact that the Democrats advocated compromise and negotiation with the rebels during the Civil War, and the Republicans regularly accused them of having treasonous tendencies. Morton waved the "bloody shirt" of the martyred Union soldiers against the Democrats during the state and presidential elections between 1866 and 1876.

When Morton died in 1877, the Republican hold on the Indiana state government began to weaken. Economic difficulties had begun to affect the national economy, and many people were out of work. Labor unrest spread through the railroads in many cities, and the Democrats were able to win the state governorship in 1878.[4]

With Morton gone, MacIntire may have felt vulnerable to the shift of political winds. However, he had been superintendent of the Indiana Institution for twenty-five years, and he hoped to stay on for many more. Regardless, his sense of vulnerability was soon confirmed.

On March 6, 1879, the Democrat-controlled state legislature passed an act to provide for appointment and confirmation of the boards of trustees in the benevolent institutions for their more efficient management and uniform government. This innocuous sounding bill created a new board of trustees at the Indiana Institution. On March 15, the new board asked for MacIntire's resignation, effective May 29, 1879.

The board appointed a dentist, William Glenn, to be the new superintendent of the Indiana Institution. Very little information is available about Glenn, aside from the fact that he was a member of the state Democratic Party and apparently had no experience with either educational administration or the needs of deaf students.

The Indianapolis *Journal* newspaper printed a blistering editorial, "An Infamous Proceeding," about this appointment. The *Journal* pointed out that MacIntire had provided long service to the Indiana Institution and held several national offices in deaf education. The editorial called the new board of trustees "an unscrupulous ring of Indianapolis Democrats whose sole object was to pelt and plunder," and asked how the dental skills of William Glenn would be useful in the instruction of deaf students. The editorial claimed that parents and friends of deaf children would remove those students from the Indiana Institution.[5]

Even though MacIntire was no longer superintendent of the Indiana Institution during the summer of 1879, he followed through with one of the most important tasks of an institutional superintendent: enrolling his pupils in the National Deaf Mute College (today's Gallaudet University). The admission process into the college during the nineteenth century was highly personal. National college examinations did not exist. For a deaf student to gain admission into the college, he (only males were admitted until 1887) had to have his school superintendent and his U.S. senator send letters of recommendation to the college president, Edward M. Gallaudet. Deaf students could receive federal scholarships to attend the college, which explained the role of the senator. Gallaudet apparently relied on the superintendents' letters of recommendation to judge applicants' abilities. Admitted students had to undertake a lengthy period of examinations at the beginning of the first year. If successful, they were judged fit for college work. In the fall of 1879, four pupils from the Indiana Institution—Charles Kerney, Oscar Osborne, Philip Hasenstab, and Nathaniel Morrow—were admitted into the college in the fall of 1879. This group was an unprecedented number of new students from one state; every year the college admitted only about fifteen students from the entire country.

Hastenstab and Morrow were unique in that they skipped their senior year at the Indiana Institution. The Institution's register of new pupils noted their departure at the end of their junior year, and they were the only two to be able to do so in the entire history of the Indiana Institution. Gallaudet must have approved this unorthodox maneuver, which indicates that MacIntire, Gallaudet, Hasenstab, and Morrow did not have any confidence in the incoming dentist superintendent. In retrospect, it is clear that the departure of MacIntire marked the passing of an era of benevolent and competent administration of the Indiana Institution.

Glenn's administrative priorities were evident in his annual reports to the board of trustees. MacIntire's annual reports usually were about thirty pages long, with general statements of expenditures, deaths and illnesses, new programs, and new needs of the institution. However, Glenn's first

annual report was 300 pages! Twenty-eight pages were given to the state
of the institution, with the remainder of the annual report devoted to day-
by-day expenditures on sundry supplies. Glenn noted that the 1879 expenditures for the institution were only $55,855 compared with $62,997 in
the previous year. A sum of $4,793 was returned to the state treasury. In
the 1880 annual report, also more than 300 pages, the expenditures were
proudly noted to be $50,005. In subsequent years, the institution's expen-
ditures reached almost $60,000, but Glenn's voluminous annual reports
still listed day-to-day expenses, even down to an expenditure of one quar-
ter for postage in one day!

The board of trustees previously had elected the superintendent for
four-year terms, but when Glenn was up for reelection in July, 1883, he
was reelected for only one year. This decision may have been a result
of the unfavorable report from a legislative investigation in 1881 that
charged him with economizing excessively and serving poor food.[6]
Glenn's term as superintendent ended abruptly on November 12, 1884,
when he was removed from his position with no explanation.

Eli Baker was chosen to be the new superintendent, effective December
15, 1884. Baker had two strange qualifications for the position: he was
once a deputy warden at the Indiana State Penitentiary, and he was a
Democratic Party worker.[7] The selection of new superintendent Baker
was certainly not good news.

At the beginning of the 1886–1887 school year, an alumni reunion took
place at the Indiana Institution, with about 200 people attending. This was
the first of a series of triennial alumni reunions, which led to the organization known as Indiana Association of the Deaf. One afternoon was devoted to a memorial service for MacIntire, who had died in September of
1885. His widow and daughter were present, and numerous tributes were
made to the departed superintendent. Those at the reunion passed various resolutions with respect to the Indiana Institution and its betterment.
One resolution called for the state to have only one state institution for
deaf students, with no other schools elsewhere in the state. However, this
resolution was too little and too late.

The Evansville Day School

Barely a week had passed since the alumni reunion when, on September
2, 1886, a new day school for deaf students was announced in the
Evansville public schools. Charles Kerney, a member of the graduation
class of 1879 at the Indiana Institution, was its founder. This event marked
the first time that another deaf school existed in Indiana, and it was even

Etching of the Evansville Day School for the Deaf in the old city library in Evansville. Source: "The Evansville School," in Edward A. Fay, ed., *Histories of the American Schools for the Deaf* (Washington, D.C.: Gallaudet College, 1893). Courtesy of the Gallaudet University Archives.

more troubling for the Indiana Institution that one of its alumni founded the day school. In the past forty years of the existence of the Indiana Institution, the most prevailing assumption had been that every deaf child in Indiana would go there without question.

Charles Kerney was born in western Kentucky in 1857, with an unexplained loss of hearing at an early age. He reportedly said that he did not know his own name until he entered the Kentucky Institution at the age of fifteen. Kerney had lost both of his parents before his graduation from the Indiana Institution in 1879, but he went on to graduate from Gallaudet College. Subsequently, he worked briefly as a file clerk in the Department of Commerce in Washington, D.C.

Kerney's establishment of a day school in the late 1880s fit a larger national trend in the United States. Before the Civil War, instruction of deaf students in America took place almost exclusively in residential institutions that served broad geographical areas, typically a state, but occasionally a region. Government funding enabled schools to construct dormitories and bear the expenses of residential facilities. However, a marked shift toward day schools took place after the Civil War.

One reason was that the state institutions used sign language as the primary communication tool. The oral method, which stressed speech training and speechreading, especially among children who had not completely lost their hearing, came from England and Germany and was gaining popularity in the late-nineteenth century. Oral instruction required small classes and frequently involved intensive parental involvement in speech training. The state institutions were distant from the majority of these parents, however, depriving parents the opportunity to receive training in oral methods that they would then use in the home.

The State of Maine provides an example of this reason for the spread of day schools. Before 1876, all deaf children in Maine were sent to the American School for the Deaf in Hartford, Connecticut, but the American School did not have speech-training classes. A woman established a small class in Portland, Maine, to teach deaf children how to speak and, thus, began the Portland Day School, an oralist school.

Not all day schools in this period were oral schools, though, and several—like the Evansville school—were started by deaf people. In 1875, for example, Philip Emery proposed to the Chicago School Board that a small day school be established. A graduate of the Indiana Institution himself, Emery established branch classes for deaf students in various Chicago neighborhoods and obtained state funding by 1879. William French, also an alumnus of the Indiana Institution, founded the Eastern Iowa day school in Dubuque in 1888. The founder of the Cincinnati day school in 1892 was Robert MacGregor, the first president of the National Association of the Deaf.[8]

A question comes up: what is the motivation for these day schools, established by these deaf people? More research needs to be done upon the histories of these individual schools. As of the Evansville day school, two major motivations appear to be the overcrowding of the Indiana Institution, and its politically appointed superintendents. However, the day schools in other states may have different motivations for their establishment.

Evansville

Evansville was Indiana's second largest city in the 1880s. It was a transportation hub on the Ohio River, with railroad connections to Chicago, Nashville, St. Louis, and Louisville. Forests nearby provided lumber for furniture manufacturers, and farms shipped grain to its mills. Tobacco came from Kentucky to be processed into cigars. The large German population of southern Indiana and Illinois ensured ample business for its breweries.

In the 1880s, Evansville was prosperous. It had an elaborate new courthouse in the Second Empire architectural style. A local group, the Business Men's Association, had constructed a five-story structure for its meetings and offices and included a grand opera house. The city had constructed a large meeting hall, Evans Hall, in honor of the city's founder, General Evans; the new hall could hold up to 2,000 people.[9]

Prominent individuals in Evansville had myriad connections with deaf education, providing support for Kerney's efforts. The editor of the *Evansville Daily Journal* was said to be the brother of James S. Brown, the former superintendent of the Indiana Institution. He was also the classmate of Philip Gillett, superintendent of the Illinois Institution for the Deaf, and he had other relatives who worked as superintendents of deaf schools.[10] Gillett's brother was the president of Citizens' Bank, a prominent bank in town.[11] The secretary of the local utility, the Gas and Electric Light Company of Evansville, had a deaf son named John D. Hall. One teacher in the Evansville Day School, Emma Macy, boarded with John Hall's parents.[12] Finally, General Evans, the founder of Evansville, had three deaf grandchildren: Silas, Emma, and DeWitt Stephens. The Stephens family were wealthy, with extensive property throughout the city. Silas and Emma Stephens were already graduates of the Indiana Institution when Kerney founded the Evansville Day School, but DeWitt Stephens was among the new school's first pupils.

The Evansville Day School opened in 1886 with twenty-eight pupils. On December 30, 1886, they gave an exhibition of skits and recitations to 1,200 people in Evans Hall. Charles Kerney also used this opportunity to make a speech, calling to convert the day school into a state institution for the deaf children in southern Indiana.[13] The Evansville Day School was thus only four months old when Kerney challenged the Indiana Institution's monopoly of state-funded education for deaf children.

Four factors suggest that Kerney's attempt to receive government support was realistic. First, private day schools in other states had been converted to state institutions or had started receiving state support. The Pittsburgh Day School, for example, had become the state-supported Western Pennsylvania Institution for Deaf-Mutes in 1876, and the Chicago Day School had begun receiving state appropriations in 1879.

Second, state institutions proliferated across Indiana after 1865. From 1867 through 1895, ten state institutions opened—from the Indiana Boys'

Reformatory in Plainfield to the Indiana Soldier's Home in Lafayette—
and only one was in Indianapolis. In *The Centennial History of the Indiana
General Assembly 1816–1978,* Justin E. Walsh describes this period well:

> [T]he asylums and prisons were major sources of patronage. . . .
> Politics, local logrolling and genuine need, combined to increase the
> number of penal and benevolent institutions after the Civil War. Politics
> were involved, because of the increased possibilities for patronage.
> Local logrolling was involved because each section of the state de-
> manded its own asylum or prison.[14]

Third, the Indiana Institution in Indianapolis was crowded. The dining
room was originally designed for 250 pupils, but it held 312 pupils with
continuous rows of tables from one end of the room to the other. The attic
above the institutional chapel was raised as a second story for a new dormitory housing older boys. Fifty boys slept there in an area of 50 feet by 60
feet. The dorms were so crowded that it was calculated that only 514 cubic
feet were available for each pupil.[15]

Finally, the Indiana Institution clearly was not meeting the needs of
all the state's deaf children. The 1880 census reported that Indiana had
950 deaf residents between the ages of five and twenty years, yet only
317 of this group—only one-third—were enrolled in the Indiana
Institution.

The arrival of the Evansville Day School had an immediate effect on the
Indiana Institution. A deaf person and former instructor at the Indiana
Institution, Orson Archibald, prepared a legislative bill that called for
stringent civil service regulations and an $80,000 new schoolhouse with
thirty classrooms for the Indiana Institution. He spent three weeks in
February 1887 lobbying for the bill—the first record of a deaf citizen directly involved in Indiana state legislative activities—but Archibald ultimately was unsuccessful.[16] He failed not because of his efforts but because the state legislators were particularly contentious that session.

> The legislative session of 1887 was chaotic and unproductive, display-
> ing the state government machine at its worst. . . . [W]hen Republican
> Lieutenant Governor Robert S. Robertson was duly elected in the fall
> general election of 1886, the Democratic controlled Senate repudiated
> him and chose one of its own members. . . . From that point on, the
> two houses, operating under mutually antagonistic party leadership, re-
> fused to cooperate with each other. The outcome was a legislative dead-
> lock; little business was transacted and few laws enacted.[17]

November 26, 1887, marked the date of the first issue of *The Indiana Deaf-Mute Journal,* the school newspaper of the Indiana Institution. Institutional newspapers were important to the deaf community in the nineteenth century. Schools had printing shops to teach boys the art of printing. As one strategy to accomplish this objective, the institutions printed weekly newspapers. The weeklies described pupil activities and news of alumni such as weddings, deaths, jobs, and so forth. Many deaf people subscribed to their institutional weeklies to keep track of school friends and developments at the state institution. The institutional weeklies comprised a loosely knit fraternity, dedicated to wider public knowledge of the deaf institutions and their activities. They were in friendly competition for correspondents and subscribers, but they reprinted excellent articles from one other. Any unfavorable publicity, however, would result in denials and rebuttals from the affected institution. The institutional weeklies also provided a platform to debate controversial topics such as oralism and the role of religion in the state institutions. Shifting alliances formed among certain papers such as the alliance of Midwestern institutional weeklies unifying in opposition to the Eastern papers. Alliances changed frequently, however, depending on the subject matter. Many younger deaf institutions preceded Indiana in establishing their institutional papers, such as the Illinois and Iowa institutions, which were already publishing before Indiana finally started in 1887.

It is conceivable that the Indiana Institution was forced to publish its own institutional weekly to present its side of the controversies surrounding the institution and the new Evansville Day School, but whatever the motivation, the initial edition of *The Indiana Deaf-Mute Journal* did not have an easy baptism. Almost immediately, other institutional weeklies gave it plenty of criticism. The first difficulty was its newspaper name, which was obviously a copy of the title of the venerable and well-respected New York Institution weekly, the *Deaf-Mutes' Journal.* Before 1887, all the institutional weeklies had created their unique names, reflecting upon their states' heritages, and did not copy one another's names. The *Deaf-Mutes' Journal* was not pleased at the Indiana newspaper's brash imitation.

Furthermore, the first few issues of the Indiana Institution weekly contained numerous typos and brought charges of plagiarism from other weeklies. The other weeklies were not pleased at its blatant disregard of journalistic principles.

Before *The Indiana Deaf-Mute Journal,* there was little record of life at the Indiana Institution, but the paper provided some clues of the turmoil the school was experiencing. For example, the February 13, 1888, issue included an editorial telling how an unscrupulous businessman sold some bad butter to a certain institution. When this businessman returned with the next shipment of butter, he was stripped of his clothing and smeared with the rancid butter from head to toe. Another editorial in the October 13, 1892, issue denied a previous newspaper article in Indianapolis that impure milk had caused many pupils at the deaf institution to become violently ill. This editorial pointed out that this incident actually happened at the institution for blind students, and the editor bitterly complained about the local press confusing the institutions. Both incidents of bad food were written in a matter-of-fact tone, as if spoiled food was an ordinary matter in the school.

The editor of *The Indiana Deaf-Mute Journal* produced many editorials criticizing Charles Kerney and the Evansville Day School, but the editor apparently overreached himself with this editorial:

KERNEY'S YOUR MAN

In glancing through the "want column" of the Indianapolis Daily Sentinel we ran across the following rather strange-looking advertisement:

> 'WANTED-A Consummate Liar. Please address with statement of ability, to Fame and Fortune, New York.'

We would recommend that the Indiana correspondent to the *New York Journal* [that is, Kerney] immediately apply for the situation."[18]

The *Deaf-Mutes' Journal* recommended that Kerney file a suit of libel against this editor, but no action was taken. What spurred this nasty editorial was a long and anonymous article in the *Deaf-Mutes' Journal* titled "Politics in Schools for the Deaf" by a fictitious person called Elna Keneta. This article claimed to describe the conditions of "one state institution for deaf mutes in certain Western and Southern states." The fictional author stated that the principal was poorly educated and knew nothing of sign language. It described broken chairs and tables in the study rooms and crumbling walls. It claimed that female instructors of the Institution knew no sign language and stayed long enough just to get married and quit.[19]

The Keneta article sparked a controversy among the institutional weeklies. The *Minnesota Companion* protested against the anonymous nature and slanderous tone of the article, but the editor of the *Deaf-Mutes' Journal* noted that it was standard practice for many correspondents of the institutional weeklies to assume "noms de plume." The *Deaf-Mutes' Journal* also noted that the Indiana Institution had been the first institution to take offense at the Keneta article and, being the first one, made it

DEAF AND DUMB INSTITUTION.

A THREATENED EVIL INDIANA SHOULD FIGHT TO THE END.

INDIANAPOLIS, IND., October 20, 1888.

Our Dear Friends:—We, deaf-mutes, of Indiana, have labored in vain since 1879, to call the attention of the Democratic Administration to the mismanagement of our State Benevolent Institutions, especially the Indiana Institution for the Education of the Deaf and Dumb. In 1879, they gave us for our Superintendent a Democrat dentist from a village, a member of the School Board of Trustees. In 1883 they gave the dentist's place to a Democrat jailer (from the town of the President of the School Board) of education below that of the Average American, now occupying the position of great responsibility. They "Gave us stones for bread!"

The Republican Party has pledged itself in its platform that all the State Institutions should be divorced from party control, managed on business principles, and only such men employed as are fitted by experience and education to perform the duties intelligently. As it is universally conceded that the institutions cannot be reformed until the Republicans control the Legislature, so we, Democrats, and Republicans, alike, are fully determined to work for the success of the Republican Party.

Please read what the newspapers throughout the country say of the Deaf-Mute Institution.

Remember a vote for the Republican ticket means a new management for our various State Institutions.   Very truly yours,

P. J. HASENSTAB, New Albany.   S. S. STEPHENS, Evansville.
C. O. DANTZER, Indianapolis.   C. E. STEINWENTER, Indianapolis.
J. C. F. WHEELER, Vincennes.   THEODORE HOLTZ, Evansville.

Prof. Charles Kerney mailed to the graduates of the Indiana Deaf Mute Institution.

EVANSVILLE, IND., April 11, 1888.

Dear Friend: I want to ask you here a question of great importance, as to our dear alma mater, now degraded by politics. We have directed the attention of the most influential citizens of Indiana to the bad management. They are so anxious to be supplied with all the needful facts which they are to lay before the legislature. But no work which includes the interest of the institution at heart, can be well done without the active, earnest sympathy and co-operation of the deaf of Indiana. To secure their close co-operation would insure for our alma mater the vigorous and successful prosecution of the approaching legislature. This effective and inexpensive organization would be the best working medium yet devised for the restoration of our dear alma mater to its former glory. Here is most keenly felt the want of intelligent co-operation which means success. None could engage in a more praiseworthy and patriotic service than of actively laboring for the advancement of the institution. Nothing promises so nearly to accomplished these results outlined herein. Courage is the one indispensable qualification for success in every association in life, be it religion, business or politics. We despise the man who has not the moral courage to set his face against the world's opinion. We have no use for those on the fence.   *   *   *   As you are one of the brainiest boys the Indianapolis Institution ever produced, what do you think of this? If you are fond of this, for God's sake take a fearless step upon every question that relates to the best interests of the whole institution. Of course jealousy, suspicion and prejudice must be avoided. Hastily,   CHARLES KERNEY.

This communication was from a sense of sympathy and duty to save our dear alma mater from party control. Prof. Kerney graduated from the Kentucky and Indiana Deaf Mute Institutions, and the National Deaf Mute College, Washington, D. C. He has always been a hard-shell Democrat, but now feels it his supreme duty to work for the success of the Republican Party. We can not do better than to quote the words of Prof. Albert Berg, one of the teachers of our institution, of Prof. Kerney, as follows: "I can say he is a man of uncommon intellectual ability and a gentleman in every sense of the word. Mr. Kerney is a keen observer of the educational dawn of the day, and has his opinions as rigidly defined now, as he occupies the proud position of being the champion of the deaf people of Indiana. What endears Mr. Kerney to his silent friends is his warm sympathy and his sincere patriotism."

D. AND D. INSTITUTION.

A Threatened Evil Indiana Should Fight to the End—A Wise and Common-Sense Communication from a Graduate Against the Management of the Indiana Deaf Mute Institution.

As a graduate of the Indiana Institution for the Education of the Deaf and Dumb at Indianapolis, I wish to direct the attention of the public to its mismanagement. An official investigation would reveal a sickening condition of affairs that makes one almost disposed to lose faith in humanity when human beings can be found who for a little paultry gain will be guilty of such barbarity to helpless deaf children. Every person connected with the institution, who can be shown to have been wilfully guilty of this mismanagement, should be subject to the utmost punishment which a violated law and an outraged humanity can inflict. The examination of the press is only a specimen of the many others in the State which seem to have been shamefully mismanaged. The subject matter of this statement is of so grave a character that a searching and impartial investigation is imperatively necessary.

The 1888 election pamphlet, written by Charles Kerney. Courtesy of the Gallaudet University Archives, Washington, D.C.

appear guilty. The *Deaf Mutes Journal* editor denied that Kerney penned that article, however. In the same issue, its Columbus, Ohio, correspondent wrote that the *Indianapolis Journal* newspaper had noted the Keneta article and demanded action from the board of trustees of the Indiana Institution, even though that article did not mention any institution by name.[20] The authorship of the Keneta article may never be known, but it contributed to the ongoing struggle between the Indiana Institution and the Evansville Day School, a struggle that had become overtly political by the fall of 1888.

In October of that year, Kerney launched a direct attack on the Indianapolis school, printing a political pamphlet titled, "DEAF AND DUMB INSTITUTION: A Threatened Evil Indiana Should Fight to the End." The document contained nine pages of tiny print, including the Keneta article from the *Deaf-Mutes' Journal* and other editorials and articles against the Indiana Institution and its board of trustees. Kerney encouraged Indiana's deaf citizens and their hearing friends and parents to vote Republican in the fall elections, suggesting that a change in the governor's mansion would result in a new board of trustees at the Indiana Institution.

The Indiana Institution also became directly involved in the election. In its November 7, 1888, issue, *The Indiana Deaf-Mute Journal* published an editorial announcing a demonstration of 150 boys marching around the institution grounds with burning effigies of Kerney and other deaf leaders. Superintendent Baker was wildly cheered by the boys, and the editor said that it was apparent that the Indiana Institution was heavily involved in state politics.

The Republicans won the governorship, but the Democrats retained control of the state legislature. It appeared that the political stalemate between the governor and the legislature would still continue. However, the winds of politics began to shift in this election. In his history of the Indiana General Assembly, Justin E. Walsh notes,

> [P]artisan committees [had] investigated charges of cruelty, extortion and fraud allegedly perpetuated by state agents against students and inmates at various state institutions. . . . By 1885, the legislature investigated major scandals at the Orphan's Home and the State Prison South; in 1887 it investigated another at the Insane Hospital in Indianapolis. . . . Reform was so obviously necessary that the Democratic General Assembly of 1889 cooperated with Republican Governor Alvin P. Hovey in conducting a thorough housecleaning. Because of such excesses, the charitable and correctional institutions were removed from politics in the 1890s and they began to be staffed by professionals operating under civil service rules instead of patronage.[21]

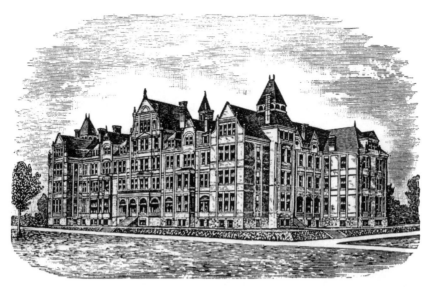

The proposed Southern Indiana Institute for Deaf Mutes to be located in Evansville, which was never built. Source: Charles Kerney, letter to Edward M. Gallaudet. Courtesy of the Gallaudet University Archives, Washington, D.C.

The previous scandals and investigations of the charitable and correctional institutions had paved the road to reform. Kerney's actions also may have played a part. Certainly, the Indiana Institution benefited because, on January 31, 1889, the state legislature approved a bill appropriating $50,000 for a classroom building, what Orson Archibald had tried to achieve two years earlier.

The 1888–1889 school year also marked important achievements for Kerney and his small school. First, Edward Miner Gallaudet, president of Gallaudet College, came as the guest speaker to the Evansville Day School for its annual exhibition in December. Gallaudet's appearance lent respectability to Kerney and his school. Two thousand people were present for his address, and almost $800 was collected in donations. After the exhibition, there was a reception for Gallaudet in Evansville's fanciest hotel.[22] A sketch of the proposed State Institution for Deaf-Mutes in Evansville also was unveiled, confirming Kerney's desire to have a state-supported school in Evansville. Second, the Evansville Day School was able to announce at its graduation ceremony that two of its graduates, Oscar Schaffer and Theodore Holtz, had been accepted into Gallaudet College. This announcement marked the first time that the college had taken students from a day school.[23]

Charles Kerney (standing at the extreme right) with his class at the Evansville Day School. His assistant, Emma Macy, stands at the extreme left. Source: The Silent Worker (April 1902): 116. Courtesy of the Gallaudet University Archives, Washington, D.C.

Changes were also occurring in the Indiana Institution in Indianapolis. The 1889–1890 school year initiated a change in the name of its institutional paper, now titled the *Silent Hoosier*. This new name effectively ended the confusion with New York's *Deaf-Mutes' Journal*, and the board of trustees appointed a new temporary superintendent, Richard O. Johnson, to replace Eli Baker, who resigned on July 1.

Johnson, who had graduated from the Virginia Military Institute and had gotten training as an attorney, was not new to the school. He had served as treasurer and secretary to the school's board of trustees since 1884. Even though Johnson had been involved with the political activities of the board of trustees, deaf people in Indiana welcomed him, and he returned the favor. At the ceremony on November 6, 1889, to lay the cornerstone for the new classroom building, Johnson signed his speech, marking the first time in ten years that a school superintendent had signed directly to the pupils.

Johnson's appointment introduced a peaceful interlude between the two deaf schools. Kerney sent a congratulatory message, which was printed in the *Silent Hoosier*. This paper also started to carry regular columns about the Evansville Day School. Various teachers from the Indiana Institution came down to Evansville as special lecturers to its deaf community.

The deaf community of Evansville benefited from the day school. Emma Macy, Kerney's assistant, set up a Sunday school class for deaf people in Calvary Baptist Church, and she served as the church treasurer during its move to a new structure. Kerney was active in the Business Men's Group, and he helped set up a literary society for deaf adults in the Evansville YMCA. By 1891, the Evansville Day School had become sufficiently popular that a legislative bill to grant it state support failed by only one vote in the Indiana General Assembly.[24]

Kerney seemed to be making progress in his personal life, too. Already materially comfortable because of a substantial family inheritance, in 1890, he married Annabell Powers, a deaf woman from a wealthy family. The *Deaf-Mutes' Journal* carried a front-page account of the Gilded Age wedding in the bride's parents' home with 150 guests. There were roses and white lilies everywhere in the house, and the wedding ceremony was held under a canopy of roses inside the parlor. Wedding gifts, including rare china, works of art, silver and gold ware, a large bronze clock, and bronze figures filled the second floor of the house. The couple honeymooned in Europe for two months, but events soon took an unexpected turn.

At the end of the 1891–1892 school year, the Evansville School Board dismissed Kerney from his position. Macy left soon after and took a position at the Arkansas School for the Deaf. The reasons for Kerney's dismissal are not clear. The Evansville newspapers do not explain it, and careful review of the school board minutes from 1886 to 1892 reveal no act of wrongdoing by Kerney. The enrollment of the day school had remained constant since 1886. However at the beginning in 1886, there were expectations of rapid growth and the school board had provided space for sixty children. Unfortunately, that growth didn't materialize in subsequent years. The removal of Kerney appeared, therefore, to be a reaction to dispelled expectations.

The Struggle Continues

Oddly enough, in June of 1892, the school board changed its mind, offering Kerney a teaching position for $100 a month. It is apparent that his removal had caused a public outcry, and the school board had to backtrack and ask him to return.[25] However, Kerney had already accepted a teaching position at the Indiana Institution in Indianapolis. In this situation, finding themselves without a teacher, the school board would have been

Paul Lange, the second teacher of the Evansville Day School. He taught at Evansville from 1892 to 1902, before moving to teach at the Wisconsin Institution. Source: "The Evansville Day School," in Edward A. Fay, ed., *Histories of the American Schools for the Deaf* (Washington, D.C.: Gallaudet College, 1893). Courtesy of the Gallaudet University Archives.

expected to hire a hearing, nonsigning, oralist woman to teach—a typical arrangement in many day schools during the 1890s, especially in Wisconsin.[26] Instead, at its August 8, 1892, meeting, the school board hired, for $70 per month, a young deaf man, Paul Lange, just graduated from Gallaudet College. This move was an amazing action during the heyday of the oralist movement in America.

The departure of Kerney apparently cost the Evansville Day School dearly and produced an ironic turn of events. Enrollment dropped from twenty-two in 1891 to eight in 1892, suggesting that Kerney was the life force behind the school.[27] In August, 1894, however, the Evansville School Board received a letter from Kerney that "requested that the Deaf Mute School of this city be closed and the pupils be sent to the State Institution at Indianapolis." No action was taken, and the letter was simply filed away.[28] However, the *Deaf-Mutes' Journal* had a fuller account in its "Indiana" article in its August 27, 1894, issue. Paul Lange had been away from Evansville for the summer, and Kerney came to town to persuade the deaf pupils to attend the Indiana Institution in the coming fall. When Lange returned to Evansville, he wrote a letter of protest to Johnson, who replied that he had had nothing to do with Kerney's actions. Johnson also defended himself against an angry article in the *National Exponent*, an independent deaf newspaper in Chicago.

It is difficult to know whether Johnson was actually behind Kerney's efforts to close the Evansville Day School in 1894, but it is plausible. Statehouse politics was still a force to be reckoned with in the Indiana Institution. But it is also true that Kerney was experiencing physical and possibly emotional difficulties. Pupil accounts in the *Silent Hoosier* recounted his frequent bouts with stomach problems. He went to a private sanitarium in Michigan for two months one fall and then to Florida in the spring.[29] In 1895, he resigned from his position because of poor health.

The *Silent Hoosier* also described attendance problems in the Evansville Day School.[30] Philip Gillet, the former superintendent of the Illinois Institution of the Deaf, was now the national president of an oralist organization called the American Association to Promote the Teaching of Speech to the Deaf, and one of his duties was to travel among schools to observe speech training. This article referred to his visit to the Evansville Day School sometime during May 1896. The school's enrollment was nine pupils, but only three were present on the first day of Gillet's visit. Efforts were made to round up the nonchalant pupils, and seven were present on the second day for Gillet's inspection. The *Silent Hoosier* commented on the difficulties of having good attendance in the day schools compared with the state institutions.

The article in the *Silent Hoosier* was not a vindictive one. There were no mandatory school attendance laws in Evansville or in Indiana. One school board superintendent had a policy that public school teachers were responsible for the attendance of their pupils, and the teachers were expected to attract pupils by sheer force of their personalities and excellent teaching. The success of teachers was measured in part by attendance figures.[31]

Lange was not pleased with Gillet's visit, even though Gillet reported that the deaf teacher was a pleasant, zealous young man from Gallaudet College. In his May 25, 1896, letter to Edward M. Gallaudet, Lange complained that Gillet wanted him to introduce articulation and speech training. Lange was exasperated at this suggestion because he had nine pupils of varying ages, grades, and intelligence. Such a medley of pupils required much individual attention and assistance from the teacher, leaving no time for speech training.

Lange continued Kerney's attempts to convert the Evansville Day School into a state institution. In its December 12, 1896, meeting, the school board passed a resolution in favor of petitioning the state legislature for this purpose. In a letter to Edward M. Gallaudet the following January, Lange enclosed a political pamphlet, calling for such an action. It had been eleven years since Kerney's first call for a state institution for deaf children in southern Indiana. This 1897 pamphlet stated that deaf children were found to have only one or two years of schooling from the Indianapolis school. Two years were inadequate. New York State had eight deaf schools; Pennsylvania had two; Ohio had three; Missouri had two; Michigan had two; and Illinois had two. There was a compelling logic in the argument to convert this day school to a state institution, but Lange was becoming disenchanted with the situation. He thought that the Evansville business leaders and politicians were novices in state politics, and he did not have much faith in this measure. In a previous letter to Gallaudet, Lange had complained of his small salary ($75 per month) and he had requested a recommendation from Gallaudet for a teaching position in the Kentucky Institution.[32]

By the late 1890s, the weakness of the Evansville Day School was obvious. Only nine pupils were enrolled, four residents of the city and five from the county. Before the 1897–1898 school year started, the school board approved a measure to convert a basement room of the high school to a classroom for the deaf school, and a rear stairway was sealed up for this purpose.[33] This arrangement was not unique for a day school. The *Deaf-Mutes' Journal* reported that deaf pupils were discovered in a basement classroom in one school in the Chicago public school system, and its poor ventilation and the health problems of the pupils caused a major scandal.[34] The Evansville School Board's action showed that the day school had lost importance since its founding in 1886. The school used to occupy two rooms in the former city library; now it was relegated to the high school basement. Frustrated, Lange resigned in September 1901 after accepting a teaching position at the Wisconsin Institution, and the school board considered closing the facility.[35]

In spite of its small size and basement location, however, the day school had surprisingly wide public support in Evansville, especially from the *Evansville Courier* newspaper. At the next school board meeting on October 7, the pupils of the day school, their parents, and their friends were present to ask the school board to continue the day school. The editor of the *Courier* spoke on their behalf and presented a petition signed by 1,140 persons. The school board let all present express their opinions, but ultimately, this effort appeared to be a useless exercise.

Two weeks before, on September 23rd, the city attorney had told the school board that the state's common school laws did not authorize a local school board to maintain a day school for deaf children. The state already maintained separate institutions for these "unfortunates." No other city in Indiana had provided for instruction of their local deaf pupils, and the funds of the common school system were not intended to be used for special schools at the local level. Thus, the members of the Evansville School Board could be liable for misuse of common school funds.[36] After the public meeting on October 7, therefore, the board met in private and decided to close the Evansville Day School.

The city attorney's rationale may have been technically correct, but it also appears that the school board's response may have been a self-serving attempt to avoid criticism. In the history of public education in Indiana in the nineteenth century, many cities and towns did not wait for the state legislature to grant authorization to establish common schools and high schools. The first schools were established by the towns themselves. It took several decades before the state legislature passed appropriate laws for these schools. If these towns had waited for specific state authorization first, no progress would ever have been made.

The school board's decision did not end the history of the Evansville Day School, however. It was converted to a private institution, and James E. Gallaher assumed charge on December 7, 1901. Well-known in the deaf community, Gallaher had taught in the Chicago Day School since its founding. He was also the managing editor of the *National Exponent,* an independent deaf newspaper, and he wrote two volumes of brief biographical sketches of deaf people, *Representative Deaf People of the United States* and *Representative Deaf People.* He seemed to have quick success in Evansville. The school had only five paying pupils when Gallaher assumed control, but he soon increased attendance to sixteen.[37] Kerney even came to the school's support, paying for a five-page insert in the April 1902 issue of the *Silent Worker,* a section that described the deaf community of Evansville and its day school.

Kerney's support was brief, however. Four months after this special edition appeared, the Evansville Day School's founder committed suicide in his father-in-law's house in Decatur, Illinois. Though one of the wealthiest deaf Americans of his day, Kerney had suffered from increasing mental and physical health problems. Several enterprises he had begun in the years before his death, including a hotel in West Virginia and a national weekly newspaper called *Once A Week,* had failed, leading the *American Annals of the Deaf* to conclude:

> The failure of his enterprises affected his mind still further; he became melancholy and finally committed suicide. He was a man of genial deposition and extraordinary energy, and during his early career showed remarkable ability as an organizer, teacher and lecturer.[38]

Now Gallaher was left alone with the Evansville Day School. In 1903, another bill was prepared for the Indiana state legislature for $3,000 every year plus $100 for each pupil in this day school. In the same year, the Maine state government assumed responsibility for the Portland Day School, creating the Maine School for the Deaf. This action must have given Gallaher some motivation.

However, at the same time the Indiana legislature had another bill under consideration that called for the relocation of the Indiana Institution to a larger campus elsewhere in Indianapolis. On March 5, 1903, the state legislature approved the bill to establish a building commission for the Indiana Institution, thus reducing the chances of passage for the Evansville bill, which failed to pass in the Senate on March 12, 1903. The Evansville Day School officially closed that day, an act that marked the end of the era of two deaf schools in Indiana, just as the Indiana Institution entered a period of unprecedented prosperity.

A New School

The time was propitious for an expansion of state educational services. As Indiana entered the twentieth century, its economy was booming. At the northwestern corner of the state, the United States Steel Corporation built an entire new town named Gary, with the world's largest steel mills. Natural gas had been discovered in the northeast portion of the state, not far from Indianapolis. As a result, numerous new towns were created there, including Anderson, Marion, Muncie, and Logansport. In the coal mines of southern Indiana, output doubled from three to six million tons from 1890 to 1900 and then went on to triple to eighteen million tons by 1910. Even the farms, Indiana's economic mainstay, participated in the unprecedented boom. The value of all farm property doubled in a mere ten years from 1900 to 1910.[39] The unexpected appearance of mineral riches in an agricultural state seemed to make Indiana a little Texas of the Middle West.

The deaf institution's physical facilities and location had been inadequate for years. The school suffered from overcrowding, and the annual reports during the 1890s listed the superintendent's complaints of obsolete bathing facilities, inadequate heating, and insufficient lavatories. An 1892 fire in the boys' dormitory highlighted safety concerns. Articles in the *Silent Hoosier* from the 1890s also mentioned the spread of cooking odors through the main building and rats in the dormitory. The industrial neighborhood that had grown up around the deaf school in the late-nineteenth century precluded expansion in its old location. The building commission therefore recommended that a new campus be found in the north side of Indianapolis.

The deaf school campus that opened in 1911 marked a significant departure from the old institution that Kerney had criticized. It was located on an eighty-acre property on 42nd Street, just behind the state fairgrounds on the north side of Indianapolis. Railroad tracks no longer bisected the school campus. Each building was only two floors tall, a tremendous improvement in fire safety. All buildings had large windows to let in sunlight and fresh air. The dormitories and the dining room were housed separately from the main building. There was ample space for 500 pupils; 700 could be squeezed in if necessary. Now, any deaf child in the entire state could attend the Indianapolis school. The main building had a new auditorium with a large stage for dramatic productions. Just below the new auditorium was a new gymnasium with modern gymnastics equipment, which resolved the old dilemma for exercise areas during rainy weather. Finally, the institutional name was changed to the Indiana State School for the Deaf. Thus, the educational nature of this institution was made clear to the general public; the deaf school was no longer to be regarded as an asylum or an institution. The appearance of the word "State" in the new school name appeared to emphasize that the deaf school was for the whole state.

Long-Term Consequences

The old Indiana Institution had been transformed to the Indiana State School for the Deaf, with a new campus on 42nd Street; Charles Kerney was dead; and the Evansville Day School was no more. Sadly, even in

Evansville, there was no building to mark Kerney's efforts. No one in Evansville or Indianapolis remembered the man Charles Kerney. His old adversaries William Glenn and Eli Baker were also nearly forgotten by the Indiana school, which does not even have their portraits among its official superintendent portraits. Nevertheless, this close examination of state-house politics of Indiana and the role politics played in the interaction between the Indiana Institution and the Evansville Day School leads to several observations that are not familiar to students of deaf history.

The first is that deaf educators had a major role in establishing early day schools. It has been widely accepted that hearing oralists were active in establishing most day schools of this era. However, a good number of day schools started with the use of sign language: Pittsburgh, Evansville, St. Louis, Cincinnati, and Dubuque, for example. The Portland school started as an oralist school, then became a day school using sign language and, finally, a state residential institution; it is striking to observe how that school moved through the entire spectrum of deaf education.

A second observation is that there was a stunning contrast between private wealth and small institutional budgets. Kerney and his wife had personal assets that must have been in the several hundreds of thousands of dollars at a time when Paul Lange was paid only $70 per month and when many teachers at the Indiana Institution were paid $100 per month. The annual budgets of the Indiana Institution ranged between $50,000 and $65,000 per year in the late-nineteenth century.

In Christmas 1899, Charles Kerney and his wife received a gift of $165,000 from his father-in-law. That was equivalent to $2,598,750 in 1990 dollars (according to the U.S. Consumer Price Index). This Christmas gift would have been sufficient to pay for three years of operation of the Indiana Institution!

The 1886 annual report of the Indiana Institution mentioned its school library with 3,350 volumes worth $4,909.98. Previous annual reports described the slow growth of the school library. Small fancywork made by the girls was sold for funds to buy additional books.

The third observation, an offshoot of the second, is that, although the situation of the Indiana Institution represented great institutional poverty amid incredible individual wealth, the school never exploited this opportunity to enhance its well-being. Considering the assets of Kerney and those of Evansville's Stephens family, it appears that a great opportunity was lost in soliciting funds for the library. It would have taken one donation of only $5,000 to double this library's holdings in 1890, and that sum would represent only 3 percent of Charles Kerney's Christmas present! But the Indiana State School for the Deaf had a long tradition of receiving full

support from the Indiana state government, without any private donations
and bequests from wealthy people. In contrast, the New York Institution
actively received private funds to erect new buildings and improve school
facilities.[40] If the New York Institution could have done that, there is no reason why the Indiana Institution could not have done the same.

A fourth observation is that the personalities of the state institutions for
deaf children shifted in the last decades of the nineteenth century, becoming more bureaucratic and less interested in educational challenge and social improvement. Thomas MacIntire, superintendent from 1852 to 1879,
had advocated in his annual reports for educational innovations such as
the education of "feeble-minded" children. During his superintendency,
the women's reformatory was built on land originally owned by the
Indiana Institution. MacIntire was an ordained Presbyterian minister, but
he welcomed Catholic Masses in the school chapel for the benefit of deaf
Catholics—an amazing example of liberality amid anti-Catholic feelings
of the nineteenth century.[41] Furthermore, most of the institutional weeklies in America were founded during the 1870s and 1880s, and they freely
conducted debates on educational issues and carried news of the deaf
communities across the country, reflecting the progressive nature of their
state institutions.

The annual reports of the Indiana Institution during the 1890s, by contrast, reflect the change in institutional personalities. Budgetary issues
were the main concerns, and defensive positions were taken on the affairs
of the institution. No more mention was made of any educational innovations. As the twentieth century wore on, most of the institutional weeklies
were placed under strict control by the school superintendents, and their
news coverage became more focused on the institutions themselves and
their superintendents' achievements.

A related observation is that partisan politics was playing an ever-
increasing role in school governance in the late-nineteenth century. In
1852, MacIntire was appointed to the superintendency, based on his work
experience at the Ohio and Tennessee Institutions. The backgrounds of
William Glenn and Eli Baker, however, showed no relationship to education or deafness, as described previously. They were political appointments, presumably to reward partisan supporters. Richard O. Johnson
was somewhat of an anomaly. Although trained to be an attorney, he had
been involved with the board of trustees at the Indiana Institution, and he
knew some sign language. Civil service reforms of the 1890s ensured
placement of more competent and better trained employees at the Indiana
school, presumably, but superintendents nevertheless continued to be political appointees.

Johnson was removed from his position in 1919, for reasons that have never been explained, and he was replaced by Oscar Pittenger. Pittenger at least was familiar with education, having been an elected public school superintendent in a rural county. He knew nothing about sign language or educational processes for deaf students. He claimed that he never applied for the superintendency of the Indiana school. Supposedly, it came out of the blue.[42] Perhaps his most important characteristic was that he was a staunch Republican, and not surprisingly, he was abruptly removed from his position in May 1935, after the election of a powerful Democratic governor. The new superintendent of the deaf school was Jackson A. Raney, a Democrat and a county school superintendent. Again, Raney did not know sign language or deaf education methods beforehand.

When Raney retired at the Indiana school in 1956, William McClure was appointed to be its next superintendent. McClure had been principal of the Kendall School on the Gallaudet campus, and then also became superintendent of the Tennessee school. McClure also came from an old family of deaf educators. He was neither a Democrat, a Republican or even an resident of Indiana! McClure's appointment in 1957 ended almost 80 years of politically appointed superintendents at the Indiana school.

Indiana was not alone in suffering from political interference with deaf education during this period. During the statewide elections in Illinois at 1892, superintendent Philip Gillet endorsed one candidate for governor. Unfortunately this candidate did not win the election.[43] In spite of Gillet's excellent service at the Illinois Institution for thirty-seven years; and in spite of outpouring of statewide and national support for Gillet's continued superintendency, the new governor immediately fired him.[44]

In its first forty years of its existence (between 1861 and 1901), the Kansas Institution had fifteen superintendents. That resulted in an average term of less than three years for each superintendent. In contrast, the Indiana Institution had only five superintendents in its first seventy five years of existence (between 1844 and 1919).[45]

The Ohio, Iowa, and Texas Institutions also experienced problems caused by political appointments.[46] These political manipulations and the disruptions that ensued were noted in the deaf press, but they continued in some states well into the twentieth century.

Finally, evidence suggests that Kerney's criticisms of the Indiana Institution were justified. He and other writers in the *Deaf-Mutes' Journal* claimed that the school was degraded and ruined by state politicians. The MacIntire superintendency, by contrast, was often referred to as a golden age by its alumni.[47] Sentimental memories themselves do not make history, however. Educational quality is difficult to measure, but nevertheless,

Table 1.
Teachers and Leaders Who Graduated from the Indiana Institution

Role	Teachers and Leaders Who Graduated from the Indiana Institution before 1885	Teachers and Leaders Who Graduated from the Indiana Institution after 1885
Ministers	Austin Mann (1867)	—
	Philip Hasenstab (1879)	
	Charles O. Dantzer (1881)	
School Founders	Philip Emery (1856)	—
	Charles M. French (1879)	
	Charles Kerney (1879)	
Teachers (with a college degree)	Vollantine Holloway (1869)	Arthur H. Norris Sr. (1895)
	Orson Archibald (1870)	
	Henry Bierhaus (1876)	
	Nathaniel Morrow (1879)	
	Albert Berg (1881)	
National Organization President	H. Carrington Anderson (1883)	Robert Lankenau (1930)

some data suggest that during the late nineteenth century the Indiana Institution was not producing high caliber graduates.

The number of students admitted to Gallaudet College provides one measure of educational success. These data have to be used with care because education is a process that takes many years to complete. When a superintendent leaves an institution, he or she still has an effect on its students for a few more years after his or her departure. Still, the trend in the Indiana Institution seems clear: MacIntire sent twelve pupils to Gallaudet from 1864, when the college opened, until 1879, when MacIntire was forced out. For the next three years, a few more students went to Gallaudet—but they were taught mainly under MacIntire's superintendency. MacIntire's successor, Glenn, sent four pupils during his five years; Baker sent none; and Johnson, who served from 1889 to 1919, saw only two graduates in thirty years attend Gallaudet College.[48]

Public comment on the lack of college-bound pupils received some discussion in the *Silent Hoosier*. An Indianapolis newspaper in 1897 criticized the Indiana Institution, and the editor of the *Silent Hoosier* prepared a defense. The school newspaper's editor claimed that the lack of Indiana students in Gallaudet College was simply because of poverty and the costs of

Table 2.
Number of Pupils Admitted to the
Indiana Institution at the Beginning
of the School Year

Year	Number of Pupils
1880	390
1885	372
1890	355
1895	355
1900	384
1905	387
1910	347
1915	335
1920	388
1925	409

attending college.[49] This argument seems weak, though, because earlier Gallaudet students from Indiana, for example, Albert Berg, an 1885 graduate of Gallaudet, were able to find ways to pay his college expenses. Furthermore, the Indiana economy was booming well through much of this period of decline in attendance at Gallaudet. The Indiana institution's sensitivity to this matter is apparent. A *Silent Hoosier* editorial in 1902 discounted the value of a college education and insisted that deaf people had to learn a trade first.[50] Articles in 1903 and 1904 discussed farming as an ideal occupation for deaf boys and servant work for deaf girls.[51] This attitude was hardly likely to push students toward college.

During the long period of its politicization, Indiana failed not only to produce students who would go on to Gallaudet but also to produce deaf leaders, as table 1 shows.[52]

One might argue that there were fewer opportunities for deaf people to become teachers during the period of oralist domination in the early twentieth century, but that would not explain the inability of the Indiana Institution to produce a significant number of ministers or organizational leaders. Furthermore, the number of pupils at the school showed some decline after 1880, as table 2 shows.[53] Between its founding in 1843 and 1880, the Indiana Institution showed consistent growth in enrollment, except for the Civil War years and the state's financial crisis in 1857.

The failure of the Indiana Institution to meet the needs of all the state's deaf children is obvious from these numbers. The 1880 enrollment high

mark was not surpassed for forty years, despite mandatory school attendance laws passed in 1907 and despite the construction of a new campus
that was supposed to eliminate the capacity constraints of the old school.
Ironically with the presence of the new campus on 42nd Street in 1911, enrollment actually declined from 1905 through 1915.

Charles Kerney saw the need for a local school for deaf children and
tried to fill it with the Evansville Day School. The Indiana Institution, because of political meddling and perhaps because of the unwillingness of
parents to send children far from home for their education, not only did
not provide an education for many deaf children in Indiana but also
seemed increasingly unable to produce the educated and successful deaf
adults that the school's early success would have predicted. A school that
at one point was able to send two students from the junior class directly to
Gallaudet College, bypassing their senior year, was hardly able to send
anyone at all, even graduates, on to Gallaudet for nearly three decades.
This study of the Evansville Day School's challenge to the Indiana
Institution's monopoly of deaf education suggests that attention needs to
be focused on institutional governance and goals to understand the vital
role of state residential schools in the lives of most deaf Americans in the
late-nineteenth and early twentieth centuries.

Notes

1. Charles Whisman, *Highlights of the History of the Indiana School for the Deaf: 1843–1944* (Indianapolis: Pipps Publishing), 17.

2. During the nineteenth century, many state governments created "benevolent institutions" to educate their blind, deaf and mentally retarded populations. Sometimes
they were clustered together with prisons, veterans' orphanages and state hospitals.
This term "benevolent institutions" was commonly used in this time period.

3. Whisman, *Highlights of the History of the Indiana School for the Deaf*, 17.

4. Emma Lou Thornbrough, *Indiana in the Civil War Era: 1850–1880* (Indianapolis:
Indiana Historical Society, 1968), 225.

5. Editorial, "An Infamous Proceeding," *Indianapolis Journal*, May 17, 1879.

6. Amy Warner Wilhelmena, "Indiana State School for the Deaf" (master's thesis,
University of Chicago, 1930), 60–61.

7. "Removal of Superintendent Glenn," *The Indianapolis Journal*, December 6, 1884, 3.

8. Compiled from Jack Gannon, *Deaf Heritage: A Narrative History of Deaf America*
(Silver Spring, Md.: National Association of the Deaf, 1981) and various issues of the
journal *American Annals of the Deaf*.

9. "Items from Evansville, Ind.," *Deaf-Mutes' Journal*, August, 14, 1890, 3.

10. "Evansville," *Deaf-Mutes' Journal*, February 16, 1888, 1.

11. "A Metallic Badly Cracked," *Deaf-Mutes' Journal*, January 12, 1888, 3.

12. "The Evansville Exhibition," *Deaf-Mutes' Journal*, January 13, 1887, 4.

13. Ibid.

14. Justin E. Walsh, *The Centennial History of the Indiana General Assembly, 1816–1978* (Indianapolis: Indiana Historical Society, 1968), 251.

15. Assorted annual reports of the Indiana Institution, 1871 through 1898, (Indianapolis, Indiana, the Indiana Institution) and Indiana Board of State Charities, *Annual Reports, 1889–1912* (Indianapolis: Indiana Board of State Charities).

16. Association of Graduates & Former Pupils of the Indiana Institution, *Proceedings of the First Triennial Reunion* [supplement] (Indianapolis: Indiana Association for the Deaf, 1890), 3.

17. Clifton J. Phillips, *Indiana in Transition: The Emergence of an Industrial Commonwealth 1880–1920* (Indianapolis: Indiana Historical Society, 1968), 24.

18. Anon, Editorial, *The Indiana Deaf-Mute Journal,* March 26, 1888, 3.

19. Anon. (Elna Keneta), "Politics in Schools for the Deaf," *Deaf-Mutes' Journal,* March 8, 1888, 4.

20. Editorial, *Deaf-Mutes' Journal,* April 3, 1888, 2.

21. Walsh, *The Centennial History of the Indiana, General Assembly,* 252–53.

22. Untitled announcement, *American Annals for the Deaf* 34(1889): 71.

23. "Evansville, Indiana," *Deaf-Mutes' Journal,* October 17, 1889, 3.

24. Untitled announcement, *American Annals of the Deaf* 37(1891): 74.

25. Evansville School Board minutes, meeting of June 27, 1892, in *Board of School Trustees Minutes, 1886–1902* (Evansville, Ind.: Evansville-Vanderburgh County School Corporation), 406.

26. See "The Academic Integration of Deaf Children in Historical Perspective" by John Vickrey Van Cleve in this volume for a detailed discussion of the Wisconsin situation.

27. Compiled from pupil statistics found in Charles Anglin, "History of Education in Evansville" (master's thesis, Indiana University, 1948).

28. Evansville School Board minutes, meeting of August 16, 1896, 197.

29. Brief news item, *Deaf-Mutes' Journal,* November 21, 1895, 2.

30. Unknown author, "Evansville Day School," *Silent Hoosier,* May 21, 1896, 2.

31. Charles Anglin, "The Development of Education in Evansville, Indiana, 1819–1900" (master's thesis, Indiana University, 1948), 66.

32. Paul Lange letter to Edward M. Gallaudet, January 21, 1896, EMG correspondence files, Gallaudet University Archives, Washington, D.C.

33. Evansville School Board minutes, meeting of August 17, 1896, 206.

34. "Neglect for Deaf Pupils," *Deaf-Mutes' Journal,* April 3, 1902, 2.

35. Evansville School Board minutes, meeting of October 1, 1901, 428.

36. Evansville School Board minutes, meeting of October 7, 1901, 431.

37. "James E. Gallaher," *The Silent Worker,* April 1902, 115.

38. "The Evansville Day School," *American Annals of the Deaf* 47(1902): 478.

39. Economic data compiled from Phillips, *Indiana in Transition.*

40. Untitled editorial, *Deaf-Mutes' Journal,* January 15, 1894, 2.

41. Unknown author, "Thomas MacIntire," *American Annals of the Deaf* 31, no. 1(January 1886): 10.

42. Oscar Morton Pittenger, "Oscar Morton Pittenger: Autobiography," *Silent Hoosier,* December 5, 1930, 1.

43. Unknown author, "Chicago," *Deaf-Mutes' Journal,* November. 12, 1896, 2.

44. See "Chicago Mission for the Deaf" by Kent R. Olney in this volume for more discussion of this matter.

45. Data compiled from the book *Some Bits of Kansas School for the Deaf History* (Kansas Association of the Deaf, Olathe KS, 1984).

46. Untitled editorial, *Silent Hoosier*, May 12, 1892, 2; Untitled editorial, *Deaf-Mutes' Journal*, August 25, 1887, 2; "Texas School for the Deaf," *Deaf-Mutes' Journal*, November 10, 1887, 2.

47. "Proposed Willard Memorial," *The Indiana Deaf-Mute Journal*, March 5, 1888, 2; "What Our Visitors Say," *The Indiana Deaf-Mute Journal*, October 31, 1888, 2.

48. "Indiana Pupils at Gallaudet: 1869–1944," table, from Whisman, *Highlights of the History of Indiana School for the Deaf* (Indianapolis: PIP Publishing, 1988), 63.

49. "The Institution Discussed," *Silent Hoosier*, March 3, 1897, 2.

50. Untitled editorial, *Silent Hoosier*, May 29, 1902, 2.

51. Untitled articles, *Silent Hoosier*, April 9, 1903, 2; and also in *Silent Hoosier*, February 11, 1904, 2.

52. Data compiled from *Silent Hoosier* back issues and from Whisman, *Highlights of the History of Indiana School for the Deaf.*

53. Data compiled from Whisman, *Highlights of the History of Indiana School for the Deaf.*

Bibliography

Sources of Indiana State History

Phillips, Clifton J. *Indiana in Transition: The Emergence of an Industrial Commonwealth 1880–1920.* Indianapolis: Indiana Historical Society, 1968.

Thornborough, Emma Lou. *Indiana in the Civil War Era: 1850–1880.* Indianapolis: Indiana Historical Society, 1968.

Walsh, Justin, E. *The Centennial History of the Indiana General Assembly.* Indianapolis: Indiana Historical Society, 1968.

Sources of Indiana Deaf History

Association of Graduates and Former Pupils of the Indiana Institution. *Proceedings of the First Triennial Reunion.* Indianapolis: N.p., 1890.

Indiana Board of State Charities. *Annual Reports, 1889–1912.* Indianapolis: Author.

Indiana Institution for the Education of the Deaf and Dumb. *Annual Reports, 1875–1912.* Indianapolis: Author.

Indiana Institution for the Education of the Deaf and Dumb. *The Indiana Deaf-Mute Journal* school paper, Indianapolis, 1887–1889.

Indiana Institution for the Education of the Deaf and Dumb. *The Silent Hoosier* school paper, Indianapolis, 1889–1912.

Johnson, Richard O. "A Semi-Centennial Account of the Indiana Institution of the Deaf & Dumb." Chapter in *Histories of the American Schools for the Deaf.* Washington, D.C.: The Volta Bureau, 1893.

Kerney, Charles. "Deaf & Dumb Institution." Political pamphlet, Evansville, Ind., 1888.

Lange, Paul. "The Evansville School for the Deaf." chapter in *Histories of the American Schools for the Deaf.* Washington, D.C.: The Volta Bureau, 1893.

"Some Salient Reasons Why an Institution of the Deaf & Dumb Should be Established in Southern Indiana." Political pamphlet, Evansville, Ind., 1897.

Warner, Wilhelmena Amy. "Indiana State School for the Deaf." Master's degree thesis, University of Chicago, Ill., 1930.

Whisman, Charles. *Highlights of the History of Indiana School for the Deaf: 1843–1944.* Indianapolis: Pip Publishing, 1988.

Sources of American Deaf History

American Annals of the Deaf quarterly (following selected articles), Gallaudet University, Washington, D.C.:

"Arguments for a Day School," 20, no.1(January 1875): 34–36.

"The Pittsburgh & Boston Schools for the Deaf & Dumb," 20, no. 1(January 1875): 164–70.

"Thomas MacIntire," 31, no. 1(January 1886): 1–22.

"Celebrating 150 Years: Illinois School for the Deaf 1839–1989." Newspaper supplement, *Jacksonville Journal-Courier*, 1989.

Deaf-Mutes' Journal weekly (following selected articles), New York Institution for the Deaf, New York, N.Y.:

"Revolution in Indiana Benevolent Institutions," 8, no. 26(August 26, 1879): 4.

"A Free School for the Deaf," 16, no. 32(August 26, 1886): 3.

"The Evansville Exhibition: Gallaudet's Birthday," 17, no. 2(January 13, 1887): 4.

"Politics in Schools for the Deaf," 17, no. 10(March 8, 1888): 4.

Gallaher, James E. *Representative Deaf Persons of the USA.* Chicago: James E. Gallaher, 1898.

———. *Representative Deaf People.* Chicago: E. S. Waring, 1902.

Gannon, Jack R. *Deaf Heritage: A Narrative History of Deaf America.* Silver Spring, Md.: National Association of the Deaf, 1981.

Edward Miner Gallaudet correspondence files, Gallaudet University Archives:

Charles Kerney letter to Edward Miner Gallaudet, November 13, 1888, EMG correspondence files, Gallaudet University Archives.

Charles Kerney letter to Edward Miner Gallaudet, May 24, 1892, EMG correspondence files, Gallaudet University Archives.

Paul Lange letter to Edward Miner Gallaudet, January 8, 1897, EMG correspondence files, Gallaudet University Archives.

Paul Lange letter to Edward Miner Gallaudet, May 26, 1896, EMG correspondence files, Gallaudet University Archives.

Gallaudet, Edward Miner. Journal of Edward Miner Gallaudet, daily entries from December 11, 1888 to December 20, 1888. EMG correspondence files, Gallaudet University Archives.

Gallaudet, Edward Minor. Notes for a lecture in Evansville, December 18, 1888. EMG correspondence files, Gallaudet University Archives.

Sources of Evansville History

Anglin, Robert A. *The Development of Education in Evansville Indiana 1819–1900.* Master's thesis, Indiana University, 1948.

Evansville Courier newspaper (following selected articles), Evansville, Ind.:

"Deaf Mutes: The Exhibition at Evans Hall and Reception at the St. George's Hall," December 19, 1888, 4.

"Charles Kerney Takes His Life Because of Ill Health," August 2, 1902, 1.

Evansville Journal newspaper (following selected articles), Evansville, Ind.:

"The Deaf Mutes—A Novel & Interesting Entertainment Last Evening," December 31, 1886, 4.

"Evansville Deaf Mute School," May 10, 1888, 1.

"Charles Kerney Left Out," May 20, 1892, 1.

Evansville-Vanderburgh County School Corporation. Board of School Trustees minutes, 1886–1902, Evansville, Ind.

6

The Academic Integration of Deaf Children: A Historical Perspective

John Vickrey Van Cleve

Editor's Introduction

The following essay argues that deaf adults historically have opposed the mainstreaming of deaf children in public schools, and yet hearing parents, school administrators, and politicians have successfully lobbied for mainstream programs, ignoring the collective voice of the American deaf community. Detailed historical examination of the development of coeducation for deaf and hearing students leads to several conclusions about it. First, mainstreaming has a long history in the United States. By 1920, twice as many deaf children were mainstreamed in the state of Wisconsin, for example, than attended the state residential school. Second, a consistent reason for mainstreaming's popularity is that it is seen as being cheaper than the residential school alternative. Finally, mainstreaming also has been driven by strong ideological beliefs. Among these are the propositions that putting deaf children in public schools serves society by encouraging cultural homogeneity, by strengthening parent-children relationships, and by stressing the overall goal of "normality" for deaf children.

"Theoretically considered," Alexander Graham Bell wrote in 1905, "the best school for a deaf child, is a school with only one deaf child in it . . . one deaf child with an environment of hearing children."[1] Bell was not alone in this belief. Attempts to separate deaf children from each other

Originally published in Renate Fischer and Harlan Lane, eds, *Looking Back: A Reader on the History of Deaf Communities and Their Sign Languages* (Hamburg, Germany: Signum, 1993).

and integrate them with hearing children during their school years have formed a consistent theme in the history of deaf education. Within 50 years of the first public attempts to educate deaf children, schools in various German-speaking European states were endeavoring to educate together deaf and hearing children.[2]

By the end of the 20th century, support for academic integration—termed "mainstreaming" in the United States—was nearly ubiquitous.[3] In 1990 almost three-fourths of all deaf school children in the United States, for example, attended classes in an integrated setting. The numbers for the state of Illinois are illustrative: in 1990, 1200 deaf students were enrolled in Chicago's public schools, but only 270 attended the state residential institution.[4] Even American state-supported residential schools, such as Illinois', however, are so overwhelmed by the ideological and political imperatives of deaf-hearing coeducation that nearly all offer mainstreaming programs for their students.[5] Yet, ironically, the benefits of academic integration have been and remain a chimera.

The first major study of such attempts made this point unequivocally. Joseph C. Gordon, a professor at the National Deaf-Mute College (today's Gallaudet University) and later superintendent of the Illinois School for the Deaf, carefully reviewed the literature related to German, French, and English endeavors to co-educate deaf and hearing children. In 1884 and 1885 he reported his findings. Gordon discovered that European parents, educators, philanthropists, and government officials in the early 19th century all "advocated the education of the deaf in more or less intimate connection with the public schools." Almost no one defended residential institutions that segregated deaf from hearing students.[6] Nevertheless, Gordon concluded, "disappointment and failure" of coeducation programs were so uniform that "systematic and organized efforts in this direction [were] abandoned" in Europe by the mid-1880's.[7]

Gordon's study was well-known in the United States. He presented it orally at an unusual session of the convention of the National Education Association (NEA) in 1884. The following year he published an extended version in *the American Annals of the Deaf*, at that time an authoritative and widely-read journal. Gordon, moreover, was an intimate of Bell, the most articulate and forceful American proponent of academic integration. Bell was at the NEA convention; yet neither he nor anyone else ever tried to refute Gordon's findings directly, choosing to ignore European experience and the conclusions Gordon drew from it. There is no evidence that Deaf people themselves have advocated coeducation with hearing children, either. To the contrary, those who have articulated a position have nearly always supported separate educational facilities for deaf children.[8]

The following account places this seemingly paradoxical situation—the unremitting pursuit of the academic integration of deaf and hearing children despite abundant evidence of its failure as an educational model—into historical perspective by examining closely the early record of American efforts at deaf-hearing coeducation.

Private Schools

The overriding ideological goal of most of these efforts has been to accustom deaf children to the mores and communication methods of persons who hear and thus to prevent them from developing a culture apart from the hearing community. The complexity and frustrations inherent in the objective, however, have led to a plethora of schemes in both the United States and Europe. These have ranged from totally coeducational experiences, where students at all ages and all grade levels were integrated in the same classrooms, to various efforts to place self-contained deaf classes in the same building with hearing children. Some programs integrated young hearing and deaf children and then sent the older deaf ones on to deaf residential schools; others commenced deaf children's education in segregated schools and then transferred them to integrated public schools for advanced studies.[9] One remarkable American school, however, had an entirely different objective than the others: David Bartlett's Family School sought to acculturate hearing children to those who were deaf.

Bartlett operated a small, integrated primary school at various locations in New York and Connecticut from 1852 until 1861. His ostensible objective was to extend education to very young deaf children who had not yet reached the age of admission to residential institutions, usually 10 or 12. Yet his school in fact pioneered revolutionary ideas. It challenged two important ideological presumptions: first, that deaf people must become as similar to hearing people as possible if they are to be happy or successful, and second, that a weak minority—in this case deaf people—must always adapt their culture to meet the cultural preference of the stronger majority.

Bartlett suggested that hearing families could adapt to their deaf children, rather than vice versa, and he placed deaf and hearing pupils on a truly equal footing. He encouraged his deaf pupils to be joined in the school by their hearing siblings, so that the latter could acquire the language of signs and assist their deaf brothers and sisters in communicating with members of their families.[10] Deaf alumnus Henry Winter Syle wrote that at Bartlett's "there was perfect equality in every respect" between the deaf and hearing pupils, prayers were conducted in signs, and in class, Syle emphasized, "all recited manually."[11]

Bartlett's model for an integrated education for deaf and hearing children was unique. A former and future teacher in residential schools, Bartlett was comfortable with sign language. He recognized its importance to deaf students, and he believed that it could form the basis for shared experiences among deaf and hearing people. Rather than force his deaf charges to try to imitate their hearing fellows by communicating with speech and speechreading—which would necessarily put the deaf children at a social and educational disadvantage—Bartlett expected the hearing students to conform to the communication requirements of those who could not hear, which put no one at a relative disadvantage. Fingerspelling and signs (apparently in English word order) were used throughout his school.[12]

Bartlett's, like most small private schools, was a failure financially, but educationally his approach apparently was successful. Educated deaf contemporaries commented on the academic and social skills of the school's alumni, who included not only Syle, the first deaf Episcopal priest in the United States, but also Gideon Moore, the first deaf American to earn a doctoral degree.[13] Other 19th century private schools that integrated deaf and hearing children, however, followed a completely different course, attempting to force the Deaf minority to accommodate to the hearing majority and rejecting the idea that a manual language could be shared by deaf and hearing people.

Alexander Graham Bell's experimental school in Washington, D.C., and F. Knapp's Institute in Baltimore, Maryland, both attempted to achieve integration by encouraging their deaf pupils to adapt to the communication methods used by hearing people. Knapp's, a large bilingual private school offering German and English instruction for the children of German immigrants, began admitting a few deaf students in the 1870's. Their education commenced in a "Deaf Department," where they were taught speech and speechreading. When the deaf children "attained sufficient command of articulate speech and facility in reading the lips" they were dispersed into regular classes with hearing pupils.[14] The rationale for this approach was the founder's belief, in his son's words, that the more "the deaf commingled with the hearing, the less would they notice their defect."[15] Sign language and fingerspelling were absolutely forbidden. Hearing children who motioned or gestured to a deaf child were sent out of the classroom, and both deaf and hearing children who used "signs or the manual alphabet" were gloved, as evidence of stupidity and punishment.[16]

Bell did not encounter such problems in his tiny school. A maximum of four deaf students were enrolled at one time; all were very young; and Bell was careful to admit only children who had never learned formal signs.[17] The Bell school's integration efforts differed somewhat from Knapp's, in that the deaf and hearing children were kept in separate classes within the same building but only mingled during playtime and for certain other activities.[18] Bell's underlying assumptions and motivations, though, were the same as Knapp's. He planned to open the school, in his words, because the "best plan that has yet been devised to educate deaf children was the method of bringing together deaf children in small numbers in the midst of hearing children in large numbers."[19] Furthermore, the school would present Bell with an opportunity to "prove empirically that all deaf children can be taught to speak-and understand speech by the eye."[20] A failure, the school closed after two difficult years, but its experience did not dim the enthusiasm of Bell or other theorists of academic integration.

Public Schools

American advocates of deaf-hearing coeducation focused their efforts on public schools as the 19th century progressed. Large scale academic integration of American deaf students could never result from the efforts of private schools such as Bartlett's, Knapp's, or Bell's. Only governments have been able to provide consistently the financial resources necessary to educate deaf children. Thus state and local governments (and in the late 20th century the United States federal government) have become the loci for academic integration efforts. The state legislature of Wisconsin, in particular, provided the arena in which deaf-hearing public coeducation received its first and most important impetus in the United States.

Wisconsin's importance to deaf education resulted primarily from the state's ethnic characteristics, the working of the state's political system, and the convincing presence of Alexander Graham Bell at crucial moments. An attempt to secure public funding for a private school for the deaf children of Milwaukee's many German immigrants eventually became the key to a wide-ranging experiment in state support for a particular kind of academic integration.

In 1878, recent German immigrants opened the Milwaukee Day School for their deaf children. Like German parents in cities such as Detroit, Baltimore, and New York, they wished their deaf children to preserve German cultural traditions and envisioned private schooling as a means to that end. Consequently, they employed a German teacher who followed German educational methods, using speech and speechreading rather than sign language as the basis for communication. Overseen by a charitable foundation called the Wisconsin Phonological Institute, which sought donations to support the endeavor, the Milwaukee Day School nevertheless soon ran short of money and asked the state for assistance.[21]

The Wisconsin legislature, however, balked. An initial deaf education bill, proposed in 1881, would have given support only to the Milwaukee school. This was seen as narrow, self-interested legislation, lacking any broader purpose than relieving a group of German-American parents of private school tuition. To gain more support, supporters rewrote the bill to extend state financial aid to any municipality that might wish to establish its own school for deaf children. In 1881 and 1883, however, the legislature still refused to approve the bill.[22] Taxpayers already supported the Wisconsin School for the Deaf, a residential institution at Delavan, and most lawmakers saw no reason to support other educational options for deaf children. They changed their minds, though, after Bell twice visited Madison and explained the practical and ideological underpinnings of academic integration.

Bell became involved with Wisconsin at the request of Robert C. Spencer, the first English-speaking head of the Wisconsin Phonological Institute and the proprietor of a Milwaukee business college.[23] Desperate to secure state support for the Milwaukee Day School, he wrote to Bell, whose ideas about academic integration were already known, and asked for the famous inventor's assistance.[24] Fortuitously, in 1884 the NEA planned to hold its national meeting in Madison, Wisconsin. At Spencer's urging, Bell arranged with the NEA's president to schedule a special session addressing the issue of "Deaf-Mute Instruction in Relation to the Work of the Public Schools."[25] In the summer of 1884, the NEA held its unusual session in the Wisconsin State Senate Chamber in Madison. Governor Jeremiah Rusk attended to hear Bell talk about the importance of educating deaf children within the context of a hearing environment.[26] Here Gordon also first presented his study of deaf-hearing coeducation's failure in European schools.[27] But it was not Gordon that Governor Rusk heard.

At the opening of the Wisconsin state legislature in 1885, Rusk recommended the passage of a law to provide state support for "day schools" in Wisconsin's cities and towns. He used information provided by Bell to support this request, arguing that locally operated day schools would prepare deaf children to "enter the common schools and receive the same education as other children."[28] He also asked Bell to visit Madison again and to speak directly to the education committees of the state legislature about the need for day schools. Bell had privately made this suggestion to Rusk and readily accepted the public offer.[29] Thus the stage was set for a clear and unambiguous statement of the ideology of academic integration of deaf children.

Bell presented his argument to the state legislators in terms that they could understand and appreciate. Day schools, he argued, would reach deaf students who were not attending the state residential school because of their parents' desire to keep them at home. Without education, he warned, deaf children would grow up in ignorance and possibly be a threat to the community. Bell stated that the day school option would please parents, for they would be able to keep their children under their daily tutelage and supervision, and yet the children would still receive the education they needed. Furthermore, day schools would be cheaper than a new or expanded state residential institution, and Wisconsin would benefit by showing itself a pioneer in an important new philanthropic endeavor.

The heart of the academic integration position, however, was more subtle. Day schools, Bell told the lawmakers, embodied "a principle of dealing with the deaf and dumb that has long been seen to be advisable from a theoretical point of view. . . . The principle involved may be tersely described as the policy of decentralization,—the policy of keeping deaf-mutes separated from one another as much as possible."[30] Bell was particularly emphatic in his desire to achieve "decentralization" because of his eugenic concerns, but the continuing appeal of academic integration lies elsewhere.[31] Genetic knowledge and the 20th century horrors perpetrated in the name of eugenics have largely discredited that aspect of the academic integrationist position.[32]

What has not been discredited is the belief Bell also articulated that both individual deaf people and the nation as a whole benefit when deaf children are placed in an environment of coeducation with their hearing peers, in which the dominant language is that of the hearing majority. Bell told Wisconsin legislators that "every means that will bring the deaf child into closer association and affiliation with hearing children of his own age will promote his happiness and success in adult life."[33] In other words, deaf people's road to life satisfaction was that followed by hearing people as well. Bell, a hearing man, believed that he knew what was best for those who were deaf, and what was best for them was to conform to the ways of the hearing community. Although not everyone would agree with this conclusion—as will be discussed below—Wisconsin legislators did and enacted day school legislation in April of 1885.

Wisconsin's experiment in academic integration provided cities or towns with $100 for each deaf pupil they placed into their own day school.[34] Later, the level of state funding increased several times; eventually the state even paid for the costs of boarding non-resident pupils with local families so that they might attend day schools.[35] Within a few years, 18 Wisconsin cities, many of them quite small, had created day school.[36] The number of students in day schools steadily increased subsequently, while the number in the residential school fluctuated but never exceeded the total present in 1885, when the first day school bill was enacted. More than twice as many deaf children attended day schools as attended the residential institution at Delavan by 1920. A new trend had begun in America's education of her deaf children.[37]

Following the Wisconsin victory, Bell and his integrationist supporters extended their success to other states. Bell personally became involved in legislative discussions of hearing-deaf coeducation in Illinois, Ohio, Michigan, and Minnesota, while closely observing the situation in California.[38] Soon each of these states and Missouri as well followed Wisconsin's example of voting for public support of day schools.[39] Integrationist zealots tried to prevent deaf teachers from employment in day schools, and in Wisconsin at least, also attempted to have the residential institution closed.[40]

The day schools resulting from this flurry of activity were not uniform in every respect, but each followed a pattern designed to facilitate integration of deaf and hearing children without burdening the latter. They all copied the integrationist model of F. Knapp's Institute and Bell's private school, rejecting the Bartlett school's attempt at integration through modifying the behavior of hearing students.

Although in contemporary terminology these experiments in deaf-hearing coeducation were called "day schools," most today would be characterized as "day classes," rather than "schools," for they usually consisted of a single classroom for deaf children within a public school.[41] A hearing teacher, female and trained at a normal school connected with a large urban day school, taught all the deaf students by means of speech and speechreading.[42] The children were placed into classes with hearing pupils for activities such as art and physical education where precise communication was assumed to be unnecessary. Another important assumption was that the day school experience, with gradually increasing integration of educational activities, would prepare the brighter deaf children to take their place in completely integrated classrooms with hearing children. This could happen at any time, but was expected to occur no later than the completion of eighth grade.[43]

Legislation creating day schools in various states carefully avoided comments about sign language or communication. To raise this issue, Bell argued, would create unnecessary complications in the attempt to establish coeducation.[44] "The promoters of this bill," he told Wisconsin legislators, "have wisely abstained from restricting in any way the methods of instruction to be used in the schools. . . . The State may rest assured, that, when the interests of their afflicted children are at stake, the parents will be apt to make a careful choice."[45] Bell surmised that hearing parents, isolated from the adult deaf community and vulnerable to the promises of oralism, would support education by speech and speechreading only. His surmise was correct; sign language was not used by the teachers or students. Indeed, attempts were made in the day schools, as in Bell's experimental school in Washington, to prevent students familiar with sign from enrolling.[46]

One of the most compelling arguments of integrationists, then and now, was that placing deaf children in local public schools kept them under beneficial parental influence. Ironically, however, by the turn of the century nearly 40 percent of Wisconsin's day school students outside of Milwaukee did not live at home but boarded with strangers in day school towns. Twenty years later the proportion had risen to almost one-half.[47] The low incidence of deafness and its intermittent character should have made the need for boarding obvious. Furthermore, experience with day classes in hearing schools in densely populated London, England—organized before those in Wisconsin—demonstrated the necessity for boarding deaf day school students, even under optimum conditions.[48]

Integration Criticized

The unpleasant reality of boarding provided one basis for criticism of day schools. Boarded deaf children lived away from their parents while school was in session, as did students at the residential schools. But boarders, unlike their residential school counterparts, were not in a closely supervised environment surrounded by other deaf children and both hearing and deaf adults; rather, they lived with a hearing family that agreed to provide the deaf child with food and sleeping accommodations in exchange for a fee paid by the state. Strong parental bonds that might have helped to lessen the inevitable communication difficulty between hearing adults and a deaf child were absent in the boarding relationship, which was, at its core, a pecuniary one between the state and the individuals providing the boarding service. For older children, particularly those entering adolescence, the boarding arrangement raised a host of problems. These were especially acute for deaf females boarded outside of their homes and often unable to communicate easily and accurately with adult women in the household or in the school.[49]

As day schools spread in the United States, other objections mounted. Frequently these challenged the practical realities of academic integration; less frequently they attacked its fundamental ideological basis. The strongest critics tended to be residential school administrators and deaf adults, neither of whom had been invited to address the Wisconsin State Legislature as it discussed the future of the state's deaf children.

School administrators and deaf adults raised the practical objection that day schools or classes precluded grouping deaf students by grade or skill level.[50] The number of deaf students in each town or city with a public school was insufficient for such classification, which was one of the reasons why residential schools were believed necessary in the early 19th century. Outside of Milwaukee, the average enrollment in a Wisconsin day school in 1901, for example, was less than nine deaf students in all age groups combined.[51] Even in a metropolis like London, England, similar problems had emerged when deaf students were put in day classes of public schools. There were not sufficient numbers in each age category to allow each teacher to instruct simultaneously more than one or two pupils.[52] Without classification according to age and ability, academic progress beyond the most elementary level was impossible. Teachers were spread too thinly and could do no more than try to familiarize students with basic, common skills, which most frequently meant focusing on oral work-speech and speechreading to the exclusion of academic subjects.

Similarly, specialized vocational training was not practical in an integrated academic setting. This issue was of particular concern to deaf adults as they contemplated America's rapidly changing and more competitive industrial climate of the late 19th century.[53] Residential schools for deaf children had been ahead of public schools in developing vocational training and making it a significant part of their curriculum, usually encompassing half of each day's school activities. School administrators believed that skilled trades offered the best employment possibilities for deaf persons. In the 19th and early 20th centuries, deaf adults accepted this rationale for vocational education and were loath to see an employment advantage lost if deaf children attended public schools.[54]

Deaf adults and residential school administrators also believed that coeducation with hearing students hampered the academic achievement of deaf children. The primary reason for this, deaf people argued, was that deaf pupils could not accommodate themselves to the communication method used by hearing children, which was, and is, the model of academic integration followed by American public schools. In an official publication of the National Association of the Deaf, Olof Hanson—deaf architect, Gallaudet College graduate, teacher, and Episcopal priest—insisted in 1901 that deaf students would fall behind academically in any situation where they had to rely on speech and speechreading to communicate with their teachers or with each other. In an oral environment, he wrote, deaf children took so long to acquire "a fair command of language" that they did not have the time or the ability to learn other subjects.[55]

Residential school administrators provided evidence to support this charge. In 1896 the superintendents of the Michigan and Illinois residential schools toured the day schools of Wisconsin, testing students as they went along. They reported that they were appalled by the students' unfamiliarity with the most elementary subjects. Furthermore, they were struck by the students' inability to speak intelligibly or speechread their instructors, although this seemed to be the major focus of teachers' efforts.[56]

A 1902 report on Wisconsin's day schools, conducted by a coeducation advocate, provided support for the belief that academic integration was not meeting the needs of many deaf students. Warren Downs Parker, the report's author and the state inspector of day schools, stated that only 109 of the 208 day school pupils he examined could read lips, and yet this was the primary basis for communication from teacher to student, since the schools all prohibited formal signs.[57]

Elmer Walker, for many years superintendent of the Wisconsin School for the Deaf at Delavan, summarized the situation well. He reported that of 118 pupils who had transferred to his school from integrated settings none was "able to keep up grade for grade with those who had been in our school for the same length of time."[58] "As it is now," he wrote in 1905, "most of the children who go through the day schools are left stranded. They are given no industrial training and they are not taken far enough in their academic work either to provide what could be called a fair education or to fit them for college."[59]

Such objections have never addressed the wider ideological context of academic integration, however. As Bell argued to the Wisconsin legislature, the purpose of educating deaf children in an environment dominated by hearing people was to acculturate them. For integrationists the cultural imperative was more important than academic achievement or occupational success, although they seemed to believe that one necessarily would follow the other. Socialization to the hearing world would be accomplished in the home, Bell said, where hearing parents would ensure that their deaf children adapted to the ways of their hearing families, and in the schools, where the presence of overwhelming numbers of hearing children and hearing adults would force deaf students to speak, to speechread, and to become—figuratively—hearing persons. "The tendency of educational progress in regard to [disabled children]," Bell insisted in 1898, "is to keep to the normal environment of the child as closely as possible."[60] If this were not done, if deaf children instead were allowed to grow up among their deaf peers and in the presence of signing deaf adults, the president of the NEA argued in 1911, "they would become social outcasts, freaks."[61] Academic integrationists insisted that both society and deaf individuals ultimately would profit from the coeducation of deaf children, preferably in their local schools.

Some critics countered that appeals to the value of parental influence and the family home rested on a weak foundation and demonstrated ignorance of the typical family situation confronting deaf children. Beginning with Edward Allen Fay, a number of people in the 19th and early 20th century challenged Bell's sentimentalization and idealization of the home environment. Fay, vice president of Gallaudet College, contemptuously argued in 1882 that for deaf children the home provided "no beneficial influences whatever. Friends and relatives of deaf children," Fay went on, "cannot or will not—certainly, in most cases, do not—learn to converse with them except . . . by rude and elementary gestures."[62] The WSD's Walker argued that deaf children with hearing parents have no family existence as hearing people understand it.[63] The deaf child "may be loved and fed and clothed and sheltered but he is not part of the intellectual life of the home."[64]

Whether academically integrated deaf children became part of the intellectual or social life of the local schools they attended is questionable as well. Hearing children were not encourage to sign to their deaf classmates; on the contrary, except in Bartlett's school the rule in integrated settings has been that the deaf children must conform to the needs of spoken English, even if it is a communication medium for which they are physically unsuited.

Reports from various sources indicated that true integration, in the sense of equal social intercourse among hearing and deaf children, did not occur in day school settings. A Wisconsin mother wrote that during the integrated recesses of her local day school the deaf children stood around and watched the hearing children play. They simply have a recess with no pleasure in it, she concluded, and sent her deaf daughter to the residential school.[65] William Stainer, who organized eight London day schools and was strongly committed to the belief that deaf people must be socialized to the hearing world, noticed the same phenomenon. On the playground, he wrote, deaf children seem "to mix, but they are not assimilated" with their hearing schoolmates.[66]

The strongest condemnation of academic integration came from deaf people who experienced it themselves. George Wing and Elizabeth Fitzgerald were particularly articulate critics of the coeducation of deaf and hearing children, at a time when the system had just begun to evolve in the United States. Both were hard-of-hearing, with easily understood speech and, by their own measure, excellent speechreading abilities. Both had begun their education in integrated settings; both were skillful in written and spoken English, and yet both found academic integration a humiliating and destructive experience. Wing wrote in an 1886 article that placing deaf children in a classroom with hearing children—as he had been placed—was a cruel experiment sure to be "barren of good results."[67] Fitzgerald said in a 1905 speech, published in 1906, that day schools "believe it a good plan to place their pupils . . . in schools for the hearing. That is the way I was educated and I would give a great deal had it not been so." She described her experience in an integrated academic setting as one of social isolation, embarrassment, and lack of enthusiasm for subjects that depended on class discussions she could not follow.[68]

Yet supporters of coeducation in the United States did not solicit the views of deaf people or even listen to them when offered, either by individuals or by organized groups such as the National Association of the Deaf. To have done so would have been to recognize the autonomy of deaf culture and to surrender the superiority hearing people felt toward those who were deaf. Walker, the enlightened and compassionate Wisconsin superintendent, wrote to a Minnesota correspondent that the latter should heed what deaf people in his state had to say about academic integration. "I suggest," Walker stated in a sentence remarkable for its time, "that the educated deaf, themselves, are more familiar with what is best for them and their kind than are the educated hearing."[69] More typical, however, was the attitude of the Chicago Board of Education.

In 1904 that body refused even to permit a group of deaf adults to address them about the city's day schools. The deaf petitioners were certainly qualified to speak to a school board: they included a Methodist minister, a chemist, and a newspaper publisher. All were college graduates in an era when high school diplomas were not common among hearing people. The Chicago Board of Education, while advocating academic integration as a eugenic measure to prevent deaf intermarriage and the production of deaf offspring, nevertheless (and apparently without irony) told the deaf adults that their testimony about education of deaf children would have no relevance because they were not themselves parents.[70]

The Chicago Board of Education was typical of the many states and local governments that have followed the advice of integrationists and ignored other voices. Indeed, by 1975 the United States federal government had given its legal and financial support to academic integration with the passage of the Education for all Handicapped Children Act, which made no clear distinctions among children with various kinds of disabilities, instead mandating mainstreaming "to the maximum extent appropriate" for all disabled school children.[71] A lobbyist and frequent advocate for deaf rights rhapsodized in 1983 that this law "precipitated great improvements in the education for the handicapped. Millions of handicapped children have been brought into the schools or given new special programs" since its enactment.[72] Reviewing the effects of the Education for All Handicapped Children Act, two American scholars concluded in 1987 that "few other pieces of social legislation affecting children have conferred so many benefits on a needy group and done so without unintended negative consequences."[73]

The Continuing Appeal

Why has the academic integration of deaf children grown from its weak roots in Wisconsin's public schools to become the most significant factor in deaf education today, not only in the United States but throughout much of the world? The historical record in the United States does not yet provide easy answers. Part of the difficulty lies in the decentralized structure of American education. Local school boards, state legislatures, and today the federal government, all are participants in defining the school experience for both deaf and hearing children. Archival research needs to examine closely individual instances of legislative discussions of this issue. As a review of Wisconsin's experience demonstrates, the drive to integrate deaf and hearing children there actually began from an unrelated issue, that is, an attempt to secure state support for a private school. Furthermore, decisions by legislative bodies (including school boards) are often compromises, supported by different groups for a plethora of sometimes unrelated reasons, frequently poorly articulated and documented. Despite these limitations, however, tentative suggestions can be made.

Certainly one consistent factor in encouraging the academic integration of deaf children has been cost. Joseph Gordon reported the relevance of this for European efforts at coeducation in the first decades of the 19th century. German states in particular, he wrote, were impoverished by efforts to defeat Napoleon, and consequently turned to academic integration as one small cost-cutting step in public expenditures.[74] As early as

1881, a publication of the United States Bureau of Education urged public schools to enroll more deaf children in order to reduce the expenses associated with the segregated residential institutions.[75]

Individuals who wished other states to copy Wisconsin's day school experiment emphasized its financial benefit. The Wisconsin Phonological Institute's Robert Spencer, for instance, claimed that day schools saved the state over $100,000 in their first ten years.[76] A state-funded study in 1902 supported this claim, reporting that the average cost per pupil per year at the Wisconsin School for the Deaf was $180, but it was only $134 at the day schools.[77] These numbers surely impressed lawmakers.

Economic incentives, however, cannot be the whole explanation. Legislative bodies work within an intellectual framework, a system of beliefs, that defines the boundaries of their actions. If legislators had thought—or think today—that academic integration was destructive of their values or contrary to the wishes of articulate constituents, they would not have supported it, whatever its financial advantages. Bell and other savvy advocates of coeducation understood this point. They carefully stressed the ideological aspects of their preferred method of educating deaf people.

Academic integrationists make at least three significant arguments that have resonance within modern society. One is that the nation functions most smoothly and to the benefit of the greatest number of individuals when it is not torn by cultural conflicts, when it is culturally homogenous. This argument was particularly appealing in the United States at the turn of the century when large numbers of immigrants were arriving, bringing unfamiliar languages, religions, and cultures to American shores. Bell emphasized it again and again. Unless deaf people were educated with hearing people, and socialized to use their language, he said, they would become a class apart and therefore threaten social harmony.[78] One might suggest that this argument also is appealing in modern times as the United States and other nations try to resolve problems related to ethnic tensions, and one way of doing so is simply to deny minorities the right to use their own language, which almost inevitably results from academic integration.

A second powerful argument is that daily parental care and supervision provides all children, including those who are deaf, with advantages not available in a boarding school. In the 19th century some people publicly challenged this position, arguing that non-signing, hearing family members and friends could not provide the communication richness and social interaction deaf children needed to mature, whereas the residential institutions could. In the early 21st century, however, with the continued sentimentalization of children and the unquestioned acceptance of the value of child rearing within nuclear families, this issue seems muted. Both in law and public feeling, a child is nearly always presumed to be better off in the hands of his or her parents than in an institution. Educational integration of deaf children with those who hear provides a means to keep the former out of residential institutions and with their biological families.

Finally, integrationists argue that deaf children raised among hearing peers will be figuratively if not actually "normal." The appeal of this promise has been recognized for decades: parents fervently desire "normality" for their children. As a group of deaf adults wrote in 1904, hearing parents wish "to get as far away as possible from the fact that their children are grievously afflicted." Thus the parents "become easy victims to almost any suggestion . . . that seems to hold out the possibility of their children attaining to an equality with the hearing."[79] Few would argue that equality with the hearing is not a laudable goal for parents and educators and friends of deaf children.

Historians might ask, however, "What is 'normal' for deaf people?" Nora Groce has suggested in *Everyone Here Spoke Sign Language* that sign language-using deaf people on Martha's Vineyard were considered "normal" until the 20th century, although, when given the opportunity, they chose segregated education among other deaf children.[80] Further, when residential schools were founded in the United States, Thomas Hopkins Gallaudet, Laurent Clerc, and others believed that segregating deaf children and educating them by means of signs was "normal." Deaf minister Philip Hasenstab and his deaf cohorts argued in 1904 that nothing could be more "normal" for deaf adults than to wish to segregate themselves from those who hear, in order to feel comfortable and not be exposed to ridicule and the difficulty of communicating with non-signers.[81] If the definition of "normal" has changed historically, then, it is a socially-determined label, not one defined by biology.

Historians can add perspective to discussions of academic integration by looking at change through time, examining what has been meant by "normal" and how that has affected the ways that deaf people have lived, have viewed themselves, have been viewed by non-deaf people, and have been educated. They also can examine and discuss historical alternatives to current models of academic integration, such as that proposed and briefly carried through by David Bartlett. Such studies, together with detailed examinations of the immediate causes and long-term results of academic integration, may provide useful data to those who question the value and direction of this seemingly ubiquitous and ideologically appealing policy.

Notes

1. Alexander Graham Bell [hereafter AGB] to F.H. Haserot, 5/16/1905 in Alexander Graham Bell Family Papers, Manuscript Division, Library of Congress, Washington, DC, [hereafter AGBFP] container 178.

2. Joseph C. Gordon, "Deaf-Mutes and the Public Schools from 1815 to the Present Day," in *The American Annals of the Deaf* [hereafter, *Annals*] 30 (April 1885), p. 123.

3. See "La Integracion en el mundo," in *PROAS: Promocion y Asistenca a Sordos* (1985) 35–37 for a review of European movements toward the academic integration of deaf children in the late 20th century.

4. "Schools and Classes for the Deaf in the United States," *Annals*, 135 (1990) 99–100

5. In 1990, residential schools in every state except Missouri, New Jersey, and West Virginia reported having mainstream options. ("Schools and Classes," 88–134).

6. Gordon, "Deaf-Mutes," p. 123.

7. Gordon, "Deaf-Mutes," pp. 141–2.

8. For a good review of the perspective of many contemporary Deaf Americans, see Mary C. Malzkuhn, *Listening to the Deaf: An In-Depth Case Study and Policy Analysis of Board of Education V. Rowley.* (Unpublished PhD Dissertation, University of Maryland, College Park, 1988).

9. Both were tried in mid-19th century France; the latter has been more common in the United States and is practiced by many residential schools today. For France, see Gordon "Deaf-Mutes," pp. 123–4, pp. 128–9.

10. Edward Allen Fay, "Mr. Bartlett's Family School," in Edward Allen Fay, ed, *Histories of American Schools for the Deaf, 1817–1893,* vol. 3 (Volta Bureau: Washington, DC, 1893) p. 4.

11. Quoted in Fay "Bartlett's," p. 6.

12. See the Comments of George Wing in Fay, "Bartlett's," p. 7.

13. Jack R. Gannon, *Deaf Heritage: A Narrative History of Deaf America* (Silver Spring, MD: National Association of the Deaf, 1981) p. 7.

14. William A. Knapp, "The Department for the Deaf of F. Knapp's Institute," in Fay, ed. *Histories,* Vol. 3, p. 4.

15. Knapp, "Department," p. 11.

16. Knapp, "Department," pp. 11–12.

17. AGB to Miss Littlefield (10/11/1884): "Journal of Private School for Deaf Children," in AGBFP, cont. 191.

18. Gertrude Hitz Burton, "Dr. A. Graham Bell's Private School: Line Writing and Kindergarten," p. 10. pamphlet (no date, no place of publication) in AGBFP, cont. 191.

19. AGB to Mary True (1/11/1883) in AGBFP, cont. 191.

20. AGB to Edward J. Herman (11/2/1883) in AGBFP, cont. 173.

21. Robert C. Spencer, "The Wisconsin System of Public Day Schools for Deaf Mutes," in Fay, ed., *Histories,* Vol. 3, pp. 3–6. in National Education Association, *Journal of Addresses and Proceedings of the Thirty-Seventh Annual Meeting.* (Chicago: University of Chicago Press, 1893).

22. *Journal of Proceedings of the Thirty-Fourth Annual Session of the Wisconsin Legislature* (Madison: David Atwood, 1881) pp. 454–55, 550, 578, 656, 686, 693, 744. *Journal of*

Proceedings of the Thirty-Sixth Session Annual Session of the Wisconsin Legislature (Madison: Democrat Printing Co, nd), pp71, 595–6.

23. "Robert Closson Spencer," *The National Cyclopedia of American Biography.* Vol 8, Reprint, (Ann Arbor: University Microfilms, 1967) p 11.

24. AGB to Robert C. Spencer (9/28/1883) in AGBFP, cont. 171.

25. Robert C. Spencer to AGB (12/29/1883) in AGBFP, cont. 179; Robert C. Spencer to AGB (4/28/1884) in AGBFP, cont. 171.

26. A. J. Winnie, compiler, *History and Handbook of Day Schools for the Deaf and Blind* (Madison: Democrat Printing Co, 1912), p. 11.

27. This meeting is discussed in "The National Educational Association," *Annals,* 29 (October 1884), p. 339.

28. *Journal of Proceedings of the Thirty-Seventh Session of the Wisconsin Legislature* (Madison: Democrat Printing C0,1885) p. 14.

29. AGB to Jeremiah Rusk (12/26/1884) in AGBFP, cont 178; "Mabel Hubbard Bell's Journal" (2/7/1885) in AGBFP, cont. 34.

30. AGB, "Open Letter to Committees on Education of the Senate and Assembly of the Legislature of Wisconsin," (2/18/1885) in AGBFP, cont. 179.

31. Bell's most emphatic statement of his eugenic beliefs is in his *Memoir Upon the Creation of a Deaf Variety of the Human Race, presented to the National Academy of Sciences at New Haven, Connecticut* Nov. 13, 1883; Reprinted by the Alexander Graham Bell Association for the Deaf (Washington, DC, 1969) For a review of Bell and eugenics see Richard Winefield, *Never the Twain Shall Meet: Bell, Gallaudet, and the Communication Debate* (Washington, DC: Gallaudet University Press, 1987) esp. pp. 82–96.

32. Daniel J. Kevles, *In the Name of Eugenics: Genetics and the Uses of Human Heredity* (New York: Alfred A. Knopf, 1985) is the best study of this issue.

33. AGB, "Open Letter."

34. *Laws of Wisconsin 1885,* Chapter 315, pp. 293–5.

35. *Laws of Wisconsin 1893,* pp. 498–499; *Laws of Wisconsin 1909,* p. 203; *Laws of Wisconsin 1917,* p. 598; *Laws of Wisconsin 1919,* p. 583.

36. Warren Downs Parker, *First Annual Report of the Inspector of Schools for the Deaf* (Madison: Democrat Printing Co, 1902) pp. 7, 14, 21–22. Schools opened and closed with some regularity. Thus precise numbers of either students or cities have little significance.

37. A. B. Cook to T. Emery Bray (12/6/1920) Public Instruction, Bureau for Handicapped Children, Wisconsin School for the Deaf, Archives of the State Historical Society of Wisconsin, Madison, Wisconsin [hereafter PIBHC, WSD].

38. ABG to Mabel Hubbard Bell (2/14/1886) in AGBFP, cont. 38; Jeannie Bright Holden to AGB (3/11/1903) in AGBFP, cont. 178; W.C. Martindale to AGB (6/14/1905) in AGBFP, cont. 178; AGB to Andrew W. Smith (1/10/1906) in AGBFP, cont. cont. 178; Adolph O. Eberhart to AGB (1/20/1914) in AGBFP, cont. 178.

39. Parker, *First Annual Report,* p. 19; Jay C. Howard, "The Minnesota Plan of Education the Deaf," *Companion,* (November 15, 1916).

40. Robert C. Spencer to AGB (3/5/1896) in AGBFP, cont. 198; Elmer W. Walker to Annie E. Scheffer (4/15/1903) in PIBHC, WSD; "Draft of Assembly bill #412, A" Elmer W. Walker to A.J. Winnie (3/4/1909) in PIBHC, WSD; A.J. Winnie to Elmer W. Walker (2/25/1896) in PIBHC, WSD; Elmer W. Walker to M.C. Potter (8/12/1913) in PIBHC, WSD. For a variety of reasons, Bell refused to support attempts to close residential institutions.

41. Parker, *Report,* p. 15.

42. Parker, *Report,* pp. 18, 41–2. See Elizabeth Van Adestine to AGB (11/19/1903) in AGBFP, container 178, for the situation in Michigan.

43. Robert C. Spencer, "The Wisconsin Public Day Schools for the Deaf," in *Journal of the Proceedings and Addersses of the Thirty-Seventh Annual Meeting* (Chicago: University of Chicago Press, 1898) p. 1056; Winnie, *History and Handbook*, p. 30.

44. AGB to Andrew W. Smith (1/10/1906) in AGBFP, cont. 178.

45. AGB, "Open Letter."

46. Robert C. Spencer to Fred C. Larson (2/14/1907) in PIBHC, WSD.

47. Parker, *Report*, p. 24; A.B. Cook to Emery Bray (12/6/1920) PIBHC, WSD.

48. David Buxton, "Day Schools," *Annals*, 30 (Jan. 1885) pp. 76–77.

49. For the comments of a woman day school supervisor in Wisconsin who was worried about molestation of deaf girls in boarding households, see L.H. Lowell to Elmer W. Walker (n.d.) PIBHC, WSD.

50. Olof Hanson, "Day Schools for the Deaf," *Circular of Information* (National Association of the Deaf, 1901); Elmer W. Walker to H.C. Buell (5/5/1903) PIBHC, WSD.

51. Parker, *Report*, pp. 7, 14.

52. Gordon, "Deaf-Mutes," pp. 139–40.

53. See John Vickrey Van Cleve and Barry A. Crouch, *A Place of Their Own: Creating the Deaf Community in America*. (Washington, D.C.: Gallaudet University Press, 1989) pp. 155–63 for a more thorough discussion of employment concerns during this period. The advent of vocational programs in public schools is discussed in David John Hogan, *Class and Reform: School and Society in Chicago, 1880–1930* (Philadelphia: University of Pennsylvania Press, 1985).

54. Hanson, "Day Schools." "To the Legislature of Wisconsin in Session Assembled," a petition by "present and former deaf citizens of Wisconsin" July 15, 1914, PIBHC, WSD.

55. Hanson, "Day Schools."

56. S. T. Walker to J. W. Swiler (5/7/1896) PIBHC, WSD ; Francis D. Clarke to J. W. Swiler (5/8/1896) PIBHC, WSD.

57. Parker, *Report*, p.24.

58. Elmer W. Walker to E. L. Michaelson (10/28/1913) PIBHC, WSD.

59. Elmer W. Walker to G. D. Jones (3/18/1905) PIBHC, WSD.

60. AGB "Closing Address," National Education Association, *Journal of Addresses*, pp. 1058–9.

61. Carol G. Pearce, "The Oral Teaching of the Deaf," *Nebraska Journal*, 40 (Jan. 30, 1912) pp. 2–3.

62. Edward Allen Fay, "Day Schools Compared with Institutions," *Annals* 27 (July 1882) p. 185.

63. Walker to H. C. Buell.

64. Walker to M. C. Potter.

65. G. H. Jones to Elmer W. Walker (3/17/1905) PIBHC, WSD.

66. Quoted in Gordon, "Deaf-Mutes," p. 139.

67. George Wing, "The Associate Feature in the Education of the Deaf," *Annals* 31 (January 1886) pp 22–35.

68. Elizabeth Fitzgerald, "Echoes of the Morganton Convention," *Annals* 51 (March 1906) pp. 167–9.

69. Walker to M. C. Potter.

70. P. J. Hasenstab, G. T. Dougherty, Wm. O'Donell, O. H. Regensburg, and C. C. Codman, "Petition to the Board of Education of the City of Chicago" (11/15/1904) PIBHC, WSD.

71. For a discussion of this law see Sarah S. Geer, "Education of the Handicapped Act," in John V. Van Cleve, ed., *Gallaudet Encyclopedia of Deaf People and Deafness*, Vol. 1

(New York: McGraw-Hill, 1987) pp. 380–383. For deaf peoples' role in its enactment, see Malzkuhn, *Listening to the Deaf*.

72. Jack Tweedie, "The Politics of Legalization in Special Education Reforms," in J. C. Chambers and W. T. Hartman, eds., *Special Education Politics: Their History, Implementation, and Finance* (Philadelphia: Temple University Press, 1983) p. 48.

73. Judith Singer and John Butler, "The Education for All Handicapped Children Act: Schools as Agents of Social Reform," *Harvard Educational Review* 57 (1987) p. 125.

74. Gordon, "Deaf-Mutes," p. 125

75. Edward Allen Fay, "Notices of Publications," *Annals* 27 (1882) pp. 123–124.

76. Spencer, "Wisconsin ," p. 1057.

77. Parker, *Report*, p. 21; for similar data for Massachusetts, see Mabel Ellery Adams, "Day Schools and Institutional," *Volta Review* 12 (1910) pp. 354–357.

78. This idea is developed most strongly in Bell, *Memoir*.

79. Hasenstab et al., "Petition."

80. Nora Groce, *Everyone Here Spoke Sign Language* (Cambridge: Harvard University Press, 1985).

81. Hasenstab et al., "Petition."

7

Taking Stock: Alexander Graham Bell and Eugenics, 1883–1922

Brian H. Greenwald

Editor's Introduction

Brian Greenwald has studied Alexander Graham Bell's relationship with the American Deaf community more intensely than any other historian. In the article below, his subtle and complex arguments reflect both careful scholarship and the ambiguity of Bell's legacy. Greenwald argues that mainstream historians and students of deaf history have overlooked Bell's role in racist programs and eugenics. Mainstream scholars have emphasized Bell's scientific contributions and his iconic stature as an American hero. Deaf community historians have demonized Bell for his support for oralism. Greenwald argues, though, that Bell was a key player in the American eugenics movement, and that he could have caused the American Deaf community irreparable damage if he had allowed zealous eugenicists to classify deaf people among those who represented a serious threat to America's biological well-being. Despite Bell's interest in and support for eugenics, and despite his studies of deafness and genetics, Greenwald writes, he consistently refused to advocate any programs that would limit the rights of deaf people to marry whom they pleased or that would other-

---

This article represents a portion of my dissertation, *Alexander Graham Bell through the Lens of Eugenics, 1883–1922* (George Washington University, 2006). I would like to thank Nathaniel Comfort for guidance. In addition, I wish to acknowledge Susan Burch for sharing incisive comments. Also, thanks goes to Janey Greenwald-Czubek for her editorial work. The Gallaudet University Press provided valuable suggestions. The research was supported by funding received from Gallaudet Research Institute. Finally, special thanks goes to John Vickrey Van Cleve for the support and willingness to value historical discussion over information technology work.

wise—such as through sterilization—take away deaf reproductive rights. Greenwald attributes Bell's moderation to his familiarity with and respect for deaf individuals.

To Deaf people, Alexander Graham Bell is best known for his opposition to Deaf culture and American Sign Language, but Bell was also deeply involved in eugenics. His colleagues and professional collaborators included several of the most important American eugenicists, notably Charles Benedict Davenport, Henry H. Goddard, and David Starr Jordan. Davenport was arguably the most influential figure in the American eugenics movement of the early twentieth century. Goddard, made famous for his work on the Kallikak family, was a well-known psychologist. Jordan was president of Stanford University during the rise of eugenic activity in the United States, and his intellectual contributions helped shape the first organization exclusively devoted to eugenics. Alexander Graham Bell was a zealous eugenics participant along with his better known colleagues.

Bell's mother and wife were both deaf, although paradoxically neither Bell nor Davenport mentions this fact in any of their correspondence with each other. The paradox continues in that, although America celebrates Bell as a true hero, the signing Deaf community spurns him, often identifying Bell as a tyrant, guilty of committing "linguistic and cultural genocide" against the Deaf community.[1] Those Deaf voices, however, remain suppressed and largely unheard in the mainstream intellectual community. Although specialized Deaf history studies contain accounts of Bell and his attitudes toward the Deaf community, nearly all broad examinations of Bell ignore his racial and eugenic attitudes.[2] Even scholars in Deaf studies tend to focus on Bell's advocacy of oralism or to review the debates about Bell's mission to discourage matrimonial unions among Deaf people. A more concise analysis of Bell's relationship with Davenport, who was his primary contact with the eugenics movement, will help fill a void overlooked by other scholars. First, a brief historical background is necessary before studying Bell's eugenic work.

Bell's father, Alexander Melville Bell, devoted much of his life to educating deaf children, and his son initially followed in his footsteps. Melville Bell pioneered the use of "visible speech," a system he invented, which correlated all speech sounds with particular visual symbols as a way to assist deaf children to learn to speak. Bell began his professional involvement with deaf children by first teaching visible speech and then promoting oralism, the belief that deaf children should to be taught to speak and read lips—without using sign language—and that deaf children could be trained to lead resourceful, independent, and productive lives.

Alexander Graham Bell worked with deaf children during a period of national controversy over language varieties and uses that sparked the interest of educators, parents of deaf children, and the Deaf community. In the late-nineteenth century, prominent leaders of the American Deaf community watched Edward Miner Gallaudet—the president of Gallaudet College and the son of Thomas Hopkins Gallaudet and his deaf wife, Sophia Fowler Gallaudet—and Alexander Graham Bell engage in an intellectual debate about language issues and deaf education, driven by their lifelong passion for educating deaf children. Gallaudet and Bell vehemently disagreed with each other in letters, articles, and speeches.[3]

Bell was living in an intellectually fertile environment. The Gallaudet-Bell debates took the central stage before he shifted his interests to racial thought, eugenics, and possible applications of the new science of human improvement to the American Deaf community.

The American Deaf community watched in horror as Bell forged ahead in the communications debate, radically altering the characteristics of American education for deaf children. Oralism became increasingly popular in the United States, and a growing number of hearing women were being trained in "normal schools" to teach deaf children, often replacing deaf male teachers. During the 1870s, normal schools were teacher-training programs that came to emphasize professionalism and academic knowledge in educating children.[4] Women were exploited as a source of cheap labor, as they supposedly possessed the characteristics necessary for educating Deaf children with oral methods. Male principals and superintendents of deaf schools believed that women were far better teachers in an oral environment because they were patient, gentle, kind, and motherly. By 1910, oralism and its female teaching corps had made such strides that the vast majority of deaf schools in the United States had banned sign language from the classroom.[5]

Francis Galton coined the term *eugenics* in 1883, the same year in which Bell presented to the National Academy of Sciences in New Haven, Connecticut, his first study of heredity and the American deaf community.[6] Galton, known for his numerical and phrenological fascinations, recorded his eugenic ideas in his *Hereditary Genius* in 1869. Galton wanted his eugenic ideas to improve English society whereby selective human breeding could be used to address the social and political problems of

England during the late-nineteenth century. Procreation of the intelligent became his utmost concern. Galton wanted to curb the procreation of criminals, handicapped people, institutionalized individuals, and those deemed to be less intelligent or more dependent on government support than most, and, instead, encourage the procreation of people who were brilliant and successful.[7]

Bell's 1883 paper, *Memoir Upon the Formation of a Deaf Variety of the Human Race*, outlined his thoughts on Deaf marriages and dovetailed neatly with Galton's ideas. This polemical document noted aspects of Deaf culture—such as isolation from the hearing majority, institutional-ization during childhood (in residential schools), the use of sign language, and intermarriage between Deaf people—that he believed would increase the size of the Deaf population in the United States. Bell argued that his advocacy of oralism was beneficial to prevent this expansion from occur-ring because increased use of speech and speechreading, he believed, would lead to a more mainstreamed life for Deaf people. If the current trends continued, wherein a Deaf culture encouraged Deaf people to choose others who were also Deaf as their marriage partners, the result would be obvious: "[I]f the laws of heredity that are known to hold in the case of animals apply to man," Bell wrote, "the intermarriage of congeni-tal deaf-mutes through a number of successive generations should result in the formation of a deaf variety of the human race."[8] One option to pre-vent this evolution was to enact legislation to prohibit the intermarriage of congenitally deaf people. A second choice was to adopt "preventive measures" through the systematic elimination of deaf residential schools (hence the rise of oral day schools), the removal of sign language from the educational environment, the firing of deaf teachers and superintendents, and the replacement of them with hearing teachers (most of whom would be women).[9] Bell himself observed that legislation prohibiting deaf inter-marriage would be difficult to pass and enforce and would probably be ineffective.

Eight years after speaking to the American Academy of Sciences, Bell emphasized the role of personal marital decisions in an address to the Literary Society on the Kendall Green campus of today's Gallaudet University in Washington, D.C. Bell bluntly told the audience that on their graduation, they would go into the "world of hearing and speaking peo-ple" and could not use sign language. Bell attempted to dismiss the myth that he wanted to prevent deaf people from marriage, however, stating:

I have never done such a thing, nor do I intend to; and before I speak upon this subject I want you to distinctly understand that I have no intention of interfering with your liberty of marriage. You can marry whom you choose, and I hope you will be happy. It is not for me to blame you for marrying to suit yourselves, for you all know that I my-self, the son of a deaf mother, have married a deaf wife.[10]

Bell's address to the Deaf college students on Kendall Green revealed that he was concerned that in the future, "in a hundred years or so," there would be an identifiable deaf variety of the human race, separate from the hearing community and, presumably, a drain on that community's re-sources. Bell emphasized that his scientific work was significant because he would be able to identify those would who would be likely to have deaf offspring. According to Bell, this knowledge would allow Deaf peo-ple themselves to be responsible for increasing or *diminishing* (emphasis is Bell's) the number of Deaf children by selecting their partner with full knowledge of their genetic characteristics. Bell used the data from his re-search to outline the probabilities for having Deaf offspring. He empha-sized to the students that he did not wish to interfere with their liberty of free choice, but he firmly opined that the ideal marriage would be with a hearing person because

> the chances are infinitely in your favor that out of the millions of hear-ing persons in this country you may be able to find one with whom you may be happy than that you should find one among the smaller num-bers of the deaf. I think the sentiment is hurtful that makes you believe you can only be happy with a deaf companion. That is a mistake, and I believe a grave one. I would have you believe that the welfare of your-self and your children will be greatly promoted by marriage with a hearing partner, if you can find one with whom you can be happy.[11]

Bell was nervous that the audience would take his address out of context and brought a stenographer with him for verification. Eventually, Bell de-livered a printed version of his address to the members of the Literary Society.

Bell's interpreter for the Kendall Green address was Edward Allen Fay, who would later publish *Marriages of the Deaf in America: An Inquiry Con-cerning the Results of Marriages of the Deaf in America*. Although Fay's study was funded by the Volta Bureau, an organization that Bell founded and controlled, it challenged some of Bell's conclusions about deaf mar-riages.[12] In his *Memoir Upon the Formation of a Deaf Variety of the Human Race*, Bell stated that "deaf-mutes marry deaf-mutes" and claimed that people with congenital deafness in deaf-deaf marriages tended to pro-duce a higher percentage of deaf offspring than hearing people. Fay's data agreed with Bell on his point that deaf people marry other deaf people, but Fay's careful research suggested that deaf-deaf marriages did not produce a higher proportion of deaf offspring than deaf-hearing marriages. Eugenicists found Bell's *Memoir Upon the Formation of a Deaf Variety of the Human Race* more useful for their efforts than Fay's study.

Eugenics became increasingly important for Bell as the nineteenth century ended and the twentieth began. He became a zealous participant in the American eugenics movement and allied himself with Charles Benedict Davenport. Davenport had taught zoology at Harvard during the 1890s but left for a position at the University of Chicago in 1899. In 1904, he successfully lobbied the Carnegie foundation to establish a station for Experimental Evolution at Cold Spring Harbor, on Long Island, New York.[13] Along with other eugenicists, Davenport advocated stringent immigration laws, arguing that people from Northern and Western Europe were genetically more advanced than Southern and Eastern Europeans. Likewise, Davenport detested government intervention in assisting people who were categorized as insane, mentally retarded, or criminals.[14] Sterilization of such individuals became an option for some mainline eugenicists. Bell, an American hero and world famous inventor who was interested in discouraging the intermarriage of deaf people, was a powerful ally for the eugenicists.

During the heyday of the Progressive Era, the eugenic gospel—as a social reform movement—spread across the United States through the efforts of Davenport and his collaborators, among others. Even England's Eugenics Education Society was impressed with the speed and magnitude of Davenport's work. Sterilization of those individuals alleged to be genetic defectives became common in many states, and Eugenic Education Societies proliferated in states such as California, Minnesota, and Wisconsin and in cities such as Chicago and St. Louis.[15] On the federal level, immigration laws reflected the influence of eugenic and racist thinking. The Chinese Exclusion Acts of 1882 and 1902 and the Gentleman's Agreement of 1907, for example, were based on widespread assumptions about the genetic basis of behavior and the genetic characteristics of national groups. The National Origins Act of 1924 (also known as the Johnson Laws), enacted shortly after Bell's death, showed even more clearly the extent to which eugenic beliefs had become accepted. Influential groups such as the Galton Society that met periodically at the American Museum of Natural History in New York and the Race Betterment Foundation that was established in Battle Creek, Michigan, showed significant support among America's educated citizens. Elite Americans, supported by supposed scientific expertise, by wealth, and by influence, unabashedly promoted eugenics. Within this context, then, Bell's research on Deaf people and heredity and, more broadly, on the inheritance of genetic traits, found a receptive audience.

Bell did not confine his interest or his studies to humans and deafness. Indeed, he once wrote to Davenport inquiring about deafness in white cats with blue eyes. Bell had two cats himself, a male and female. Although the cats never reproduced, Bell observed that they "seemed to be totally deaf and appeared to be peculiar in other ways also. For example, they could not climb about with the facility displayed by ordinary cats, exhibiting a marked instability of gait. In walking along the top of a sofa for example they used their tails as balancing poles."[16] Bell advised Davenport, if he was interested, to consult a Dr. W. F. Black who reportedly had a deaf breed of white cats for several generations in Calais, Maine.

Davenport responded two weeks later, stating that he was planning to contact Dr. Black, not to obtain cats, but to satisfy his insatiable curiosity. "Darwin says he once thought the rule invariable that white blue-eyed cats are deaf but has learned of a few authentic examples. From inquiries among the cat ladies I find that they still get a good many deaf offspring but feel that they are eliminating the tendency."[17] Davenport lamented that he had not had the opportunity to examine the behavior of his four deaf cats. Davenport's wife commented that the cats' voices were "decidedly peculiar."[18] Davenport offered to ship his four cats to Bell for further study, but mentioned that he had "already been obliged to destroy a number."[19] Whether Bell saved these deaf white cats is unknown.

Bell was much influenced by the works of Charles Darwin and tried to study whether certain physical anomalies in animals might produce evolutionary advantages. For example, on his Beinn Bhreagh estate on Cape Breton Island in Nova Scotia, Bell kept numerous pairs of rams and ewes to determine whether multinippled sheep were more fertile than the normal two-nippled variety. Bell worked to determine whether twin sheep produced extra nipples and a greater quantity of milk. Bell killed all of his four-nippled rams, keeping six-nippled rams for breeding.[20] Davenport was equally interested, purchasing some of Bell's ewes, and had the sheep shipped to Cold Spring Harbor for further study. Bell was thorough and meticulous in his data, identifying each sheep by number, recording sheep weight in the fall and winter months, measuring nipples, and even tracking deformed sheep. Bell did not trust Mr. McKillop, his shepherd, with record keeping: "[the record] is very unreliable unless checked and verified; he does his best but he has educational limitations that interfere with accuracy of records."[21] Bell continued his fascination with sheep experiments on his estate until his death. The most important result of his sheep experiments was that it propelled Bell into the genetic science elite circles, particularly through his contact with Davenport, who led Bell to become closely linked with the American Breeders Association (ABA) and subsequent eugenic work.

Mendelian genetics became popular when it was "rediscovered" circa 1900 with groundbreaking research into corn, bread molds, and the fruit-fly. During the 1860s, Austrian monk Gregor Mendel had conducted breeding experiments with pea plants. Mendel cross-pollinated the pea plants and concluded that certain traits were passed on to the subsequent generation in specific ratios, depending on whether the trait was domi-nant or recessive. The work of Mendel became popular with American hereditarians. Although later scientists would discover flaws in Mendel's work, American eugenicists in the early twentieth century applied Mendel's ratios without regard to environmental factors or other com-plexities of genetics.[22] American eugenicists argued that the physical, behavioral, and intellectual development of human offspring were based on their inheritance of patterns of dominant and recessive parental genes. They argued that it was now possible to "predict" the characteris-tics of offspring by studying their parents, and therefore, it was feasible to improve American society—and the human race—through selective breeding.

The ABA provided organizational support for this goal. Agriculturists and biologists established the ABA in 1903 with the intention of improv-ing the quality of plants and animals in the United States. In 1906, the ABA established a Committee on Eugenics to resolve breeding issues. In a short time, this committee would be charged to exclusively examine efforts to improve the human race, and it would be chaired by David Starr Jordan, president of Stanford University. Historian Mark Haller recog-nizes this organization as the "first group in the United States to advocate eugenics under the name of eugenics."[23] In 1910, the constitution of the ABA was modified to include "man" by adding a section relating to breeding in humans, known as the eugenics section.[24] At the invitation of James Wilson, who was then the Secretary of Agriculture, Bell attended an ABA convention in Washington, D.C., in 1908 and presented his thoughts on eugenics.

In his speech, which was also published in the *National Geographic* mag-azine, Bell considered whether the laws of heredity could be applied to humans through social changes: "Can we formulate practical plans that might lead to the breeding of better men and better women? . . . [The] solution depends upon the possibility of controlling the production of offspring from human beings."[25] Bell feared that offspring in inferior condition—sickly and defective in physical and mental capacity—would undermine the human race. Bell considered imposing legislative restrictions on marriage, but he knew he would then be violating the inalienable rights claimed in the Declaration of Independence.[26]

Bell stated that the procreation of undesirable children would weaken the community but that measures to curtail offspring from genetically defective individuals should be carefully evaluated. Parents, Bell reasoned, should not have children if they could not offer support and care for the duration of the child's life. Bell stated, however, that "legal prohibition of marriage should only be resorted to in cases where there could be no manner of doubt that the community would suffer as a result of the marriage. . . . [P]ublic opinion, and the desire of all persons to have healthy offspring, would, in my judgment, be a more powerful deterrent to the production of undesirable offspring than a compulsory process of law."[27]

Bell's statement begs the question of exactly *what* alleged genetic conditions or characteristics of any two individuals would leave "no manner of doubt that the community would suffer" from their marriage and childbearing. Even though Bell does not explicitly mention deaf people in this category, it can be inferred from his papers and his association with the subcommittee on eugenics (within the ABA) that he believed that the larger community—and ultimately the human race—would suffer if deaf individuals were permitted to procreate. Finally, Bell suggested that Congress provide an ethnical survey of the people of the United States. Bell feared the mixing of races, thought it could be controlled by "suitable immigration laws tending to eliminate undesirable ethnical elements," and advocated that the "final result should be the evolution of a higher and nobler type of man in America, and not deterioration of the nation."[28]

Shortly after Bell's presentation, Davenport was a guest at Bell's home. He later wrote Bell, stressing the importance of the Committee on Eugenics within the ABA. Eugenicists, reasoned Davenport, must work alongside students of eugenics, stating "it would be very unfortunate for a group of students of human inheritance and race improvement to segregate themselves from the students of the same subjects."[29]

By December of 1908, Davenport reported to Bell on the establishment of subcommittees on feeblemindedness and insanity within the ABA eugenics committee. Davenport also wanted to study hereditary deafness. He thought it possible to discover the "proportion of offspring of a particular mating of deaf strains which will be particularly liable to deafness." Davenport reasoned that this information would enable eugenicists to "discover a precise law of mating ensuring normal offspring from a parent with hereditary tendency toward ear defect."[30] He offered Bell the chairmanship of the subcommittee on deafness of the ABA's Committee on Eugenics. Bell wholeheartedly accepted the nomination, breaking his vow two years earlier not to serve in an official capacity.

Bell was both a wealthy man and an American celebrity, thus increasing his potential to contribute significantly to eugenics efforts. Davenport recognized this resource and tried to draw the telephone inventor into assisting with fund-raising. He wrote Bell that he was courting Mrs. E. H. Harriman of New York City. Davenport wanted Bell to meet Mrs. Harriman and secure funds for the Eugenics Record Office. Harriman's late husband, Edward Henry Harriman, was involved in the railroad industry and had left a huge fortune to his widow. Davenport met Mrs. Harriman through her daughter, Mary Harriman, who believed in the importance of eugenics. Davenport wrote Bell that Mrs. Harriman intended to turn over some property to the Eugenics Office.[31] An excited and motivated scientist, Davenport also eyed the Rockefeller Foundation for funds.

By this time, Davenport was well-established as the premier American scientist on eugenic work, and he maintained contact with prominent individuals such as John D. Rockefeller and J. H. Kellogg, the cereal magnate, who could advance his cause. Kellogg was linked to the Race Betterment Foundation and organized three conferences between 1914 and 1928. Located in Battle Creek, Michigan, that foundation became an important center for the dissemination of medical research that had racial implications.

The movement was gaining support outside of Cold Spring Harbor and Battle Creek. Numerous letters came in, and people donated money to advance the "cause." Arba N. Lincoln, an attorney, wrote from Fall River, Massachusetts, "I am much interested in eugenics and would like to advance the cause what I can and I enclose herewith $2.00 for I do not fully understand the nature of the society. . . . The fact that the association is in some way advocating the cause of eugenics seems to be sufficient warrant for me to join it."[32] Numerous people sent similar letters and money to Davenport and the Cold Spring Harbor laboratory between 1910 and 1913.

Bell's increasing interest in and involvement with eugenics was apparent by 1911. In that year, the ABA's eugenics committee met at the Volta Bureau in Washington, D.C., at Bell's invitation. Named for the Volta Prize, which the French government awarded Bell for the invention of the telephone, this institution was central to Bell's efforts to expand oralism in deaf education.[33] Bell had used the Volta Prize funds (50,000 francs, or $10,000 at the time) to establish the Volta Laboratory and conduct experiments in sound transmission and recordings. This work led to a recording patent that Bell and other colleagues later sold. Bell then turned his profits from the Volta laboratory work over to support the Volta Bureau as an institution "for the increase and diffusion of knowledge relating to the deaf."[34] In 1908, the Volta Bureau and another group Bell founded and supported, the American Association to Promote the Teaching of Speech to the Deaf (today's Alexander Graham Bell Association for the Deaf and Hard of Hearing), merged.[35] The Volta Bureau provided the oralist organization with office and meeting facilities as well as an extensive library collection of deafness-related materials. Bell used this ABA forum to talk with the Eugenics Committee about the work of the Volta Bureau.

Nearly a year after this meeting, Bell emphasized the importance of eugenics and praised his friend Davenport, writing "You have started a great work, of vast importance to the people of the United States and to the world, by the establishment of the Eugenics Record Office, and I can assure you of my hearty co-operation as one of the Board of Scientific Directors."[36]

Furthermore, the Eugenics Record Office would encourage the "study of the consequences of close marriages and the study of new blood introduced to America by immigration."[37] Bell had moved from the theoretical application of eugenic thinking reflected by his *Memoir Upon the Formation of a Deaf Variety of the Human Race* to more practical work with his sheep-breeding experiments on his Beinn Bhreagh estate, on to public advocacy of eugenic measures throughout society. The Deaf community in the United States, however, failed to recognize Bell's new interest in eugenics and his influence with important American eugenicists.

Most, if not all, leaders of the Deaf community assumed Bell's work on eugenics was limited to his *Memoir Upon the Formation of a Deaf Variety of the Human Race* and his talk to the Literary Society on the Gallaudet campus in 1891. Deaf leaders missed the larger implications of the eugenics movement. They never pieced together how oralism fed on eugenic ideas as it reflected popular social ideals during the early twentieth century.

They may also have missed Bell's particular approach to eugenics, one that seemed compatible with American political traditions and individual self-determination. Bell espoused a position that is often called "positive" eugenics. He wrote to Davenport in 1912 that the

> whole subject of eugenics has been too much associated in the public mind with fantastical and impracticable schemes for restricting marriage and preventing the propagation of undesirable characteristics, so

that the very name 'Eugenics' suggests, to the average mind, insanity, feeble-mindedness, and an attempt to interfere with the liberty of the individual in his pursuit of happiness in marriage. If we make the promotion of desirable marriages our chief aim, and relegate interference with marriage to a subordinate position, the problem will gain a truer conception of the aims and purposes engaged in eugenical work.[38]

Bell had made a similar point more than twenty years earlier in his speech on the Gallaudet campus when he attempted to respond to the charge that he supported legal limitations on the right of deaf people to marry.

Davenport was eager to keep Bell within the eugenics fold and was concerned when "negative eugenics" grabbed the spotlight. For example, when a 1915 article about an alleged plan of the Eugenic Record Office to sterilize fourteen million Americans circulated in the Hearst papers, Davenport rushed to assure Bell. He wrote to him saying that this report was a "very sensational fake article" and apologized that it disturbed the "placid waters about Beinn Bhreagh."[39] Bell immediately responded, writing that it is a "great relief, as I was naturally disturbed over the newspaper notices,—even though I didn't believe them."[40] In his *Memoir Upon the Formation of a Deaf Variety of the Human Race,* delivered to the American Academy of Sciences in 1883, Bell avoided any discussion of such radical steps as sterilization of Deaf people, and he remained consistent in his ideology thirty-two years later.

Bell's publications and addresses raised concerns among the elite members of the Deaf community, but his relationship to Davenport, and its potential significance, seems not to have surfaced among Deaf people. Correspondence between Bell and Davenport demonstrates that each sought to benefit from the other's work. Bell capitalized on Davenport's scientific connections as well as his work at the Cold Spring Harbor laboratory. Likewise, Davenport forged an alliance with Bell to exploit his personal wealth and celebrity status. Their correspondence shows that Davenport had a strong influence on Bell personally and intellectually. Yet Deaf leaders knew Bell almost exclusively through his polemics in support of oralism and his visit to the Literary Society on the Gallaudet College campus.

The elite members of the Deaf community underestimated, or were unaware of, Bell's influence and the status of the individuals with whom he was associated in promoting eugenics. John D. Rockefeller Jr. and J. Pierpont Morgan, for example, both supported Davenport and his eugenics work, and President Theodore Roosevelt was well aware of the existence of a laboratory at Cold Spring Harbor. Had prominent leaders of the Deaf community known about these contacts and Bell's influence with the Eugenics Committee of the ABA, they might have been far more worried about the possible consequences of a eugenics program than with attempts to preserve the purity of sign language on film, a major concern of the National Association of the Deaf in the early twentieth century.

George Veditz, a member of the intellectual elite of the American Deaf community during this period, led that NAD effort to combat the assault against sign language through attempts to preserve it on film. Veditz became the seventh president of the NAD in 1907. A prolific writer, he well articulated the signing Deaf community's fear and dislike of Bell's actions. Veditz claimed that Bell was the "most powerful and influential figure in American deaf-mute education for thirty years past."[41] Veditz accused Bell of violating the liberties of Deaf people by preventing marriage and procreation of their own kind, but he conceded that "deaf [people] are today more alive, perhaps, to the dangers of intermarriage of certain cases among them than any others."[42]

Rather than express concern about eugenics, though, Veditz was angry about Bell's "interference" in the educational system for deaf children. Veditz charged that Bell and the Volta Bureau deceived the public with the notion that the oral method was a new science when, in fact, it was an old philosophy that could be traced to German antecedents. According to Veditz, Bell was guilty of ignorance by declining invitations to conferences and meetings where he might have better understood the lives of signing Deaf people. "He literally sought to Prussianize our deaf school system," Veditz exclaimed. Sign language would always survive, though, because Bell has been "blind to the fact that even in 'pure' oral schools a sign-language always exists, used surreptitiously when the taskmasters are not looking."[43] Veditz believed that Bell was guilty of trying to destroy Deaf culture and devoted his time and energy to defending the Deaf community from this attack.

Bell could have inflicted even more damage on Deaf people and the American Deaf community, however, if he had used his influence and contacts to encourage an active eugenics program against deafness, a course that he never followed. Though he wrote and spoke against marriages of congenitally deaf individuals to each other, he seemed to draw the line at that, using persuasion and what he believed were accurate data to call attention to the matter, but he never did more than present argument—never suggested prohibitions on marriage, never advocated sterilization or even social ostracism of people who were born deaf and wanted to marry.

It is likely that Bell refrained from any repressive measures against genetic deafness because he was familiar with Deaf people and with their lives. He knew that they were not any more feebleminded or any less capable of learning than hearing people. Bell's very accomplished and well-read wife was deaf, as was his mother. Bell also had many friends and acquaintances in the American Deaf community, even including George Veditz and Albert Ballin. These factors seem to have humanized his view of deafness, despite the sometimes extreme language he used to describe the fate of signing Deaf people in American society.

Bell tendered his resignation as chairman of the Board of Scientific Directors of the Eugenics Record Office at a meeting on December 15, 1916. He was nearly seventy years old. At the same time, he began reducing his contacts with Davenport. The latter wished to keep Bell involved in eugenics, however, and invited Bell to present a paper at the Second International Eugenics Congress, originally scheduled for New York City in the fall of 1915. The conference was repeatedly postponed, however, because of the First World War. It was not until October of 1919 that a London meeting of eugenicists decided to hold the Second International Congress on Eugenics in New York City in 1921.[44] Bell was declared the honorary president of this meeting, and Davenport encouraged him to exhibit the results of his research either on the longevity of offspring or on the deaf families of Martha's Vineyard.

Bell had sought to answer questions about the inheritance of deafness by using Martha's Vineyard, which had a high concentration of deaf island-born residents, as his laboratory. By hiring research assistants and creating elaborate genealogical materials, Bell attempted to reconstruct the genetic patterns of deafness on Martha's Vineyard. Although he amassed much data, Bell never resolved the question of why some hearing parents had deaf children whereas other hearing parents with similar genealogies did not.[45] Bell did not understand Mendelian genetics or the workings of recessive genes and therefore could not ascertain why deafness appeared and disappeared in family lines. At one point, he even suggested that the cause of deafness was due to the subsoil that was made of "variegated clays" around the Gay Head part of Martha's Vineyard.[46]

Bell chose not to take his research on the genetic basis of deafness to the Second International Congress on Eugenics. Instead, he sent an exhibit on the inheritance of longevity that displayed "six stereograms showing the relation between Age of Fathers at Death, Age of Mothers at Death, and Longevity of Offspring."[47] In the published proceedings of the conference —which were edited by Bell's old collaborator, Davenport, and three of his colleagues—Bell was recognized as the honorary president and a "pioneer investigator in the field of human heredity."[48]

Less than one year after the Second Congress, on August 2, 1922, Bell passed away from complications of diabetes and anemia. Every AT&T telephone in North America was silent for a full sixty seconds in homage to the inventor. Ironically, deaf leader George W. Veditz wrote an editorial praising Bell for his telephone achievement:

> He was one of the great benefactors of the human race. Through his invention he added to the span of life of every inhabitant of civilized countries where the telephone is used. . . . [T]he fundamental idea of conveying speech and sound over long distances was Bell's, and for this conception the world will everlastingly remain his debtor. . . . It should be added that a more courteous, affable gentleman never existed, nor one possessed of a character more flawless.[49]

Bell always said his greatest accomplishments were teaching deaf children to speak and speechread as his father had endeavored. For the most part, scholars, too, have marginalized Bell's eugenic views, preferring to celebrate Bell for his telephone invention and spawning a revolution in the telecommunications industry.[50] However, allied with Davenport, the most famous American eugenicist of the first part of the twentieth century, Bell helped propel not only the success of eugenics but also oralism in deaf education in modern America.

Notes

1. Barry A. Crouch. "The People of the Eye," in *Reviews in American History* 26 (1988): 403.

2. For accounts of Bell and his attitudes toward the Deaf community, see John Vickrey Van Cleve and Barry A. Crouch, *A Place of Their Own: Creating the Deaf Community in America* (Washington, D.C.: Gallaudet University Press, 1989), 142–54; also see Harry G. Lang, *Silence of the Spheres: The Deaf Experience in the History of Science* (Westport, Conn.: Bergin & Garvey, 1994), 81–90; Douglas C. Baynton, *Forbidden Signs: American Culture and the Campaign against Sign Language* (Chicago: The University of Chicago Press, 1996), 6, 30–31; Susan Burch, *Signs of Resistance: American Deaf Cultural History, 1900 to 1942* (New York: New York University Press, 2002), 133–45; Richard Winefield, *Never the Twain Shall Meet: Bell, Gallaudet, and the Communications Debate* (Washington, D.C.: Gallaudet University Press, 1987), 82–96; Harlan Lane, *When the Mind Hears: A History of the Deaf* (New York: Vintage Books, 1984), 340–41; 353–75. For accounts of Bell's advocacy of eugenics, see Robert V. Bruce, *Bell: Alexander Graham Bell and the Conquest of Solitude* (Boston: Little, Brown and Company, 1973), 417–20, 469; Mark Haller, *Eugenics: Hereditarian Attitudes in American Thought* (New Brunswick, N.J.: Rutgers University Press, 1963), 31–33; Daniel J. Kevles, *In the Name of Eugenics: Genetics and the Uses of Human Heredity* (Cambridge, Mass.: Harvard University Press, 1985), 59, 63, 85.

3. Richard Winefield, *Never the Twain Shall Meet*. This book is an excellent introduction to the Edward Miner Gallaudet-Alexander Graham Bell debates. See also Baynton, *Forbidden Signs*.

4. Margaret Winzer, *The History of Special Education: From Isolation to Integration* (Washington, D.C.: Gallaudet University Press, 1993), 230–47.

5. Baynton, *Forbidden Signs*, 56–82.

6. Baynton, *Forbidden Signs*, 30–31; Bruce, 417.

7. Daniel J. Kevles, *In the Name of Eugenics*, 3–19; Francis Galton, *Hereditary genius: an inquiry into its laws and consequences* (New York: D. Appleton, 1871).

8. Alexander Graham Bell, *Memoir Upon the Formation of a Deaf Variety of the Human Race*, 1884; reprint (Washington, D.C.: Alexander Graham Bell Association for the Deaf, 1969).

9. For a good discussion, see Baynton's *Forbidden Signs*.

10. Alexander Graham Bell, "Marriage: Address to the Deaf" (Washington, D.C.: Gibson Brothers, 1891), 3–4.

11. Ibid, 12.

12. E. A. Fay, *Marriages of the Deaf in America: An Inquiry Concerning the Results of Marriages of the Deaf in America* (Washington, D.C.: Gibson Brothers, 1898), 11. Although the Volta Bureau set aside funds for Fay's work, he called it "purely a labor or love."

13. Haller, *Eugenics*, 63–66; Kevles, *In the Name of Eugenics*, 54–56.

14. Kevles, *In the Name of Eugenics*, 41–56.

15. Kevles, 59.

16. Alexander Graham Bell to Charles B. Davenport, Cold Spring Harbor in Long Island, NY, September 14, 1906, Charles B. Davenport Papers, B/D27, American Philosophical Society (APS), Philadelphia, Pennsylvania.

17. Davenport to Bell, September 22, 1906.

18. Ibid.

19. Ibid.

20. Bell to Davenport, March 11, 1904. Charles B. Davenport Papers, B/D27, APS.

21. Bell to Davenport, September 20, 1904. Charles B. Davenport Papers, B/D27, APS.

22. Hamilton Cravens, *The Triumph of Evolution: The Heredity-Environment Controversy, 1900–1941* (Baltimore: The Johns Hopkins University Press, 1988), 34–45.

23. Haller, *Eugenics*, 22.

24. "The American Breeders Association to Its Parent, The Association of American Agricultural College and Experimental Stations Greetings," Davenport notes, May 10, 1910, Folder 2. Charles B. Davenport Papers, APS.

25. Alexander Graham Bell, "A Few Thoughts Concerning Eugenics," *The National Geographic Magazine*, (February 1908): 119.

26. Ibid, 123.

27. Ibid, 123.

28. Ibid, 123. Eventually, Congress passed the Johnson-Reed National Origins Act of 1924, which imposed immigration laws. See Cravens, *The Triumph of Evolution*, chap. 7, "Mental Testing."

29. Davenport to Bell, January 29, 1907. Charles B. Davenport Papers, B/D27, APS.

30. Davenport to Bell, December 8, 1909. Charles B. Davenport Papers, B/D27, APS.

31. E. H. Harriman purchased 75 acres of property to support Davenport's work and provided funds for expenses, overhead, and operating budget. See Jonathan Marks, "Historiography of Eugenics," *American Journal of Human Genetics* 52 (1993): 650–52; Haller, *Eugenics*, 65–67; Kevles, *In the Name of Eugenics*, 54–56 for insight related to Harriman's financial contributions on which Davenport clearly was dependent.

32. Arba N. Lincoln to Davenport, December 24, 1912. Charles Davenport Collection, Cold Spring Harbor Laboratory Archives.

33. Bruce, *Bell: Alexander Graham Bell and the Conquest of Solitude*, 340.

34. Ibid, 413.

35. Ibid.

36. Bell to Davenport, December 27, 1912. Charles B. Davenport Papers, B/D27, APS.

37. Ibid.

38. Ibid.

39. Davenport to Bell, September 25, 1915.

40. Bell to Davenport, September 30, 1915.

41. George W. Veditz. "De Mortuis Nil Nisi Bonum." *The Jewish Deaf* (October 1922), 13.

42. Ibid, 14.

43. Ibid, 15.

44. Committee members selected: L. F. Barker, E. A. Hooton, R. M. Yerkes, Stewart Paton, A. G. Bell, Raymond Pearl, D. W. LaRue, and Charles B. Davenport as chairman. Davenport to Bell, March 17, 1920. Charles B. Davenport Papers, Folder B/D27, APS.

45. Alexander Graham Bell, "The Deaf-Mutes of Martha's Vineyard," *American Annals of the Deaf* 31 (3): 282–84. For additional information on deafness on Martha's Vineyard, see Nora Ellen Groce, *Everyone Here Spoke Sign Language: Hereditary Deafness on Martha's Vineyard* (Cambridge, Mass.: Harvard University Press, 1985), 46–48.

46. Groce, *Everyone Here Spoke Sign Language*, 121.

47. Alexander Graham Bell, *Eugenics, Genetics and the Family: Scientific Papers of the Second International Congress of Eugenics*, vol. 1, ed. Charles Benedict Davenport (Baltimore: Williams & Wilkins, 1923), Plate 4.

48. Ibid, 2.

49. George W. Veditz, "De Mortuis Nil Nisi Bonum," *The Jewish Deaf* (October 1922): 13.

50. For an early example of this tendency, see Harold S. Osborne, *Biographical Memoir of Alexander Graham Bell, 1847–1922*. National Academy of Sciences of the United States of America. Biographical Memoirs (vol. XXIII).

8

Deaf Autonomy and Deaf Dependence: The Early Years of the Pennsylvania Society for the Advancement of the Deaf

Reginald Boyd and John Vickrey Van Cleve

Editor's Introduction

Reginald Boyd, who grew up with family stories about the Pennsylvania Society for the Advancement of the Deaf (PSAD), and historian John Vickrey Van Cleve reviewed a collection of PSAD papers and discovered that the organization's early history challenged many of their assumptions about deaf history in the late-nineteenth and early twentieth centuries. The deaf leaders they uncovered in the PSAD's early history were uncommonly successful and shrewd as they manipulated a hostile oralist environment. When necessary, they put aside commitment to the use of sign language in education to achieve other goals that seemed more attainable and, perhaps, more important to them at the time. This study reveals the importance of examining local deaf history to achieve a more complete and nuanced understanding of deaf agency and deaf concerns in America's past, and it argues that historians of the deaf community need to move beyond their preoccupation with issues surrounding sign language use if they are to appreciate the richness of deaf lives.

Deaf college student Robert Ziegler wrote to Governor Henry Hoyt of Pennsylvania in the spring of 1881.[1] Identifying himself as chairman of

---

This article first appeared in the *American Annals of the Deaf* 139, 4 (October 1994).

the state committee of the Pennsylvania School for the Deaf (PSD) alumni association, he requested permission to use the Hall of the House of Representatives in Harrisburg, the Pennsylvania capital, for a convention of deaf Pennsylvanians.[2] Hoyt's assent cleared the way for Ziegler to launch the organization that became the Pennsylvania Society for the Advancement of the Deaf (PSAD), one of the largest, wealthiest, and most successful deaf organizations in America.

Historians have not studied the PSAD or other state-level, deaf-controlled institutions, despite the generally acknowledged significance of local organizations in deaf people's lives.[3] One factor in this oversight is limited historical sources: generally, the internal documents of such groups either have not been preserved or have been closed to public scrutiny.[4] This is not the whole explanation, however, for the deaf press—which is accessible to students of deaf history—has chronicled many local organizations. Another reason for this neglect is suggested by the PSAD's surviving records.

Pennsylvania's most important organization of deaf people did not follow the agenda of today's activists but rather its own imperatives, those of Pennsylvania's deaf leadership in the late nineteenth century. Although the PSAD grew to prominence during an era when sign language was under attack in America as never before or since, the organization shunned the emotional and divisive communication and culture debates that animate today's scholars and advocates for the deaf community. Its public positions on sign language and education do not fit the simplistic historical paradigms with which we are most familiar. Neither does its experience support the interpretation that deafness was characterized historically as either culture or pathology, in a stark dichotomy, as hypothesized by some writers.[5]

Examination of the PSAD's early years reveals ambiguity and complexity in hearing-deaf relations, and it points out that the concerns of deaf people were wide-ranging. Furthermore, hearing individuals both assisted and oppressed their deaf counterparts, the PSAD's records indicate, while deaf people disagreed among themselves on questions of strategy in dealing with the hearing majority. PSAD members certainly were not compliant victims of a hearing-dominated culture, but they recognized the weaknesses inherent in their minority status. Thus organizational debate was often vigorous but invariably concluded in cautious actions, as leaders responded creatively but conservatively to needs perceived and articulated by Pennsylvania's deaf community.

Pennsylvanians founded the PSAD during a period of perilous developments for America's deaf population. Late nineteenth century educational changes and social attitudes threatened fundamental rights deaf persons had developed over previous decades. Oralists tried to prohibit their language of signs; hearing chauvinists denigrated their culture; and eugenicists questioned their right to bear children.[6] Simultaneously, deaf individuals labored to strengthen their community, organizing at a rapid pace during the nineteenth century's waning years. Deaf leaders, however, operated within the limits of a complex, constantly shifting level of interaction with and dependence on hearing people.

During the PSAD's early years, for example, deaf officers struggled over the issue of hearing people's roles in conventions and on committees. Hearing men with deaf parents, such as Francis Clerc, Thomas Gallaudet, and Frank Booth, were active participants. The PSD's superintendent, A.L.E. Crouter—ironically a staunch oralist and vocal opponent of sign language in education—was even more involved in PSAD activities. These hearing people had the respect of many of their deaf colleagues and friends, to be sure, but deaf leaders also depended on these very same hearing individuals (especially Crouter) for their livelihood. The PSD was a major employer of PSAD stalwarts: Ziegler and his fellow Pennsylvania state committee member Samuel Davidson, for instance, eventually made careers there under Superintendent Crouter; Brewster Allabough, the third member of the Pennsylvania state committee, became a teacher at the Western Pennsylvania School for the Deaf, which also was headed by hearing superintendents.

PSAD leaders nevertheless circumscribed and limited the influence of hearing people within the society. They created and modified administrative structures frequently. Depending upon their goals at particular times, they enlarged or reduced the rights of hearing people within the organization, while attempting to maintain ultimate deaf authority. They adjusted to the complex and changing relations among the hearing and deaf communities and eventually (in the mid-twentieth century) entirely eliminated hearing persons from decision-making positions.

Within this milieu, the PSAD's members focused on several projects. The most important established a home for aged deaf persons, but the organization also attempted to influence the Pennsylvania Legislature to enact various laws of benefit to deaf people, lobbied for increased educational opportunities for deaf Pennsylvanians, raised money for a statue honoring Thomas Hopkins Gallaudet and Alice Cogswell, and resisted National Association of the Deaf (NAD) attempts at federation. Together, these efforts demonstrate deaf Pennsylvanians' particular concerns as the nineteenth century drew to a close, and they illuminate their leaders' strategies for dealing with the hearing world.

The First Convention

Ziegler's letter of 1881 marked two years of frustration with the older and less ambitious deaf leadership in Philadelphia. A small cadre of deaf Philadelphians had conducted "literary and social meetings" since 1857, and in 1865 organized themselves into the Clerc Literary Association, an elite, males-only group.[7] They were not, however, interested in expanding their organization to encompass a more diverse membership. An 1879 proposal from younger members (including Ziegler) that the Association sponsor a general, state-wide meeting of deaf people failed.[8]

In the fall of 1880, Ziegler tried another tactic. He summoned to his room at the National Deaf-Mute College (33 College Hall) twelve students who had graduated from PSD and suggested the desirability of an alumni association.[9] This gathering supported his motion and selected a state committee composed of Ziegler and two other students, Brewster Allabough and Samuel Davidson. They then sent a letter to the *Deaf-Mutes' Journal* calling for a general convention in Philadelphia to found a PSD alumni organization. In early 1881 Ziegler's effort again failed, however, because of continued dissension among the deaf Philadelphians, who could not agree to work together to sponsor a statewide meeting.[10]

Ziegler and his state committee colleagues Davidson and Allabough finally took charge themselves, and Ziegler wrote the governor on their behalf. His letter persuaded Hoyt, who then asked the Pennsylvania legislature to grant Ziegler's request. The State committee announced in the *Deaf-Mute's Journal* of July 26, 1881, that a convention would be held in Harrisburg, Pennsylvania, on August 24–26. "The paramount objective of which," Ziegler stated, "will be the forming of an alumni society."[11]

Ziegler and his youthful cohorts succeeded in gathering an impressive group of luminaries in the Pennsylvania capital. The featured orator was sixty-eight year old John Carlin. A deaf painter and essayist who lived in New York, Carlin was raised in Philadelphia and was the only surviving male from the first PSD class. Though his parents and six children were hearing, he had a deaf brother (as did Ziegler) and a deaf wife.[12] Carlin has been ridiculed in a modern historical study for being "a hearing person in everything but fact," and yet his willingness to travel from his home in New York City for this convention of deaf people and the comments he made in his keynote speech suggest that his own attitudes were more complex.[13] Perhaps more importantly, his deaf contemporaries revered and respected Carlin and thus were pleased at his acceptance of this invitation.

Similarly, deaf people in Pennsylvania looked up to Philadelphian Henry Winter Syle. One of the first of two deaf persons ordained as an Episcopal priest, Syle was chosen president of the convention, although he was not a PSD alumnus.[14] Indeed, the group decided not to create an alumni association but a general, state-wide association of and for all deaf Pennsylvanians.

No hearing teachers attended this initial meeting, despite the significant and often life-long relationships between teachers and their former students common in the nineteenth century.[15] Other than local dignitaries, the only non-deaf individuals present were Syle's fellow Episcopal priests Francis Clerc, son of deaf parents Laurent Clerc and Eliza Boardman Clerc, and Thomas Gallaudet, son of Thomas Hopkins Gallaudet and his deaf wife, Sophia Fowler Gallaudet. As was frequently the situation in mixed deaf-hearing gatherings in the late nineteenth century, Gallaudet served as the convention's primary interpreter for the hearing guests.[16]

The turnout was respectable. About 135 deaf people participated in the convention, lured in part by Ziegler's wise decision to charge no admission fee and to pay convention expenses out of his own pocket.[17] Forty-two attendees—thirty-four men and eight women—paid dues and became members of the new Pennsylvania Deaf-Mute Association, the PSAD's original name.[18]

The convention set a conservative yet provocative tone and presaged many of the PSAD's future concerns and attitudes. Carlin's oration, for instance, emphasized the importance of deaf self-determination in education. Referring to vocational teachers in schools for deaf children, he argued that "deaf-mutes and semi-mutes [persons deafened after learning to speak] of known proficiency in their respective callings, are far more suitable than speaking persons, even of equal proficiency in the same occupations, for these reasons-they are conversant with the method of colloquial intercourse, and as a general rule, have common feeling with others of their own class." Carlin concluded that "speaking persons, as instructors, are . . . deficient in . . . fellow-feeling toward the mutes."[19]

In a carefully measured and documented speech, Syle suggested that Pennsylvania was not doing enough for its deaf children and that deaf adults were uniquely qualified to recognize this fact. Syle began by arguing that deaf people alone knew the actual numbers of deaf children in neighborhoods, were aware of the number of deaf adults who had reached maturity without education, and understood the value of education to a deaf person. "Hearing people in general," Syle claimed, know "little or nothing of the true number of deaf-mutes." Syle compared the number of deaf children in Pennsylvania schools with those in New York schools and reported that although the general population of New York was only about 25% larger than the population of Pennsylvania, New York enrolled almost three times as many deaf students as did Pennsylvania. Furthermore, Pennsylvania state law required financial support for hearing pupils' schools, but funding for special schools for deaf or blind children was "left to special appropriations, which might be refused, reduced, or delayed." Finally, although hearing children could begin school at age six, Pennsylvania institutions were not allowed to admit deaf children before age ten. The Commonwealth of Pennsylvania, Syle summarized, was "not doing for her deaf children two-thirds as much as for the hearing; not one-half of what she ought."

Rather than bitterly criticize the state or its hearing politicians, though, Syle concluded on a note of self-help, which also would characterize the PSAD: "Let us who know best of all the blessings that education is to the deaf, exert ourselves to secure it for others." He suggested working through friends, influential persons, and Senators and Representatives in the Legislature to secure this goal. "Urge them to do their duty by your brethren," Syle told his deaf compatriots.[20]

Jacob Koehler, too, emphasized that deaf people could—indeed, must—help themselves, that they were not mere pawns of hearing society. This future minister and long-time PSAD officer supported a convention resolution urging the legislature to modify the state's tramp law of 1879. That ordinance exempted "deaf or dumb" persons from laws against begging. The tramp law, Koehler argued, "implies that deaf-mutes are incapable of self support; and serves to strengthen the impression that deaf-mutes are subjects for asylums." In reality, though, "deaf-mutes are rational beings, equal in all respects, save the lack of hearing and speech, to the rest of mankind."[21]

This first state-wide gathering of deaf Pennsylvanians passed several resolutions that are illustrative both for what they did say and what they did not. In the latter category, there was no call for support of sign language or for condemnations of oral methods in deaf education, although this meeting was held one year after the important Milan conference, at a time when the PSD was beginning to experiment with oral classes, and although no hearing teachers—whose presence might have been intimidating—were in attendance.[22] In the calculated voice typical of PSAD positions during its first three decades, one resolution merely stated that the convention had "the utmost confidence in and gratitude to all engaged in the good work of the education of the deaf and dumb of this State, and congratulate them on the success they have so far attained.[23] The overlooking of the communication controversy, the refusal to take sides in this issue, was not a mere fluke of the first convention. It would be a consistent policy of the PSAD well into the twentieth century.

Equally consistent was the first convention's and subsequent meetings' pronouncements related to the tramp law, which seemed to demean deaf people. Agreeing with Koehler, the convention unanimously declared that the exemption of deaf people was "a slight and insult," prompted by "mistaken feelings of benevolence" among hearing persons. Deaf people are "a class fully capable of self-support," the resolution stated; therefore, the convention urged the state legislature to remove the exemption and to apply to deaf individuals the same standard of work expectations and behavior as it did to hearing people.[24] Other resolutions endorsed "high classes" in deaf schools, and recommended that Pennsylvania open another state-supported school for deaf pupils.[25]

The convention's resolutions indicated areas of educational and social concern that deaf Pennsylvanians hoped to influence but could not, because of their minority status, control. To school boards and to the state legislature deaf people were only another special interest group, and a numerically small and poor one at that. The convention's creation of a structure for the new organization, however, reflected autonomous action, demonstrating what deaf people would do within the sphere of their own self-determination.

In 1881 the PSAD's deaf founders established an organizational scheme which subordinated hearing people to those who were deaf. Under the first constitution, a Board of Managers, composed of the group's officers and four managers, decided on everyday matters between conventions, but hearing people were not permitted to be officers or managers. This was accomplished by defining association membership in two classes: members, who had to be deaf; and honorary members, who could be hearing. Honorary members would have all the rights of members, the constitution said, "except voting and holding office." Hearing persons thus were excluded initially from all formal authority within the PSAD.[26]

This simple structure of deaf autonomy, with its unambiguous assertion of deaf authority, would not persist, however. In future years as the PSAD defined its purpose more clearly and as its leadership struggled with deaf-hearing relationships within the organization, deaf self-determination was seen as less important than other goals.

A Philanthropic Purpose

From the conclusion of the first convention in Harrisburg in 1881 until the second met in Philadelphia in 1884, the PSAD accomplished little. President Syle, whose Protestant conscience was troubled by organizations with a purely social purpose, complained that the PSAD had no function except to arrange its next convention. His presidential address in Philadelphia recommended therefore that the PSAD develop "some practical plan of usefulness," a philanthropic purpose, to unite the deaf people of Pennsylvania."

Syle envisioned a "Benevolent Fund" to assist "blind deaf-mutes." To operate this fund, he proposed the creation of five persons, "and they need not all be deaf," he said. Three of the trustees, Syle continued, should be members (and thus deaf) and two could be "free from such a requirement."[27] For reasons that are not shown in the documents, though, the final arrangements stipulated that only two trustees of the Benevolent Fund had to be members, thus permitting a hearing majority of trustees. The trustees themselves, however, were to be selected first by the Board of Managers and then by the members of the association in a general vote, indicating that the final authority—the power to appoint and remove trustees—was intended to remain in deaf hands.[28] The Benevolent Fund thus created an opening for hearing influence within the PSAD, but it was tempered by deaf people's ultimate control.

The PSAD's second convention undertook other important business in keeping with the organization's emphasis on deaf people's essential equality with those who hear. Since nothing had been done about the onerous exemption of deaf people from the tramp law, for example, the convention voted to establish a committee of three to continue to lobby for the law's modification. It voted as well to urge the state legislature to pass a compulsory school attendance law for deaf children, since, according to Koehler, three-fifths of the state's deaf children were kept at home by their parents.[29] Yet no project better shows the energy and creativity of the PSAD than its work on the Gallaudet Memorial Fund.

At the Philadelphia meeting, the PSAD authorized its first fundraising committee. This was to assist in a nationwide effort to finance a statue honoring Thomas Hopkins Gallaudet and Alice Cogswell, a work that today graces the front of Gallaudet University's Kendall Green campus. The empowering resolution stated that the committee's goal would be to raise at least $300 as the appropriate contribution of Pennsylvania's deaf citizens.[30] In fact, over the next six years the PSAD's committee raised nearly seven times that amount—$2,000, a sum greater than any other state and disproportionate to the size of Pennsylvania's deaf population.[31]

Deaf persons composed the entirety of this remarkable PSAD committee. Jerome Elwell, then a PSD teacher and vigorous proponent of deaf autonomy, chaired it; Ziegler was its secretary and general collector; Allabough managed collections in western Pennsylvania. Thomas Jefferson Trist, like Elwell a PSD teacher, William Cullingworth, a printer, and engraver James Reider completed the committee.[32] The frequently made assumption that hearing persons were necessary for fundraising, which some PSAD leaders later accepted as self-evident truth, was proven wrong by the success of the all-deaf committee.[33]

Excellent strategy, planning, and management—rather than large donations from wealthy hearing persons—accounted for the PSAD's fundraising success. The committee organized collectors in nearly every Pennsylvania county and encouraged them to gather donations from ordinary people. The counties' contributions became a source of pride. Competition was lively, particularly between deaf people around Pittsburgh and those in the Philadelphia area. PSD students and graduates collected subscriptions in their hometowns from among friends, relatives, and acquaintances. The committee sold alphabet cards, and it charged admittance to debates and lectures by deaf Gallaudet College professor Amos Draper, Gallaudet College president Edward Miner Gallaudet, and Francis Magnin, an Irish deaf leader.[34]

Fundraising for the Gallaudet Memorial occupied most of the PSAD's official efforts for six years. Attempts to save money for the Benevolent Fund, on the other hand, made no progress during that period, while efforts to revise the tramp law continued, as they would for at least another half century.[35] At the same time, the PSAD continued to define itself and to discover how, as an organization of minority individuals, it could best achieve its goals. There was no unanimity on these questions, for the PSAD worked in unchartered territory.

Autonomy and Paternalism

Jerome Elwell and Jacob Koehler articulated two different approaches, recommending two conflicting PSAD paths, for dealing with the oppression and dependence confronting deaf Americans 100 years ago. Elwell, who left his teaching job at the PSD when that school converted to oral methods, was more confrontational. He tried to steer the PSAD away from accommodation with powerful hearing people and toward an

independent position. Koehler, by contrast, seemed willing to accept a paternalistic relationship with hearing people if so doing would bring tangi-
ble benefits to deaf Pennsylvanians. The resolution of their conflict reveals
much about the PSAD's ambivalent relationship with hearing patrons.

The designated orator at the 1886 convention, Elwell broke an unwrit-
ten PSAD rule in his keynote address and openly criticized oral methods
in deaf education. He insisted that there was "unanimity" among deaf
people regarding the negative effects of "the pure oral system."[36] He believed so strongly that the PSAD should take a position on this issue that
he even proposed a resolution commending the governor for vetoing a
bill to support a new oral school in Scranton, even though previous PSAD
conventions argued that Pennsylvania needed another school for deaf
children.[37]

Koehler directly challenged Elwell's stance. He moved a resolution
stating specifically that the PSAD was not opposed to the Scranton oral
school and that Elwell's remarks did "not represent the sentiment of the
Convention." Henry Winter Syle, Koehler's fellow Episcopal priest and a
well-respected conservative voice within the PSAD, then offered a substi-
tute resolution for Koehler's. Syle's action would defuse any direct conflict between Elwell and Koehler and yet accomplish Koehler's accommo-
dationist objective.

Reflecting previous PSAD positions and anticipating PSAD's neutral-
ity as the sign language-oralism debate became more heated, Syle proposed two resolutions: (1) "That the Association as a body is not responsible for the opinions expressed by one speaking at its meetings." (2) "That
the Association wishes all success to every well-meant effort to promote
the education of the Deaf in the state, and desires a fair trial of all systems." These resolutions, with their acceptance (though not endorsement)
of oral methods, carried at the 1886 convention.[38] They were reaffirmed
and even strengthened in 1899 at the York convention, long after the death
of the influential Syle, when the PSAD appeared to endorse both sign and
oral methods. The latter convention declared that it would not meddle
with "the affairs of any other institution" and that the PSAD "believes
that good is being accomplished by every method of instruction."[39]

Elwell had not stopped with his criticism of oralism, however, but went
on in his 1886 oration to chastise "deaf mute societies" (such as the PSAD)
for their dependence on hearing people. He railed against the supposed
dominance of hearing speakers at conventions of deaf people and against
the practice of allowing hearing people to become honorary members of
deaf associations, as they were of the PSAD. This practice, he said, was
designed to alleviate the impecuniousness in our society funds," but he

found this an insufficient argument for hearing people's prominent role. Rather, he argued let there be more deaf "self-reliance"; for "God helps them that help themselves."[40]

The Reverend Koehler could not disagree with Elwell's reference to the deity, but he reached a different conclusion about the role of hearing people and the importance of deaf autonomy with the PSAD. After serving as association president for two years, in 1888 Koehler used his presidential address as a forum for his views on the direction the PSAD should follow. He insisted that deaf Pennsylvanians themselves would never have sufficient resources to establish a home for aged or blind deaf people. He therefore recommended that the PSAD liberalize its rules, created at the 1881 convention, and allow hearing people to be regular members. They would be able to vote but not to hold office. He also recommended that the name of the organization be changed from the original Pennsylvania Association of Deaf-Mutes—which clearly implied deaf ownership and autonomy—to the Pennsylvania Society for the Advancement of the Deaf, a more ambiguous title, like the later National Association for the Advancement of Colored People, that would permit a diverse membership. He reasoned that "it would cease to be merely an association of the deaf and become a *general* society for them."[41]

Koehler was not ready to dismiss deaf autonomy completely, though. He argued that his proposed arrangement would keep "*control* of the Society in the hands of" deaf people by permitting hearing persons "equal privileges with deaf members."[42] This confusing statement aside—for hearing people would not have the privilege of holding office—Koehler's proposal revealed his belief that deaf people would have to sacrifice some self-determination in order to benefit themselves. He consciously and freely suggested that the PSAD move closer to dependence on hearing people than other PSAD leaders, particularly Elwell, had before.

Koehler's sentiments struck a responsive chord, for the convention voted unanimously (Elwell apparently was not present) to accept most of his recommendations.[43] The new constitution changed the organization's name to the Pennsylvania Association for the Advancement of the Deaf; it stipulated that "Any hearing person may be elected an Associate Member" and that these individuals would "have all the rights of membership except holding office."[44] Going even beyond Koehler's specific suggestions, the new constitution removed all limits on the number of hearing people who could be members of the Board of Trustees that would administer the "Home Fund," successor to the "Benevolent Fund." Syle's original proposal suggested a deaf majority on this board, but that was changed to require at least two out of five deaf members. Now there were no restrictions on the number of hearing trustees, although the PSAD president, must be deaf, was an ex-officio member.[45]

Establishing the Home

Throughout the decade of the 1890s the PSAD focused on its new project, the founding of a benevolent home, while continuing to experiment with organizational structures and to maintain its interest in legislation related to deaf people. Syle, who first articulated a uniting philanthropic purpose for the PSAD, died in early 1890.[46] The PSAD's charter, granted one year later, would have pleased him. It stated that the PSAD existed to advance "the interests of the deaf" and to maintain "a home for blind, aged, and infirm deaf persons."[47]

PSAD leaders supported a special home for deaf people while rejecting the common idea that deaf people were particularly liable to infirmity or were more likely than those who hear to need charity. Arguments for the home rested on other considerations. Deeply religious Syle had believed that charitable activities justified the organization, benefiting both the giver and the receiver. One secular argument posited that the home project showed that deaf people were capable of self-support. Brewster Allabough said it demonstrated "the slow and sure growth of independence" of deaf people.[48] The most revealing and culturally significant argument was, however, based on communication.

Allabough explained it well in an 1890 speech. He said that aged and infirm deaf persons, like their hearing counterparts, ended up either in the care of relatives or in almshouses. In neither case could their needs be met, however, for relatives, almshouse keepers, and other inmates were almost invariably hearing people. The managers of the almshouses, Allabough continued, were incompetent to meet the needs of infirm deaf persons, "not from a lack of administrative ability, but from an imperfect knowledge of the peculiarities of this class of dependents. Those in charge often do not know how to manage them, because they do not know how to communicate with them." The aged, infirm, or deaf-blind person, then, was confined to a peculiar hell, stuck in a place from which he or she could not leave, without resources, unable to engage in conversation with others, and unable to make his or her needs known to the caretakers. "Thus he is left to himself," Allabough said, "separated. . . . from the world."[49]

Perhaps this sense of urgency is what encouraged the PSAD's Board of Managers to put aside the important principle of deaf autonomy, which was so clearly embedded in the PSAD's first constitution, and allow the home's fate to be in the hands of hearing people during the 1890's. For most of this period, the trustees consisted of two hearing persons, A.L.E. Crouter and Francis Clerc, and one deaf, Koehler.[50] Beginning in 1896 another hearing trustee, lawyer and PSD teacher J.P. Walker, joined, creating an even greater hearing-deaf imbalance.[51] The hearing presence also may have reflected Koehler's influence, for he was PSAD president from 1886 to 1890 and again from 1894 to 1900.[52]

Yet ironically this hearing-dominated group was not able to establish a home during the 1890's. As early as 1892, when the Home Fund surpassed the $2,000 mark, the all-deaf Board of Managers exhorted the mostly hearing trustees to "take immediate steps to establish the Home." The trustees resisted. They said that it was better to hold their funds as an endowment and to acquire a building from "some benevolent person." "Several [hearing] gentlemen of wealth and prominence have expressed interest in the matter," the trustees said.[53]

Whatever interest may have been expressed, though, no building was donated. The PSAD slowly but steadily raised funds for the home, acquiring many small amounts from large numbers of people, as it had for the Gallaudet/Cogswell statue.[54] The trustees, with Koehler doing all the traveling and corresponding, continued to visit and consider possible sites for the home. Reading was investigated, as was Williamsport. In both instances the trustees believed that they would receive help locally from philanthropic hearing people, but no such help was forthcoming.[55] The new century began with the home no closer to completion than it had been ten years earlier. At its December meeting in 1900, though, the PSAD's Board of Managers replaced all the home's trustees. Within a year the home was ready to open.[56]

A majority of the trustees for 1901, the pivotal year in getting the home established, were deaf. For the first time since 1891, the chairman was not Crouter, the hearing superintendent of the PSD, but Ziegler, the deaf "father" of the PSAD. The only hearing member was Frank Booth, son of deaf parents, but a member of the Alexander Graham Bell Association and a committed oralist.[57] J.A. McIlvaine rounded out the group.[58] Although Crouter was no longer an actual member of the trustees, his influence remained considerable, for Ziegler, Booth, and McIlvaine all were PSD employees.

Surviving PSAD records do not state explicitly why the Board of Managers removed the old trustees, but they suggest that the trustees' inactivity, lack of responsiveness to the Managers, and surprising financial mismanagement explain this sudden action.[59] Successive PSAD conventions and the Managers had expected the trustees throughout the 1890s to open the home, and by 1900 their unwillingness or inability to accomplish this—despite the Managers' pressure—was putting them on the defensive.[60] New charter amendments, recommended by the reconstituted trustees in 1901 and accepted by the PSAD in 1902, made clear, in Ziegler's words, that the powers of the "governors of the Home" were "subordinate to the Board of Trustees" was lost sight of.[61] The most important failure of the old Board of Trustees, however, was their decision to loan $1,000 of home funds to one of their own members, Jacob Koehler, who defaulted, resigned his pastorate of All Souls Church of Philadelphia, and moved west. Secured only by a second trust on his property, the loan proved uncollectible.[62] A large sum of money, contributed in hundreds of small donations, thus disappeared from the PSAD's treasury due to the trustee's ineptitude.

The new majority-deaf Board of Trustees succeeded where the old hearing-dominated group had not. In the summer of 1901 Ziegler sent letters to the parents of PSD pupils, asking their help in soliciting subscriptions for the Home Fund. One of these letters reached William Stuckert, an attorney whose daughter Emma attended the PSD. Stuckert contacted PSD superintendent Crouter and told him of a house in Doylestown that might be available at a low price. Crouter, no longer directly involved, referred Stuckert to Ziegler, Booth, and McIlvaine, who then went to Doylestown to look at the property and to discuss the terms of sale with Stuckert, who represented the property's owner, Joseph Mekeal of Philadelphia.[63] Stuckert said that the large home and 1.5 acres of land had been purchased by Mekeal for $21,000 but could be acquired by the PSAD for $6,650.[64]

A flurry of activity ensued. The trustees examined a total of eleven other potential home sites within a few weeks. None was as attractive as Mekeal's.[65] It had all modern conveniences; the price was right; it was in a small town; and it was only thirty-five miles from Philadelphia, to which it was connected by fourteen daily trains and a trolley. Ziegler traveled to Pittsburgh and met with Allabough, George Teagarden, and other deaf Western Pennsylvania PSAD activists. They too agreed that Doylestown offered the best opportunity to establish the home at long last.[66] In November of 1901, eleven months after assuming control, the new Ziegler-led Board of Trustees purchased the Doylestown home for $4,150 cash and a $2,500 mortgage from the Doylestown Trust Company.[67]

With the home purchased, the PSAD again restructured the Board of Trustees, expanding it to nine members, including William Stuckert and John Hart, the president of the Doylestown Trust Company, and Allabough and Teagarden, as representatives of western Pennsylvania.

Crouter was brought back on, as was Samuel Davidson, one of the original Pennsylvania state committee members and now a PSD teacher. Ziegler, Booth, and McIlvane remained the officers of the trustees, with Ziegler continuing as president. The officers constituted the executive board, which, with Crouter, conducted most of the trustees' business.[68]

The Home for Blind, Aged, and Infirm Deaf Persons was a rapid success. It opened in 1902 with five residents: three deaf-blind sisters, whom McIlvaine described as "physically incapable of self-support, and utterly destitute"; deaf-blind Anita Silva of New Jersey; and fifty-four year old Elizabeth Heiss. The sisters' deaf-blind male sibling became a resident shortly thereafter, as did a married couple in their eighties, Susan and Robert Woodside.[69] By 1906, twenty-five years after the PSAD was founded, its home had admitted nineteen persons, eleven women and eight men.[70] In 1907 the PSAD retired the mortgage, thanks primarily to the ability of Ziegler and Allabough, once again, to raise donations from Pennsylvania's deaf citizens and their families. Although a wealthy hearing benefactor was sought, in the end self-help rather than hearing philanthropy achieved the PSAD's goals.[71] Thus deaf people established the home by themselves and for themselves but not without cost to deaf independence and autonomy, as shown by the PSAD's role in the NAD federation controversy.

To Federate?

The National Association of the Deaf began in 1880 as an organization comprised of deaf individuals throughout the United States. By the 1890s, however, it was apparent that the NAD structure contained flaws. Each person at the national conventions had one vote. Local deaf people, who attended in the greatest numbers, therefore dominated the proceedings, elected the officers, and passed the resolutions. This gave the NAD a rotating regional flavor more than a national one, and thus some leaders, such as Thomas Fox of New York and Olof Hanson of Minnesota, proposed that the NAD become a federation of state organizations, with each allotted a fixed number of votes, apportioned according to its deaf population.[72] Fox argued that this arrangement would "prevent any possible misrepresentations as to the general opinion of the deaf on any special question affecting them" and would facilitate "united action as emergency might demand."[73]

The cooperation of the PSAD, one of the most successful state deaf associations, would be necessary to make this plan reality. That cooperation was not forthcoming, however, for the PSAD operated within boundaries that were not set by deaf people alone but were negotiated with important hearing persons and institutions, specifically A.L.E. Crouter and the Pennsylvania School for the Deaf.

From shortly after its founding, the PSAD had enjoyed a close relationship with the PSD, having access to its facilities and its personnel. The PSD often provided a meeting place for the Board of Managers and the trustees of the Home, for example, and when the hearing unit at the home for the aged needed work, the PSD engineer fixed it. Most importantly, many PSD leaders—particularly Ziegler, but also Davidson, McIlvaine, and others—depended on the PSD for employment.

Crouter, the PSD head and sometime member of the home's Board of Trustees, vehemently opposed federation. In an appallingly paternalistic 1908 speech at a PSAD convention, he claimed it was his duty to warn and caution "the deaf of the State of Pennsylvania, whose welfare and happiness I have very greatly at heart." He told the PSAD it must resist federation because "the deaf" of Pennsylvania "are a conservative body." Moreover, federation might be illegal, threatening the validity of the PSAD charter (although an attorney had already said it would not do so). He went on to conjecture without evidence or logic that the federation plan was an attempt by avaricious NAD leaders to acquire money and property from the deaf people of Pennsylvania: "You have the money and you have got the property and they want to get their hands into your treasury—that is what they want."[74]

The actual reasons for Crouter's opposition to federation were quite different, though. Crouter was the individual most responsible for converting the PSD's language of instruction from the signs introduced by Laurent Clerc to speech and speech-reading.[75] NAD leadership, including Fox and Hanson, consistently and sometimes vociferously opposed the use of oral methods to the exclusion of sign language. Crouter did not want the PSAD—in which he had such a large personal and professional stake—arraigned against his communication policy for the PSD. As usual, it was Ziegler, with the interests of the PSAD uppermost in his mind, who understood Crouter's motivations and his intent.

Although a signing, non-speaking, born-deaf person, Ziegler argued against federation and against any involvement of the PSAD in the NAD's battle with oralism. In 1908 Ziegler reviewed the legal status of the PSAD, announcing that an attorney he consulted said that the PSAD could federate with the NAD given certain conditions. That was not the reason for his opposition to federation. Rather, he was opposed because the PSAD had "never tried to meddle with the management of the schools for the deaf." The PSAD existed only to "advance the interests of the deaf" and to maintain the home; it had "nothing to do" with deaf education. "The Pennsylvania Society," Ziegler emphasized, "believes that it is not good policy to criticize or attack the management of any other corporation like the Pennsylvania Institution at Mt. Airy [PSD], or the western Pennsylvania Institution at Scranton." "In return," Ziegler concluded, "the institutions should co-operate with the P.S.A.D. in carrying out the purposes for which our Society is organized."[76]

The PSAD's refusal to become embroiled in the communication argument marked an implicit agreement between deaf leaders and their hearing patrons. The PSAD would not "meddle" in educational questions except non-controversial issues, such as mandatory schooling, support for vocational training, and the establishment of more schools. Hearing people, particularly Crouter and PSD staff, would in exchange lend their support to the PSAD's benevolent activities. This pattern had been sketched out by Henry Winter Syle in the PSAD's early years, and remained, throughout the organization's first three decades, consistent policy.

Conclusion

The early history of the PSAD demonstrates deaf Americans' success in a sometimes hostile and oppressive milieu. The skill and commitment of PSAD leaders, their ability to create and maintain an organization and to raise money again and again from poor segments of the population, is obvious. So too is the success deaf people had working among themselves for themselves. The home was a project they brought to fruition and which they managed. The major contributions by hearing people were those of Joseph Mekeal, who agreed to sell his property for less than market value, and William Stuckert, the father of a deaf child, who arranged the sale. Even in this case, however, the initiative came from Ziegler, who conceived and carried out the plan of approaching parents for their assistance.

The PSAD's early history demonstrates as well that deaf people—perhaps believing society's stereotypes—often lacked complete self-confidence. PSAD leaders frequently thought wealthy hearing benefactors must be solicited and their support must be gained for the PSAD to reach its objectives. The unfortunate Jacob Koehler, in particular, epitomized that failure to appreciate what deaf Pennsylvanians could do for themselves, even though the evidence was all around him in his own organization.

The precarious position of deaf people also is shown by this brief history. PSAD leaders were creative and demonstrated foresight and energy in their actions, but they always were conscious of their dependence on hearing people, particularly on Crouter and the PSD. Hearing administrators dominated the schools and controlled middle class employment at the turn of the century, placing deaf leaders in a difficult predicament. When the interests of deaf people and those of hearing people clashed, compromises had to be made and painful judgments reached.

In the end, the leadership of Pennsylvania's deaf community was willing to put aside their concerns related to sign language and oralism in order to pursue other goals. They determined that what they achieved was more important than what they sacrificed. Though remaining aloof from the debates over pedagogical methods in deaf education, during its first twenty-five years the PSAD created a benevolent home for aged deaf persons, lobbied against laws that stigmatized deaf people, raised money for an important memorial, and worked toward the education of all deaf children. The historical lives of deaf Americans, the PSAD experience suggests, were more rich, complex, and meaningful than the current focus on communication would lead us to believe. Dependence and autonomy coexisted in an uneasy struggle as deaf people, like other contemporary minorities, tested the meaning and limits of self-determination.

Notes

1. Robert Middleton Ziegler's name is spelled Zeigler in early documents. [See, for example, "Pennsylvania Convention," *Deaf-Mutes' Journal* (July 28, 1881)] Whether he changed it later or the early records are in error, we do not know. In any case, this paper will employ the "ie" spelling, which was commonly used in later years.

2. Edwin C. Ritchie, *The Pennsylvania Society for the Advancement of the Deaf* (nd, np), 5–6.

3. Jack Gannon's comprehensive *Deaf Heritage: A Narrative History of Deaf America* (Silver Spring, MD: National Association of the Deaf, 1981), for example, has a section on homes for aged deaf persons but does not discuss the PSAD, which operated one for most of a century. The PSAD is mentioned briefly in Otto Berg and Henry Buzzard, *Thomas Gallaudet: Apostle of the Deaf* (New York: St. Ann's Church for the Deaf, 1989), 66–67.

4. The PSAD leadership has saved most of the minutes, annual reports, and other important documents since the organization's founding in 1881. They were made available to the authors for their work on this article and will be opened to researchers at the Gallaudet University Archives.

5. The most forceful and erudite statement of this historical paradigm is Harlan Lane's *Mask of Benevolence* (New York: Knopf, 1992).

6. For more discussion of these issues see John Van Cleve and Barry A. Crouch, *A Place of Their Own: Creating the Deaf Community in America* (Washington, D.C.: Gallaudet University Press, 1989), 106–154; Richard Winefield, *Never the Twain Shall Meet: Bell, Gallaudet and the Communications Debate* (Washington, D.C.: Gallaudet

University Press, 1987); and Harlan Lane, *When the Mind Hears: A History of the Deaf* (New York: Random House, 1984), esp. 376–414.

7. Clerc Literary Association, *Constitution, By-Laws and History of the Clerc Literary Association* (Philadelphia: Stager and Maxwell, 1883), 3–4

8. "History of the Pennsylvania Association," The Silent World (August 30, 1888).

9. This meeting occurred in today's room 300, College Hall, on the Gallaudet University Campus.

10. The details of this controversy are sketchy, but there was a clash between Ziegler and the president of the Clerc Literary Association, Hiram Arms, who was not a PSD graduate. Some of this may be traced in the pages of the *Deaf-Mute's Journal* [hereafter, DMJ]. In particular, see Robert Ziegler, "Exonerating the Committee," DMJ (August 4, 1991). Robert M. Ziegler, "Historical Sketch of the Pennsylvania Society for the Advancement of the Deaf [hereafter, PSAD], *Report of the Proceedings of the Twenty-First Meeting* (Philadelphia: Norwood Print Shop, 1908)

11. "Pennsylvania Convention," DMJ (July 26, 1881).

12. Pennsylvania School for the Deaf, "Pupil Record Book. 1820–1841," 2, in Pennsylvania School for the Deaf Collection, Gallaudet University Archives.

13. Lane, *Mind*, 246.

14. Syle's remarkable life is chronicled by Robert C. Sampson, "Henry Winter Syle, M.A.: Friend, Servant, Scholar and Teacher" in Berg and Buzzard, *Thomas Gallaudet*, 137–159.

15. Allspice, "Harrisburg: Echoes of the Pennsylvania Convention," DMJ (Sept. 8, 1881). For a discussion of the long-term ties between students and teachers in nineteenth century, see Phyllis Valentine, "Thomas Hopkins Gallaudet: Benevolent Paternalism and the Origins of the American Asylum," in John V. Van Cleve, ed. *Deaf History Unveiled: Interpretations from the New Scholarship* (Washington, D.C.: Gallaudet University Press, 1993) 53–73.

16. "Circular Notice," included with bound copy of Pennsylvania Society for the Deaf Convention Proceedings, 1881–1890.

17. DMJ (August 25, 1881); Allspice, "Harrisburg."

18. PSAD, *Proceedings of the First Convention of the Pennsylvania Deaf-Mute Association*, (nd, np), 12.

19. *First Convention*, 8.

20. *First Convention*, 4–6.

21. *First Convention*, 10–11.

22. For a discussion of oralism at the PSD, see H. Van Allen, "A Brief History of the Pennsylvania Institution for the Deaf and Dumb," in Edward A. Fay, ed., *Histories of the American Schools for the Deaf, 1817–1893* (Washington, DC: Volta Bureau, 1893), 20.

23. *First Convention*, 4.

24. *First Convention*, 4.

25. *First Convention*, 5.

26. PSAD, *Proceedings of the Second Convention of the Pennsylvania Deaf-Mute Association* (nd., np), 17–18.

27. *Second Convention*, 4.

28. *Second Convention*, 18.

29. *Second Convention*, 12, 15.

30. *Second Convention*, 15.

31. *Report of the Gallaudet Centennial Memorial Committee of the Pennsylvania Association of Deaf Mutes* (Philadelphia: American Printing House, 1888), 5.

32. *Memorial Committee*, 6.

33. See in particular Jacob Koehler's remarks in PSAD, *Proceedings of the Fourth Convention* (Philadelphia: 1890), 5.

34. Memorial Committee, 5–14. Ironically, Magnin later organized the meeting that founded the British Deaf and Dumb Association, which immediately rejected the PSAD's example of deaf leadership, chose a hearing minister as its president, and thus led a disappointed Magnin to withdraw from its affairs. See Brian Grant, "Francis Magnin," in Renate Fischer and Harlan Lane, eds., *Looking Back: A Reader on the History of Deaf Communities and their Sign Languages* (Hamburg: Signum, 1993), 97–108.

35. *Proceedings of the Third Convention of the Pennsylvania Deaf-Mute Association* (nd., np.), 4–5.

36. *Third Convention*, 11.

37. *Third Convention*, 12.

38. *Third Convention*, 30–31.

39. Ritchie, *Pennsylvania Society*, 41.

40. *Third Convention*, 12–13.

41. PSAD, *Proceedings of the Fourth Convention* (Philadelphia: 1890) 5–6. Italics in original.

42. *Fourth Convention*, 6. Italics in original.

43. Elwell was not listed among the active PSAD members at the 1888 convention and therefore would not have had voting privileges. *Fourth Convention*, 18, 22.

44. *Fourth Convention*, 23.

45. *Fourth Convention*, 24.

46. Sampson, in Berg and Buzzard, *Apostle*, 158.

47. "Charter of the Pennsylvania Society for the Advancement of the Deaf," Granted January 3rd, 1891.

48. R. Allabough, "The Home Project," *Silent World* (July 3, 1890), 6.

49. Allabough, "Home Project," 7.

50. The only exceptions are 1890, when the trustees included Crouter, Koehler, and Davidson, and 1891, when all the trustees—Koehler, Ziegler, and Thomas Breen—were deaf. "Minutes of the Board of Trustees of the Pennsylvania Society for the Advancement of the Deaf," January 17, 1890; February 4, 1891; in the Gallaudet University Archives.

51. "Minutes of the Board of Trustees," February 12, 1896.

52. Ritchie, *Pennsylvania Society*, 72–73.

53. "Minutes of the Board of Trustees," December 24, 1892.

54. Ritchie, *Pennsylvania Society*, 72–73.

55. "Minutes of the Board of Trustees," June 15, 1892; May 11, 1900.

56. "Minutes of the Board of Trustees," January 1, 1901.

57. For more on Booth see John V. Van Cleve, "Nebraska's Oral Law of 1911 and the Deaf Community," *Nebraska History* 65 (Summer 1984). 195–220.

58. "Minutes of the Board of Trustees," January 16, 1901.

59. That the trustees did not expect to be replaced is obvious from the notes of their last meeting in 1900, when they spoke of the time and place of their next meeting, which never occurred. "Minutes of the Board of Trustees," November 30, 1900.

60. "Minutes of the Board of Trustees," July 24, 1900.

61. "Minutes of the Board of Trustees," December 14, 1901.

62. "Minutes of the Board of Trustees," March 15, 1901; December 19, 1903; April 9, 1904; September 12, 1904.

63. PSAD, *Report of the Proceedings of the Twenty-First Meeting* (Philadelphia: Norwood Print Shop, 1908), 55–56.

64. "Minutes of the Board of Trustees," December 14, 1901.

65. "Minutes of the Board of Trustees," December 14, 1901.

66. "Minutes of the Board of Trustees," November 1, 1901.

67. "Minutes of the Board of Trustees," December 14, 1901.

68. "Minutes of the Board of Trustees," May 29, 1902.

69. "Minutes of the Board of Trustees," November 29, 1902; PSAD, "Board of Trustees Annual Report, 1904," 18.

70. PSAD, "Board of Trustees Annual Report, 1907," 24.

71. *Proceedings of the Twenty-First Meeting*, 56–57; Ritchie, *Pennsylvania Society*, 78.

72. See, for example, Olof Hanson, "How the National Association May be Made More Useful," in National Association of the Deaf, *Proceedings of the Sixth Convention* (Paola, Kansas: J.T. Trickett, 1900), 17–18.

73. Quoted in Robert Ziegler, "The Federation of the Deaf," in PSAD, *Proceedings of the Twenty-Second Meeting* (Philadelphia: Norwood Print Shop, 1909), 32, 33.

74. Quoted in *Proceedings of the Twenty-Second Meeting*, 46–48.

75. Van Allen, "Brief History," 22. For Crouter's explanation of his support for oral methods and his opposition to the use of sign language in deaf education, see A. L. E. Crouter, "The Development of Speech in the Deaf Child," in *Transactions of the American Laryngological, Rhinological and Otological Society* (1910).

76. Ziegler, "Federation." 36–37.

9

The Chicago Mission for the Deaf

Kent R. Olney

Editor's Introduction

Kent Olney's study of deaf leader Philip Hasenstab and the Chicago Mission for the Deaf is pathbreaking. Olney uses Hasenstab family documents and church records to argue that historians should examine religious institutions and the role of faith to understand deaf community maintenance and self-help in a hostile, hearing-dominated world. He concludes that the Chicago Mission was successful in the deaf community for nearly five decades primarily because it was solidly anchored in and controlled by deaf community members themselves. Furthermore, the history of the Chicago Mission indicates that the condition of deafness and the commonality of deaf experiences transcended divisions of age, gender, geography, class, and, Olney suggests, sometimes even race. Olney's study points again to the value of intensive examination of local deaf situations to illuminate larger issues in deaf history, and it eloquently argues for the historical importance of organized, institutionalized religion in deaf experiences.

President Abraham Lincoln's Gettysburg Address in 1863 reminded Americans that their country had been founded with a "government of the people, by the people, and for the people." In like manner, thirty years later in Lincoln's home state of Illinois, the Chicago Mission for the Deaf was founded as a movement *of* the deaf, *by* the deaf, and *for* the deaf. As early as 1892, the Chicago Mission was recognized as having the largest deaf congregation in the country.[1] Furthermore, untold hundreds of deaf people who were not members of the congregation benefited from its work over the years. This uniquely deaf institution transcended limita-

Reverend Philip J. Hasenstab

tions of geography, denominational affiliation, ethnicity, and even gender roles in its success.

Philip J. Hasenstab, a deaf minister, directed the Chicago Mission from the 1890s until 1941. So instrumental and enduring was his leadership that the names Hasenstab and the Chicago Mission for the Deaf were almost synonymous. This identity was especially true outside of Chicago as Hasenstab traveled to share his religious beliefs with deaf individuals scattered about the Midwest. To such people, Hasenstab was the embodiment of the Chicago Mission, and to some, he was the embodiment of God himself.[2] This article describes the efforts of Hasenstab and others to reach deaf Americans through the Chicago Mission. It shows how community insiders, nearly all of whom were deaf themselves, maintained important and influential services and upheld deaf values for half a century.

Early Efforts

The first known attempts to provide religious services to deaf people in Chicago were the result of Episcopal Church activities in the late 1870s.

The *Chicago Daily News* reported in its April 29, 1878 edition: "Of the Easter services of yesterday, those which were perhaps as impressive as any were held in the chapel of St. James Church by the Rev. A. W. Mann. The clergyman and congregation were alike deaf-mutes."[3] Austin Mann had been ordained a deacon in the Episcopal Church in Cleveland, Ohio, in 1877. As the second deaf man ordained in this country, he accepted responsibility for a parish that extended from Ohio to Iowa and from Minnesota to Missouri. Mann's early efforts in Chicago were intermittent at best; most of his time was spent working among deaf people in Ohio and Michigan. Nonetheless, the presence of an Episcopal outreach to Chicago's deaf community before 1880 was likely the first of its kind.

The advent of religious work among deaf people occurred at a time when Chicago was experiencing phenomenal growth. The city's population increased from just fewer than 300,000 in 1870 to more than one million by 1890. Chicago's deaf population around this same time had grown to an estimated 400 or 500, raising concerns about who would meet the ongoing religious needs of this expanding community with its unique communication needs.[4] Beginning in the 1880s, various leaders associated with the Illinois School for the Deaf (ISD) began to view the Chicago deaf community as a mission field close to home that needed more religious workers.

Frank Read was the first person from ISD to initiate religious work among deaf Chicagoans. A graduate of ISD in 1862 and a teacher at the school from 1863 to 1900, Read became the fifth deaf man to be ordained in the United States when the Congregational Church granted him ministerial credentials in 1883. After his ordination, "Read began at once . . . an intensive evangelistic campaign" in Chicago that lasted for five years.[5] Read carried out his Chicago efforts while initiating similar works in St. Louis, Kansas City, and other towns; all of these efforts were in addition to his regular teaching job at ISD in Jacksonville, Illinois, which was several hours by train from Chicago. Read's hectic schedule of teaching and preaching eventually caught up with him, and ill health forced him to reduce his travels. ISD's superintendent, Philip Gillett, and others connected with the school then took responsibility for ministering to Chicago's deaf people.

Gillett first addressed deaf Chicagoans on Sunday afternoon, May 5, 1889. Among the 200 attendees were newspaper reporters and curious onlookers, but most were deaf residents of Chicago who had eagerly anticipated Gillett's presence and sermon. The popularity of such a religious service for deaf people was evident by the fact that "some sixty of the leading deaf and dumb citizens of Chicago" requested that ongoing serv-

Philip G. Gillett

ices be held on a monthly basis.[6] Gillett obliged, and Deaf people responded favorably to these services; on the first Sunday of July, 150 people attended the deaf service.[7]

Gillett's appeal resulted from a combination of factors. First, he had been a father figure to many of the deaf people, now living in Chicago, back when they were students at ISD; many felt great affection and respect for him.[8] Second, Gillett, though not deaf himself, was adept at the use of sign language. Sign language was under attack and being removed from many schools at this time, and yet when Gillett addressed his deaf audience in Chicago, he stood out as "a rapid, and . . . forcible master of this language of the silent ones of earth;" deaf people could understand his message in signs with clarity and "nodded with approving smiles, or otherwise testified their approval of the sentiment by nudging their immediate neighbors."[9] Finally, Gillett delivered a positive message of hope and affirmation.[10] In a society that was becoming increasingly urbanized and industrialized, people began living closer together, and differences inevitably became more noticeable. While eugenicists began pointing out differences such as deafness and suggesting measures to eradicate them, Gillett's message of affirmation and equality was an encouragement and boost to deaf people's self-esteem.

Once school opened again in the fall, Gillett's responsibilities at ISD took precedence, though he continued his periodic weekend visits to Chicago to preach to the city's deaf citizens. Gillett then sought others who might be interested in assisting with the religious work in Chicago, and he enlisted the help of certain individuals employed at ISD. The most enthusiastic and faithful was a twenty-seven-year-old teacher, Philip Hasenstab.

Hasenstab was beginning his fifth year of employment at ISD in the fall of 1889.[11] He had just returned from a summer trip to Paris, where he had been one of two delegates chosen from ISD to attend the International Congress of the Deaf.[12] Only two years earlier, he had been converted to Methodism when a religious revival swept over the ISD campus. After his conversion, Hasenstab regularly looked for opportunities to minister among the deaf students in Jacksonville; thus, when Gillett recruited him to help with the religious work in Chicago, Hasenstab was an eager candidate. He began making monthly trips to Chicago during the fall of 1889, and he received a license to preach from Grace Methodist Episcopal Church in Jacksonville on April 17, 1890.[13] From the fall of 1889 to the spring of 1893, Hasenstab held a teaching position at ISD while ministering to deaf Chicagoans at least once a month. Other faculty from ISD periodically assisted, and soon the monthly meetings became weekly services. The travel to and from Chicago was no small accomplishment, given both the distance—a one-way trip of some 250 miles—and the demands of such a grueling schedule.

Hasenstab became so enthralled with the Chicago deaf congregation that he also gave his summer months to the work. From 1890 to 1893, each summer found him leaving his teaching job at ISD to return to Chicago for the challenge of meeting the religious needs of its deaf residents. His daughter and biographer offers a helpful perspective on these summer activities:

> During the summer months Philip organized classes for Bible study on the North, West, and South sides of the city, which met weekly in the homes of members, and he conducted Sunday services in the loop [downtown area]. He did endless calling, by street-car or on foot, for his congregation was scattered over the city. Without the use of a telephone, he was not able to make appointments and often found people not at home. Mail was used to some extent and postage was cheap—letters two cents and cards a penny, but it took time.
>
> There were from 150 to 200 in the congregation on Sundays. Collections were regular but small. Salaries were low.[14]

Hasenstab soon became the regular and preferred leader of Chicago's weekly meetings during the school year.[15] His effectiveness was the subject of a letter from Will Beadell to Georgia Elliott, who would later become Hasenstab's wife. Beadell and Elliott had apparently attended school together at the National Deaf Mute College; while traveling through Chicago, Beadell attended a service led by Hasenstab and was impressed by what he saw. He gave the following description to Elliott:

> I saw Philip in Chicago and had a real nice chat with him. Splendid fellow. Really, as I told him, I was interested more by his sermon that Sunday afternoon than by many I have seen in college. It was so original, and the method of procedure of the whole meeting was different from ours at college. There was the signing of three hymns, by a Mr. Campbell, Philip and a Miss Coe, all of which lent variety to what has often been a very dull occasion. I really think Philip will "fill a long felt want" for the Chicago deaf.[16]

Deaf Chicagoans must have felt the same because they supported Hasenstab's early work with their faithful attendance.

An average of 110 people attended these Sunday afternoon preaching services in the summers between 1890 and 1893; occasionally, attendance swelled to more than 200.[17] During July in 1893, when the World's Congress of the Deaf was meeting in Chicago, Hasenstab noted that the attendance of more than 250 was "the largest ever had here;" the following Sunday, he commented that "standing space [wa]s all occupied and the hall half filled with others unable to come."[18] Though those two Sundays were exceptions because of the number of out-of-town guests, summer services were well-attended on a consistent basis. Numbers fluctuated more during the school year when a regular pastor was not available to call on the people and the winter winds began to blow in Chicago, but even then the numbers remained impressive. For example, during a cold four-month period extending from November 1892 to February 1893, Hasenstab reported attendance ranging between forty and eighty-five deaf people.[19] Chicago's deaf church was growing, and Hasenstab was quickly becoming known as its leader and pastor.

The year 1893 proved to be a pivotal year for Hasenstab as well as for deaf people in Chicago and around the Midwest. Most Chicago historians remember 1893 as the year the city hosted the World's Fair or the year that marked the founding of the famed Sears, Roebuck and Company; both events exemplified the kind of changes and advances taking place in Chicago's commercial world. However, two other events indicated how

Chicago's deaf world was also changing at the time. The first of these events was the resignation of Gillett from the superintendency of ISD; the second was the establishment of the Chicago Mission for the Deaf as a permanent work. These related events had a profound effect on the deaf community in and around Chicago.

Gillett's resignation from ISD, after thirty-seven years of leadership, resulted from outside political pressure. In the fall of 1892, Illinois elected its first Democratic governor since the Civil War—John P. Altgeld. Leadership changes began occurring in many of the state's public institutions. For example, Altgeld soon removed the superintendent at the Hospital for the Insane in Kankakee, and other changes around the state were assumed to be imminent.[20] At ISD, which was funded and operated by the state, questions were raised about the future of their Republican superintendent, Gillett. Hasenstab, a teacher at ISD, mentioned this concern as early as November 10, 1892, when he wrote in a letter to Georgia Elliott that "we fear that [the governor] will invade our institution work with his politics, but we must wait and see."[21] The fears were realized and the wait was relatively short. Despite attempts by others to intervene and help Gillett keep his position, policies and conditions changed so quickly and dramatically that he submitted his resignation on April 11, 1893, and announced that he was moving west to accept the superintendent's position at the Colorado School for the Deaf.[22]

The pages of human history are replete with the fact that unique opportunities often grow out of predicaments. Such was the case for the deaf community in Chicago at this time. Gillett's resignation became the catalyst for establishing the Chicago Mission for the Deaf as a permanent institution. Correspondence between Hasenstab and his future wife indicates that Hasenstab had been contemplating full-time religious work in Chicago for a number of years.[23] For four years, he had devoted his summers and at least one weekend of every month to the deaf people of Chicago. The changes that took place at ISD in 1893 caused Hasenstab to seriously consider his future in a new light. He wrote to Elliott on April 12, 1893, the day after Gillett submitted his formal resignation:

> Yes, my dear, you should not worry as to what may become of me here. I let it all go on, and not worry myself. Worry will not help make matters any better. The Lord knows what the new authorities wish to do, and, I believe, allows them to do some thing wrong, only to convince them some day of their foolishness. So, whether I should remain here or not, I hardly feel uneasy, but I am feeling sorry for these children who are so

helpless and will, in their helplessness, be seriously harmed by the
change in the management of the school.

Now that Gillett was offered the superintendency of the Col[orado]
school, I could not help feeling that it was providential, indeed, to himself as well as to the national profession. So I have rejoiced over it.[24]

Hasenstab's letter reveals his concerns for ISD and his own future, but
it also shows that he saw an opportunity. He indicated that the changes at
the Illinois School might actually be the work of "the Lord." He openly
wondered whether Gillett's resignation was "providential." Frank Read
confirmed these thoughts by suggesting that the developing events might
lead to a "call" elsewhere. Although Hasenstab's immediate concerns were
the welfare of deaf students and the future of ISD, hints that a religious
calling might be leading him to a career change also surfaced. After
spending another summer of ministry in Chicago in 1893, he decided to
leave ISD and answer that call.

Several factors explain Hasenstab's decision to stop teaching and become a full-time minister. First, he was compelled by the growing needs
of the deaf community he saw in Chicago; many deaf people sought his
ongoing leadership and the religious services he provided.[25] Second, the
new superintendent might not be as sympathetic as Gillett had been toward Hasenstab's role in the Chicago ministry. Third, Hasenstab received
direct encouragement from Gillett to seize the opportunity that existed in
Chicago. Finally, the leadership of the Methodist Episcopal Church came
forward and offered Hasenstab a permanent pastoral position. Hasenstab
accepted the offer and resigned his position at ISD a week before school
was to start.[26]

Although Hasenstab and his then fiancée Elliott both expressed concern over the small $800 annual salary he was promised, Hasenstab be-
lieved that he had been "called . . . to the Chicago work."[27] On October
4, 1893, he wrote to Elliott and described some of his feelings on this mo-
mentous occasion:

Today will be remembered as the day on which I began this new work.
Before this, I have preached often and visited many persons, but that
only prepared me for this regular pastoral work. . . . I am only happy
now that I am here in answer to God's call.[28]

So it was that "on October 4, 1893, Mr. Hasenstab was appointed to take
charge of the work as . . . permanent pastor"—a position he would hold

until his death forty-eight years later on December 29, 1941.[29] The Chicago Mission for the Deaf was launched; its ministry would extend for decades to come and eventually reach hundreds of miles outside Chicago.

Success

Those who contributed to the Chicago Mission believed it was the most significant work of its kind in the world, but that belief does not address the question of why Hasenstab and his colleagues were uniquely success-ful in creating an enduring community institution. This question is espe-cially intriguing when one considers that early religious efforts among deaf people in Chicago were, for the most part, initiated by respected deaf community leaders themselves. With the exception of Gillett, who quickly turned over the ministry responsibilities in Chicago to deaf teachers, all other attempts were the work of deaf men. Obviously, then, deafness itself (i.e., being a community insider) was not the critical variable. Other fac-tors made Hasenstab's ministry more successful than other comparable religious efforts.

The Episcopalians, who had a long history of ministry among deaf Americans, were still trying to establish a viable deaf work in Chicago during the late-nineteenth century. They had maintained a presence among Chicago's deaf community since their initial work began in the late 1870s and had showed signs of expanding their influence in the 1890s. The highly respected deaf Episcopalian, Austin Mann, acquired a $20,000 church building for one dollar in 1892. The church "became known as All Angels' Church for the Deaf;" it hosted the Episcopalians' Eighth Con-ference of Church Workers among the Deaf in July 1893, drawing atten-dees from many American cities as well as from England and Ireland. By the end of the year, however, as one deaf community historian has writ-ten, the "two-church problem" in Chicago was won by Hasenstab and the Methodists.[30]

Several factors contributed to the success of the Chicago Mission. Beyond the characteristics of contemporary Methodism itself, which are beyond the scope of this paper, three factors suggest themselves as most important: the deaf church's association with the city's deaf club, the pro-viding of regular church services for the deaf community, and the leaders' strong ties to ISD.

The Chicago Mission and Chicago's deaf club were closely related from the beginning. The church supported and was located near the club's building, a gathering place where deaf community members regularly so-cialized with one another on weekends. Beginning in the late-nineteenth century, deaf clubs "provided a place where [people] could meet to share their ideas, interests, and language."[31] Some students of the deaf community and its history have suggested that "the strongest organizational bonding" to take place in the deaf community occurred at local deaf clubs.[32] Chicago's deaf club, known as the Pas-a-Pas Club, was central to the city's deaf community by the end of the nineteenth century.[33]

It could be argued that the club itself was, in part, an extension of the religious influence already present among Chicago's deaf community. Although a group of deaf people had informally banded together and used the Pas-a-Pas name for several months, the formal meeting to establish and organize the club was held on October 18, 1890, nearly a year and a half after Gillett had begun his religious work in Chicago. Furthermore, Hasenstab attended the initial organizational meeting, which took place in a church and was opened with a prayer. As a respected member of the deaf community, he was invited to address "the mass meeting of the deaf," and he spoke about "the laying aside of all prejudice" and "the importance of union and harmony."[34]

The proximity of the clubroom and Chicago's First Methodist Church, where Gillett and then Hasenstab had begun holding deaf worship services, facilitated an ongoing relationship between the club and the Chicago Mission that benefited both the Methodist deaf work and the deaf community's club. In the November 2, 1892, issue of the *Deaf-Mutes' Journal*, an interesting comparison was made between the Methodists and the Episcopalians that emphasized the role of the deaf club in the former's rise to prominence among Chicago's deaf population:

> Probably no church for the deaf in the country enjoys a larger attendance than Christian Church, at the Methodist Church block. *The location is excellent, in the very center of the city, and but a square away from the club quarters.* The attendance each Sunday averages one hundred, and not infrequently does the congregation rise to one hundred and fifty. On great occasions the room has held two hundred and fifty souls. . . .
>
> The All Angels' Church already owns a beautiful $20,000 structure, and, but for its location in the uptown district, it would enjoy a larger congregation. . . . Regular church services have not yet been arranged, but Rev. Mr. Mann, the pastor, and Rev. Mr. Cloud of St. Louis, often fill the pulpit.[35]

Hasenstab took advantage of the proximity between the Methodist Church and the city's deaf club by socializing at the club himself.[36] His early participation in the club made church recruitment relatively easy. In addition to deaf people interacting with Hasenstab at the community club, the location of the deaf church was known by club members. Potential church attendees knew where the congregation met and were able to travel there along the same route they traveled to the deaf club.

A second factor in the success of the Chicago Mission for the Deaf, where other early religious efforts struggled, was also hinted at in the aforementioned *Deaf-Mutes' Journal* article; though deaf Episcopalians owned a church building by 1892, *"regular* church services ha[d] not yet been arranged."[37] In contrast, the efforts begun by Gillett and taken over by Hasenstab quickly turned into regular services for deaf people—first monthly, then weekly. In addition, from 1890 to 1893, Hasenstab gave his summer months to the Chicago work and was available on a daily basis. The Episcopalian ministers who served in Chicago, Mann and Cloud, both had primary responsibilities in other cities and ministered in Chicago only on given Sundays. The fact that Hasenstab was able to devote his pastoral attention almost exclusively to Chicago during these formative years was critical to its early success; not until the work was firmly established there did he expand his ministry to other areas around the Midwest.

A third factor that contributed to the success of the Chicago Mission was its strong connection to and support from ISD. Gillett and Hasenstab were both associated with ISD. Because most members of Chicago's deaf community were alumni of ISD, they looked forward to renewing their ties and exchanging information with those who traveled to and from the school. Hasenstab often brought greetings and news from one local deaf community to another; he became a regular and trusted ambassador from ISD to Chicago's alumni and vice versa.

A thriving ministry to deaf people thus was born in Chicago that would influence the deaf community in significant ways for more than half a century. The work soon expanded in terms of leaders, parishioners, geography, and work load; in the process, it became one of America's most unique religious institutions. The remainder of this article looks closely at the leadership and community that marked the Chicago Mission for the Deaf.

Leadership

Deaf leaders effectively organized and managed this unique ministry for half a century. Chief among them, of course, was Hasenstab, who became the Chicago Mission's first appointed pastor in 1893 and continued in that position until his death forty-eight years later. Despite Hasenstab's distinction and popularity, however, the work in Chicago was not a one-person show. Other members of the deaf community also contributed in important ways. The most significant of these were Georgia Elliott, Hasenstab's wife; Henry Rutherford, an ISD graduate who devoted the majority of his adult life to assisting Hasenstab in an outreach ministry; Vina Smith, a deaconess; evangelist Laura Sheridan; and Constance Hasenstab Elmes, the Hasenstabs' daughter.

This group of leaders was remarkable for a number of reasons. They all gave substantial portions of their lives to the ministry in Chicago; their commitments were best measured by decades rather than by months or years. Each was a pioneer in some way, and each was deaf, with the exception of Constance Hasenstab Elmes, who grew up with deaf parents. Thus, all of them were community insiders who shared a common language and a unique perspective on the world.

Philip J. Hasenstab

The community's primary leader, Philip J. Hasenstab, was a product of his residential school experiences in Indianapolis. Born in New York City on December 22, 1861, and deafened before the age of two, he enrolled at the Indiana Institution for the Deaf and Dumb at age eight. It was there that he began formulating his ideas and building a foundation for his future work, and there, he showed the drive and intelligence that would serve him well in the future. His grades for his final term in school indicated that he had averaged 100 percent in both his "studies" and "deportment;" his courses of study for the final term included penmanship, grammar, composition, chemistry, scripture lessons, and algebra.[38] At the Indiana School, Hasenstab developed strong views about the value that deaf people placed on eyesight, the utility of sign language, and the uniqueness of the Christian religion.[39] Henceforth, his life was lived in two worlds—the deaf world and the religious world—and he would dedicate his life to bringing both worlds together.

In addition to these formative experiences at the Indiana School, Hasenstab's particular traits and his early college experiences uniquely qualified him for his work at the Chicago Mission. Though he was a man of slight stature, weighing less than 140 pounds and standing five feet, eight inches tall, he filled big shoes when he attended the National Deaf Mute College.[40] He became the quarterback and captain of the school's first football team; participated in various dramatic productions; began a lifelong friendship with the college's founder and president, Edward Miner Gallaudet; and graduated in 1885 as the valedictorian of his five-member class. His life at the National Deaf Mute College confirmed what

E. M. Gallaudet (standing in middle) and Philip Hasenstab (standing next to Gallaudet). Probably faculty (seated) and students (standing) at the National Deaf Mute College in the 1880s.

he had sensed earlier at the Indiana School: The deaf community, where people could easily "understand one another," was home.[41]

Immediately after his college graduation, Hasenstab was hired by Gillett at ISD, first as the boys' supervisor and then as a teacher. Gillett and Hasenstab quickly developed a friendship and mutual respect for one another that resulted in a number of opportunities for the latter. In 1889, Gillett engaged Hasenstab in the Chicago work on weekends. A few years later, Gillett recommended that Hasenstab address the World Congress of the Deaf on the topic of "The Moral and Religious Condition of the Deaf after Leaving School."[42] Over the years, Gillett turned again and again to Hasenstab to represent ISD and found him to be a capable, dependable, and willing ambassador.

The educational opportunities Hasenstab had at both the Indiana School and the National Deaf Mute College along with regular encouragement from Gillett at ISD, combined to provide a foundation for Hasenstab's unique position in the church. Hasenstab received his local preacher's license from Grace Methodist Episcopal Church in Jacksonville, Illinois, in 1890, thus obtaining official approval and authority to

First football team at the National Deaf Mute College, 1880s. Philip Hasenstab (holding the ball) was captain and quarterback.

preach. Subsequently, on September 30, 1894, one year after he had been appointed pastor of the Chicago Mission for the Deaf, Hasenstab became the first deaf person ordained deacon by the Methodist Episcopal Church and only the ninth deaf man to be ordained by any church in America.[43] Five years later, on October 8, 1899, in Rockford, Illinois, Hasenstab completed the ordination process by being ordained elder, the final step in the Methodist ordination system.[44]

By the early twentieth century Hasenstab's leadership extended beyond the religious world. He was an elected officer in the Indiana School for the Deaf Alumni Association, and he served as president of the Illinois Association of the Deaf (IAD).[45] In 1914, Gallaudet College, formerly known as the National Deaf Mute College, honored its 1885 alumnus with an honorary doctor of divinity degree.[46] Twenty-five years later, on June 11, 1939, Hasenstab was honored once again by his alma mater. The occasion was Gallaudet College's seventy-fifth anniversary celebration and Hasenstab, at the age of seventy-seven and one of thirteen living alumni from the school's first seventeen graduating classes, was invited to give the invocation for the event.[47]

Georgia Elliott (far left) was one of the first females admitted to the National Deaf Mute College, in Washington, D.C., 1887.

By the end of his life, Hasenstab was widely revered and fondly remembered for his multiple contributions to the deaf world. In a seventy-fifth birthday card sent from a group of deaf friends in 1936, Hasenstab was applauded for having "steered our soul" for a "full forty years." In the same card, he is remembered as the "captain and field-general of Gallaudet College's great first football team, 54 years ago" who then became "captain and field-general of the Methodist Episcopal mission in Chicago and environs."[48] The influence of Hasenstab and the Chicago Mission extended far and wide. As crucial as Hasenstab was to the success of the Chicago Mission, however, he did not work alone; several other deaf leaders assumed supporting roles.

Georgia Elliott Hasenstab

Georgia Elliott became the wife of Philip Hasenstab in 1894 and was of inestimable value to the Chicago Mission during their forty-seven years of marriage and ministry. Born on May 5, 1867, in Ohio, Georgia moved with her family to central Illinois when she was a young girl. She had two older brothers and two younger sisters. In 1873, she lost both her hearing and her eight-year-old brother due to spinal meningitis. Shortly thereafter, at the age of nine, she began school at ISD. There she met Hasenstab when he joined ISD's staff in the fall of 1885. She graduated from the Illinois School in 1887 as the valedictorian of her class and hoped to attend the National Deaf Mute College.[49]

At that time, the college admitted only male students, but Elliott wrote to the school on January 10, 1887, to protest women's exclusion and to encourage an "experiment" in coeducation:

> I hope that my long cherished desire will be gratified and that many young ladies will be happy to enter the college. . . . [Coeducation] is a progressive movement which all the best educators must approve and from which only the best results can follow. I look for nothing but success from your "experiment," which I hope you may soon have a chance to try.[50]

Elliott sent a similar letter to the National Convention of Deaf Teachers who would be meeting in Berkeley during the summer, and the matter was discussed during a business session. According to the convention's proceedings, the response was favorable.[51] Subsequently, in the fall of 1887, six females enrolled at the National Deaf Mute College as an experiment, and Elliott was among them.

After two years at the National Deaf Mute College, however, Elliott left school to accept a teaching position at the Missouri School for the Deaf (MSD) in Fulton. Elliott apparently was an effective and popular teacher, liked by students and the administration.[52] Soon engaged to Hasenstab, she regularly encouraged him to be true to his calling; she reminded him often of how the deaf people of Chicago needed him and assured him of her prayers and support.[53] In one poignant letter to Hasenstab, she wrote these words after hearing about a man who had left the ministry:

> What sad news indeed about that man who gave up his work to which he was called. I pray that the dear Lord may always keep you my dear Philip in His field to the last. . . . I do wish you to remain in your field of labor always, no matter how discouraging [sic] you often may feel. . . . Your calling is the noblest work.[54]

On June 19, 1894, she married Hasenstab and moved to his home in Chicago.

Georgia Hasenstab did more to support the Chicago Mission than would have been expected for a woman of the early twentieth century.

Certainly, she engaged in responsibilities that were common for a pastor's wife—leading church organizations focused on women's activities such as the Susannah Wesley Circle, the Epworth League (for youth), and the Ladies' Aid Society, as well as teaching a class for deaf people on the south side of Chicago for thirty-two years.[55] More remarkably, as the work of the Chicago Mission expanded and Hasenstab occasionally found himself out of the city on weekends, Georgia sometimes filled the pulpit for him, preaching the Sunday sermon and leading the church service far in advance of the Methodist ordination of women.[56]

Henry S. Rutherford

Another important leader of the Chicago Mission was Henry Sidney Rutherford, an assistant pastor to Hasenstab for some forty years. Rutherford extended the work of the Chicago Mission to deaf people who lived outside the city. He was a product of ISD and attended that institution when revival fires were sweeping the campus in the 1880s.[57] Church documents state that Rutherford was "converted [to Methodism] after attending services conducted by the Rev. Philip Hasenstab."[58] Rutherford also attended the National Deaf Mute College for one year and then returned to Illinois to work as a farmer before entering the ministry. Thus, Rutherford was influenced by the same combination of educational and religious factors that motivated the Hasenstabs.

Rutherford began assisting the Chicago Mission in September of 1900, primarily traveling to provide religious services for deaf people in areas west of Chicago. He passed the ministerial entrance examination and was admitted on a trial basis to the Rock River Conference of the Methodist Episcopal Church in 1902.[59] He was ordained deacon in 1906, becoming the third deaf man to be ordained by the Methodist Church.[60]

With the exception of an eight-month absence in 1906, Rutherford served as Hasenstab's assistant from 1900 to the latter's death in 1941. Though Rutherford made his home in Chicago and often helped Hasenstab around the city, his primary goal was extending the work of the Chicago Mission to outlying territory.[61] His itinerary grew over the years to include lengthy trips to northwestern Illinois, Wisconsin, Iowa, Nebraska, Missouri, and Kansas during which he often preached an average of more than one sermon each day. He would meet with small groups of deaf people at each stop and provide Bible readings, a sermon, and encouragement. Many of the groups met in a local Methodist Church; some met in private homes, and others assembled at the YMCA or at other convenient locations. It was not unusual for Rutherford to travel more than 1,200 miles per month, covering an area of more than 40,000 square miles in five or six states; within his area of responsibility, he would meet with up to thirty different groups of deaf people in any given month.

The success Rutherford enjoyed resulted, in large part, from the fact that he could relate well with the people to whom he ministered; he was one of them, a deaf person ministering to other deaf people. He was the product of a residential school and served a term as the president of the Illinois Association of the Deaf.[62] Deaf people recognized that he was a community insider who understood their experiences. Furthermore, he was a farmer who knew the special needs and challenges of those who worked the soil for their livelihood. An article in *The Illinois Advance* noted that Rutherford was "able to offer suggestions even to farmers, and this has been done with profit to others."[63] Rutherford's background therefore equipped him for a preaching circuit that took him primarily to deaf farmers across the rural Midwest; deafness and farming were both very familiar subjects to this traveling minister.

A few years after Hasenstab's death in 1941, Rutherford retired from his work as an assistant pastor at the Chicago Mission.[64] In 1969, at the age of ninety-four, he died in Orlando, Florida. He was eulogized for his long and "dedicated service to the deaf."[65]

Other Leaders

Three more people were particularly important to the Chicago Mission's success: Vina Smith, Laura C. Sheridan, and Constance Hasenstab Elmes. The first two women, like all the other leaders discussed thus far, were deaf and were particularly instrumental in the early years of the Chicago Mission; the third, Elmes, was the second of the Hasenstabs' four hearing daughters and contributed a great deal to the ministry in its later years. All three were well-acquainted with the deaf community, and all desired to take their religious message to that community.

Vina Smith served the Chicago Mission for a number of years as a deaconess, a "quasi-ministerial status," because women could not be fully ordained in the Methodist Church until 1956.[66] Like Hasenstab, she attended the Indiana School for the Deaf in Indianapolis, graduating in 1883, four years after Hasenstab left. She worked for a number of years as a seamstress and privately taught a young deaf girl near her home. Eventually, she felt called to the deaf work that was expanding in Chicago and enrolled in the Deaconess Training School where she studied for two years, using notes taken by her hearing classmates. She was consecrated a deaconess in 1902, likely the first deaf woman to be appointed to that office.[67]

After completing her deaconess training, Smith gave nine years to the Chicago Mission for the Deaf—living for much of that time at Chicago's designated deaconess home.[68] Her duties included calling on people, teaching Sunday School classes, helping with the Epworth League, and representing the Chicago Mission on various occasions.[69] Smith's efforts and contributions in the city were vital to the early work of the entire Chicago Mission; by her sharing routine ministerial responsibilities, Hasenstab and Rutherford were able to expand the Chicago Mission's influence and outreach to deaf people elsewhere.[70]

Even more than Smith, Laura C. Sheridan's life intersected with Philip Hasenstab's repeatedly. They first became acquainted at the Indiana School, taught together for several years at ISD, and ultimately teamed up to spread their religious beliefs in the Chicago area and throughout the Midwest. Sheridan's father, an early Methodist circuit rider, and her brother, Wilbur Sheridan, were both preachers.[71] Laura had the same evangelistic fervor that her father and brother possessed and gave her life to religious service both at and away from residential schools. However, she was also an activist in other regards. Sheridan was the first woman to present a paper at the Convention of American Instructors of the Deaf, doing so in 1882.[72] Like the other leaders who came to be associated with the Chicago Mission, Sheridan was a pioneer in the deaf world.

She provided an important and unusual service for Hasenstab, sometimes serving as his interpreter, particularly when both attended camp meetings near the Hasenstab family's home in southern Indiana. The exact nature of her interpreting is not known, but she became deaf after learning to speak and did so quite well.[73] As many as twenty deaf people would sometimes attend the camp on midsummer days; Sheridan would help others interpret the preaching and would often lead her own sessions of Bible instruction and prayer for those who were deaf.[74] Over time, Sheridan became recognized for the kind of zeal, revival emphasis, and prayer meetings that were associated with holiness camp meetings; she introduced many of these religious experiences to the Chicago deaf community.

Sheridan contributed a great deal to the Chicago Mission. She conducted a variety of Bible classes and prayer meetings both in Chicago and in Jacksonville near ISD; like Georgia Elliot Hasenstab, Sheridan filled the Chicago pulpit for Philip Hasenstab on several occasions; and she traveled to hold various evangelistic meetings in places such as Baltimore, where another deaf Methodist work was begun a few years after the Chicago Mission was established.[75]

Hasenstab respected Sheridan and her family and felt he owed much to them. Even in Sheridan's later years, a visit to Chicago often resulted in an invitation for her to address the deaf congregation; special words of recognition and gratitude in the church's monthly newsletter regularly accompanied such occasions.[76] One such visit caused Hasenstab to reflect on more than thirty years of ministry at the Chicago Mission and led him to attribute the early impetus for the work to the Sheridan family. Hasenstab wrote that the Chicago Mission could "trace its activity back to [Sheridan's] father's conversion after attending a revival in a country church."[77] When Laura Sheridan died in 1933 at the age of eighty, Hasenstab and Rutherford both officiated at her funeral and expressed appreciation for the influence she brought to the deaf communities of Illinois and Indiana.[78]

Constance Hasenstab Elmes, the second daughter of Philip and Georgia Hasenstab, in some ways broke the pattern of leadership at the Chicago Mission because she was hearing. She learned sign language and deaf community values very early in her life, however. By the age of fourteen she had begun interpreting religious events conducted by her father.[79] Over the next several years, Constance continued to interpret at various funerals, baptisms, and weddings.[80] In 1922, her involvement increased from that of interpreter to that of an official assistant to her father in the ministry. In April of that year, Constance traveled to South Bend, Indiana, where she interpreted an Easter morning service and then preached at an Easter afternoon service for deaf parishioners.[81] For the next nineteen years, until her father's death in 1941, she served as her father's assistant. After his death in 1941, Elmes inherited the role of senior pastor at the Chicago Mission.

Within the limitations imposed by contemporary Methodism, Elmes also was a preacher in her own right. In 1924, she was licensed to preach, and in 1930, she became one of the first women ordained by the Methodist Church as "a local elder."[82] Although the ordination gave her expanded rights in serving as a minister, it did not impart the full rights available to male ordinands. Finally, in 1957, Elmes was granted full ordination.[83]

Elmes' proficiency in and advocacy for sign language were her greatest contributions to the deaf community. She interpreted religious and social events long before interpreting was recognized as a profession, and "she campaigned actively and long for sign language . . . when it was considered unfashionable."[84] Her use and support of signing endeared her to deaf community members, many of whom sought assistance from Elmes when dealing with institutions or agencies that were unfamiliar with deaf people and their needs.

Leadership, then, was a key factor in the Chicago Mission's success. All the individuals profiled here were pioneers. All were deaf themselves except for one, and she grew up in a deaf family. All had a thorough understanding of the deaf world and were very involved in that world: they

Reverend Constance Hasenstab Elmes led the Chicago Mission for the Deaf for more than twenty-five years after her father's death in 1941.

participated in deaf clubs, deaf associations, and deaf alumni gatherings. All were gifted in and committed to the use of sign language. All were passionate about their faith and wanted to share their religious convictions with others. They felt a strong sense of calling, privilege, and opportunity to communicate their beliefs to other members of the deaf community. All of them started while relatively young, and the majority of them continued the work into their senior years. The length of tenure ranged from nine to fifty-one years, with four of the six leaders—Philip Hasenstab, Georgia Hasenstab, Rutherford, and Elmes—giving more than forty years each to the Chicago Mission.

Community

As noted, the Chicago Mission was *for* the deaf. As the deaf population of Chicago grew at the end of the nineteenth century, the demand for various deaf social services increased. One such service was religious instruction and worship. Monthly worship services led by Gillett and a variety of

ISD teachers grew under the leadership of Hasenstab and his assistants into an elaborate community network. A deaf community of believers formed in Chicago. Soon, that community expanded throughout the Midwest and eventually even reached around the world.

Chicago

Data indicate that the deaf community of Chicago grew from a few hundred people in the late-nineteenth century to several hundred, or perhaps even a couple thousand, some forty years later.[85] Determining what percentage of them was actively involved with the Chicago Mission is problematic. Records show that it was not unusual to have more than 100 deaf people attend worship services on given Sundays of any year and that 25 percent to 50 percent of the local deaf community attended in the first few years. The attendance rate then dropped and fluctuated between 5 percent and 25 percent during the 1920s and 1930s.[86]

The Chicago Mission was more than just Sunday services at the First Methodist Episcopal Church, however. In the early years, the preaching service was preceded by a Praying Band at 2:00 p.m. and an Adult Bible Class at 2:15 p.m.[87] Both of these activities ceased in January 1920 and were replaced by the Epworth League Devotional Meeting, which followed the preaching service at 4:30 p.m.[88] Hasenstab also frequently led other Sunday services around the city, including a service for deaf African Americans each Sunday evening at 7:30 from 1927 to 1932.[89] The Susannah Wesley Circle and the Ladies' Aid Society brought deaf women together. A "brotherhood . . . to promote the physical, social, literary and spiritual welfare of its members" served the same purpose for deaf men, and a Dramatic Club and a Girls' Athletic Class were organized.[90] During the week, "class meetings" were held around the city. Hasenstab described them this way:

> The class meeting will have the different features of both [holiness and Bible study meetings], and include testimonies and prayers on the part of those present. The chief aim is, among other things, to start and develop Christian experience.[91]

Each of these organizations and formal meetings existed to provide comradeship and assistance for deaf Chicagoans.

The Chicago Mission attempted to reach out beyond its own organizational structures and serve not only the whole Chicago deaf community but also deaf people in surrounding areas. One aspect of this outreach was participation in various associations of the deaf. Chicago Mission leaders and members actively supported the National Association of the Deaf, the Illinois Association of the Deaf, the Illinois and Indiana School for the Deaf Alumni Associations, and the Gallaudet College Alumni Association.[92]

The Chicago Mission's inclusiveness is particularly apparent in Hasenstab's outreach to African Americans. On a trip to Baltimore in 1914, Hasenstab led "an evening service . . . for the colored deaf."[93] The following year, on a trip through several southern states, Hasenstab conducted chapel services at three "separate schools for colored children."[94] A few years later, in June 1920, Hasenstab announced that Sunday evening services for black deaf people would take place in Chicago twice a month at a Methodist Episcopal Church for African Americans.[95] In 1927, the Chicago Mission began providing services for black deaf Chicagoans every Sunday evening.[96] These services lasted until 1932. Finally, records show that at least one African American joined the Chicago Mission. Hasenstab wrote that in 1926, "Ulysses Grant Kendall, a former pupil of the School for the Colored Deaf at Little Rock, Ark[ansas], was admitted into preparatory membership of the Chicago Mission on July 11th."[97] Clearly, the data with respect to the outreach of the Chicago Mission for the Deaf to black deaf people are meager, but they are not insignificant. They indicate that the Chicago Mission made attempts to extend its ministry to its African American deaf neighbors despite the pervasive segregation and prejudice of the period.

A third example of Chicago Mission outreach comes from its involvement in founding and supporting the Illinois Home for the Aged and Infirm Deaf. Although this effort was not an official project of the Chicago Mission, its leaders and members were significantly involved in supporting the endeavor from the outset. As early as 1890, Hasenstab proposed that the Indiana School for the Deaf alumni association investigate the possibility of establishing such a home in Indiana.[98] Four years later, Hasenstab reported that "the Illinois Association of the Deaf ha[d] appointed a committee of seven to look into the advisability of having a home for the aged and infirm in the state."[99] Hasenstab's dream became a reality when the local deaf community purchased a home in downtown Chicago and dedicated it on June 17, 1923.[100] Thereafter, the Chicago Mission promoted the Illinois Home's purpose and financial needs in its written publications, and many of its parishioners lived there over the years.[101]

The Chicago Mission was an indispensable part of Chicago's deaf community well into the twentieth century. It provided spiritual nurture, social services, and physical care to the city's deaf population; for the most part, these services were not available anywhere else. The mission produced its own informational publication, titled *The Story of the Methodist Episcopal Mission for the Deaf*, in which it listed worship, education, pageantry (that is, presentations in sign language or drama), recreation, social services, interpreting, and evangelism as its primary goals and services. All of these combined to build a vibrant community.[102]

As much as the Chicago Mission for the Deaf did for its local parishioners, its work and influence extended to other places beyond the city of Chicago. The organization, care, and outreach of this thriving community of believers touched the lives of deaf people throughout the Midwest and beyond.

The Midwest

As deaf people graduated from residential schools and settled in various parts of the Midwest, they often sought the religious instruction and the social interaction that they had grown accustomed to at school. Hasenstab and Rutherford obliged by traveling throughout the countryside visiting deaf people and holding church services. In the earliest years, Hasenstab responded to requests that took him to several Midwestern states. As the work expanded and Rutherford came to assist him, Hasenstab largely gave his attention to deaf people in the states of Illinois and Indiana while Rutherford assumed responsibility for the western area, consisting primarily of Iowa, Missouri, Nebraska, and Kansas.

Hasenstab and Rutherford became deaf circuit riders who each routinely traveled some 1,200 miles or more per month. Hasenstab had pastoral appointments in at least twenty states plus Canada and Washington, D.C. From 1903 to 1941, he averaged more than thirteen appointments per month outside Chicago; Rutherford averaged more than twenty such appointments during the same period. Thus, for at least thirty-nine years, these two ministers, in their combined efforts, traveled to an average of more than thirty-three locations per month to spread their religious message to deaf Midwesterners. By the end of his ministry, Hasenstab alone had held appointments in 133 different towns outside of Chicago—fifty-seven of which were in Illinois and twenty-one in Indiana. Many of these appointments occurred on a monthly basis for several decades.[103]

The travel usually took place on trains and meant long nights with interrupted sleep. Each stop was an occasion when preaching, baptism, communion, a wedding, a funeral, or a combination of these religious events might take place. Hasenstab faithfully took these monthly trips to minister to deaf Midwesterners until he was seventy-five years old, when heart trouble finally caused him to slow down.[104]

These monthly trips influenced and strengthened community bonds in at least three ways. First, rural deaf people looked forward to getting together with other deaf people on those occasions when Hasenstab or Rutherford visited. The presence of one or the other of these ministers extended the deaf community of Chicago and helped foster local or regional community life in rural areas. Second, in some of the larger towns and cities outside Chicago, the work of these ministers gave birth to deaf ministries that eventually gained enough momentum to stand independently of the Chicago Mission and, thus, establish a whole new community of deaf believers that often began to organize and function based on the pattern of the Chicago community. Third, these trips frequently took Hasenstab to state residential schools, allowing him to influence and recruit younger generations of deaf people while maintaining an ongoing relationship with those institutions that were central to American deaf community life.

Hasenstab's presence at residential schools was no small matter. By 1900, nearly all the schools had a strong oral emphasis, and many prohibited signing among their students.[105] Yet when Hasenstab visited and addressed the students, he delivered his messages in sign language. Religious services provided rare opportunities when signing was still allowed at many deaf schools.[106] Hasenstab came, then, both as a representative of religious faith and as a model of American sign language. Further, he represented an adult deaf community outside the residential schools that also used and valued signing. Hasenstab thus introduced students to important deaf community values. Although his main purpose was the recruitment of converts to the community of deaf believers, he also recruited users and supporters of sign language into the broader deaf community.

The World

The Chicago Mission's activities even reached beyond the borders of the United States, most notably in ongoing contributions that promoted missionary efforts to deaf people around the world. The major recipient of this generosity was a school for deaf children in Chefoo, China.

Annetta Thompson Mills, a Presbyterian woman, had taught deaf students in New York state before marrying and moving to China, where she founded the Chefoo School in 1898.[107] Seven years later, she visited and addressed the congregation at the Chicago Mission.[108] From that time on, the Chicago Mission became one of the biggest and most loyal supporters of the Chefoo School. In a letter to her American supporters, Mills expressed her appreciation for the generous support of the Chicago Mission:

> Every time I think of Chicago I think of Dr. Hasenstab and his faithful helpers and their help. Those Thomas Hopkins Gallaudet scholarships are splendid, and there is always something more for general expenses. They have caught the vision.[109]

The Thomas Hopkins Gallaudet scholarships that Mills referred to in her letter were two scholarships that the members of the Chicago Mission provided for the school annually beginning in 1907 and continuing throughout Hasenstab's tenure. *The Silent Herald,* a monthly newsletter published by the Chicago Mission for the Deaf, regularly listed donors and the amount of their gifts for the Chefoo School; pictures of the Chinese children who were being supported were sometimes also printed.[110]

The value placed on this enterprise can be estimated by observing the number of references to the Chefoo School that occur in *The Silent Herald* between 1902 and 1941. More than 40 percent of the available issues (189 out of 444) contain some kind of information with respect to the mission school. The references include financial pleas; letters from Mills or her niece and eventual successor, Anita Carter; pictures of students; lists of donors; and a letter from an appreciative Chinese student.[111] The fact that the Chefoo School was not under the auspices of the Methodist Church was irrelevant: deafness was the common denominator that tied American Midwesterners to Chinese students.

Chicago Mission members also investigated, applauded, and discussed other efforts to evangelize deaf people around the world. For example, they recognized a deaf woman from a Baptist Church in Georgia for her efforts in taking the gospel to deaf people in Cuba.[112] The spiritual condition of deaf people in Japan was a topic of inquiry in both 1905 and 1906.[113] Members were aware that Korea, which was reported to have 14,000 deaf people in 1911, was being targeted by a Korean Methodist for the opening of a Christian school for deaf children.[114] India and Turkey were also singled out as places where individuals were beginning deaf ministries.[115] These references illustrate that the deaf believers from the Chicago Mission identified with and were concerned over the spiritual and social welfare of other deaf individuals, no matter where they lived.

Community in Retrospect

Deafness and faith defined the boundaries of the Chicago Mission community, but Hasenstab and his assistants crossed a number of traditional social divisions in the creation of this special enclave. First, they crossed denominational lines. Although the Chicago Mission was firmly rooted in Methodism, cooperation with other religious bodies was common. Second, they traversed territorial lines. One of the remarkable features of the Chicago Mission and its leaders was the amount of travel that occurred to spread the gospel. Third, they ignored socioeconomic lines. This perspective was particularly evident in the ministry of Hasenstab, the primary leader of the Chicago Mission. Hasenstab was in high demand at places such as Gallaudet College, where he socialized with its president and addressed its faculty and student body; he was also welcomed and sought after by deaf farmers in Goshen, Indiana, or Illiopolis, Illinois. Fourth, they crossed racial lines. Hasenstab visited schools for deaf African Americans and provided preaching services for the black deaf residents of Chicago. Fifth, they broke down gender lines. This effort was most apparent among the leadership of the Chicago Mission. Although Hasenstab was the pastor in charge, in his absence, Georgia Hasenstab, deaconess Vina Smith, Laura Sheridan, or Constance Elmes performed the duties of a minister. Sixth, and finally, they overcame age barriers. The Chicago Mission was largely responsible for the success of the Illinois Home for the Aged and Infirm Deaf that was established in Chicago to serve the elderly. Its leaders were also actively involved in addressing young children at residential schools around the Midwest.

Summary

The Chicago Mission for the Deaf represented an important religious and social movement in America. A major impetus was the revival at the Illinois School for the Deaf in the 1880s. Students and faculty alike were influenced by the revival fires that spread across the residential school campus, but the uniqueness of the Chicago Mission was not in its brand of religion—evangelical Protestantism; rather, its uniqueness was found in its leadership characteristics, community composition, and communication methods.

Important social trends contributed to the shape and direction of the Chicago Mission. Chief among these trends was the attack on the deaf community and its sign language that came from oralist proponents in the late-nineteenth and early twentieth centuries. This attack from outsiders led deaf people to look not only for leaders who understood their needs but also for organizations that supported their community values. They found both in the Chicago Mission, whose leaders were all deaf community insiders, users of sign language, and familiar with the values and experiences of deaf life. The work of the Chicago Mission succeeded, and the community it formed endured, because its leaders embodied values and proclaimed a message that consistently appealed to deaf people for over fifty years.

Notes

1. Otto B. Berg, *A Missionary Chronicle: Being a History of the Ministry to the Deaf in the Episcopal Church (1850–1980)* (Hollywood, Md.: St. Mary's Press, 1984), 47; compare Beatrice E. Hasenstab Krafft, *A Goodly Heritage* (Columbus, Ga.: Brentwood Christian Press, 1989), 88.

2. While gathering information for this project in August 1997, I traveled to a small town in northern Indiana to secure some written documents from one who had met Hasenstab as a child. The woman, whose parents were deaf, recalled Hasenstab visiting in her home when she was a young child and said at the time she "thought he was God." She explained that her reasoning was based on the fact that Hasenstab had white hair, just like she expected God to have; further, Hasenstab was so revered by her parents and other members of the local deaf community that she assumed he must be God himself.

3. Cited in Berg, *A Missionary Chronicle*, 21.

4. The U.S. Bureau of the Census, in *Report on the Insane, Feeble-Minded, Deaf and Dumb, and Blind in the United States at the Eleventh Census: 1890* (Washington, D.C.: U.S. Government Printing Office, 1895), 466, estimated 450 "deaf and dumb" in Chicago in 1890. That number was corroborated by Philip Hasenstab, who told Crawford Elliott there were about 400 deaf people in the city. Crawford Elliott was a Chicago businessman and brother of Georgia Elliott. In a letter to his sister, Georgia, Crawford tells of having supper with Hasenstab when the latter "told me that there were about 400 deaf people in Chicago, but only 10 [of them were] Christians." Crawford's letter is undated, but is included in a letter from Georgia Elliott to Philip Hasenstab, August 4, 1890, Elliott Collection of Personal Letters (private collection).

5. Utten E. Read, "Reverend Frank Read: Farm Boy, Teacher, Editor, Missionary Evangelist, Pastor, *The Illinois Advance* 75 no. 7(April 1942): 12.

6. "Service for Deaf Mutes in Chicago," *Deaf-Mute Advance*, May 11, 1889, 2; Laura C. Sheridan,"Tenth Anniversary of the Chicago Mission for the Deaf," *The Illinois Advance,* November 14, 1903, 5.

7. "A Service for the Deaf," *Deaf-Mute Advance,* July 13, 1889, 2.

8. See the comment of a former student, Oscar H. Regensburg, in "Unpublished Letters of Dr. Philip G. Gillett," *Illinois Advance* March 28, 1908, 1; and another student's poem: Angelina Fuller Fisher, "Thoughts for the Seventy-Fifth Birthday of Philip Goode Gillett," *The Silent Herald,* April 1908 (edited by Philip J. Hasenstab).

9. "A Sermon in Sign Language," *Deaf-Mute Advance,* August 31,1889, 2.

10. "Speech by the Dumb," *Deaf-Mute Advance,* August 31,1889, 2.

11. Hasenstab came to ISD in 1885 as a supervisor of boys, a position he held for one year. In 1886, he joined ISD's teaching faculty. See Krafft, *A Goodly Heritage.*

12. For further information on the 1889 International Congress of the Deaf and Hasenstab's trip to Europe, see Krafft, *A Goodly Heritage*, 52–68. Also see various documents preserved in the Hasenstab Family Scrapbook, n.d., p. 29 (private collection).

13. Determining the exact date of Hasenstab's involvement through existing documents is difficult. Hasenstab's personal journals (1882–1915, private collection) do not include entries from the year 1889, and only a few letters from Hasenstab before August 1892 have been preserved. Nevertheless, clear references to Chicago begin appearing in Elliott's letters to Hasenstab in December 1889. Particularly, see letters from Elliott to Hasenstab dated December 3, 1889, and December 15, 1889 (Elliott, Collection of Personal Letters, 1889–1893), which speak about the desire and need to minister to deaf people in Chicago. Elliott's letters suggest that Hasenstab became involved in the Chicago work during the fall of 1889.

14. Krafft, *A Goodly Heritage*, 81–82.

15. In a letter from Georgia Elliott to Philip Hasenstab, December 15, 1889, p. 11 (Elliott Collection), she writes the following: "I have learned from Mr. Gross that the deaf mutes out in Chicago prefer you to all others (not counting Dr. Gillett). . . . [T]hey think Mr. Cloud [deaf Episcopalian clergyman who was also on the faculty at ISD] too cold. . . . They told Mr. G. while he was in Chicago that it is so different with you."

16. Beadell's letter was dated July 6, 1890, from Duluth, Minnesota, and it is enclosed in Elliott's July 14, 1890, letter to Hasenstab (Elliott Collection). Also see Hasenstab, Personal Journals, June 22, 1890 (Hasenstab Collection) where he refers to Beadell's visit and comments.

17. Hasenstab, Personal Journals (1890–1893).

18. Hasenstab, Personal Journals, entries dated July 16, 1893, and July 23, 1893, respectively.

19. These numbers come from reports that Hasenstab gave to Elliott in his personal letters. The Sunday attendance figures and the date of each letter containing the figures are noted here: 80 people (November 20, 1892); 85 people (December 12, 1892); 40 people (December 25, 1892); 40 people, on a day when the temperature was two below zero (January 16, 1893); and 45 people (February 20, 1893) in Hasenstab Collection.

20. See Hasenstab to Elliott, March 9, 1893, Elliott Collection of Personal Letters, in which Hasenstab tells of the change at the Kankakee Hospital and wonders whether "Dr. Gillett may perhaps share the same fate."

21. Hasenstab Collection of Personal Letters.

22. "Dr. Gillett's Resignation," *Deaf-Mute Advance*, April 15, 1893, 2. Although Gillett ultimately decided to remain in the Midwest rather than accept the Colorado offer, his departure from ISD was nonetheless a blow to deaf people in Illinois, many of whom now resided in Chicago.

23. For examples of references to moving to and ministering in Chicago, see Elliott to Hasenstab, Elliott Collection of Personal Letters, December 3, 1889; December 15, 1889; March 16, 1890; April 24, 1891; and March 16, 1892. Also see Hasenstab to Elliott, Hasenstab Collection of Personal Letters (private), April 15, 1892.

24. Hasenstab to Elliott, Hasenstab Collection of Personal Letters, April 12, 1893, 1–2.

25. See the August 6, 1893, letter from Gillett to Hasenstab, Hasenstab Family Scrapbook, 31; also printed in Krafft, *A Goodly Heritage*, 87–89.

26. Hasenstab to Elliott, Hasenstab Collection of Personal Letters, August 28, 1893, indicates that school was to open on September 20th.

27. The issues of salary and calling are discussed together in a letter dated September 22, 1893, from Hasenstab to Elliott, Hasenstab Collection of Personal Letters. In an earlier letter (Elliott to Hasenstab, Elliott Collection of Personal Letters,

January 6, 1891), reference is made to Hasenstab's teaching salary of $950 at ISD and Elliott's teaching salary of $400 at MSD; both of these salaries were for the 1891–1892 school year. Elliott (to Hasenstab, May 24, 1892, Elliott Collection of Personal Letters) hoped her salary would increase to $500 the following year. Obviously, Hasenstab's new job meant a significant reduction in income. Financial stability was an early and ongoing concern as Hasenstab and Elliott planned to get married (e.g., see letters from Elliott to Hasenstab, January 29, 1890; February 1, 1890; and March 16, 1890, Elliott Collection of Personal Letters). This concern was exacerbated by Elliott's mother and older brother, both of whom predicted financial disaster if Hasenstab and Elliott quit their teaching jobs, married, and began pastoral work in Chicago (e.g., see Anna Elliott to Georgia Elliott, January 24, 1890, and Crawford Elliott to Georgia Elliott, February 5, 1890, both in Elliott, Collection of Personal Letters).

28. Hasenstab, Collection of Personal Letters.

29. *Celebration of the Tenth Anniversary of the Call of Philip J. Hasenstab to Take Charge of the Chicago M. E. Mission for the Deaf* (Chicago, Ill.: Press of the Silent Herald, 1905,) 6.

30. Berg, *A Missionary Chronicle*, 47.

31. Charlotte Baker and Dennis Cokely, *American Sign Language: A Teacher's Resource Text on Grammar and Culture* (Silver Spring, Md.: T. J. Publishers, 1980), 331.

32. Harlan Lane, Robert Hoffmeister, and Ben Bahan, *A Journey into the DEAF-WORLD* (San Diego, Calif.: DawnSign Press, 1996), 134.

33. The name Pas-a-Pas, a French term meaning "step by step," was adopted by the Chicago deaf club as early as the 1880s (see "Pas-a-Pas Club," *Silent Worker* 6 [5]: 3). For a more thorough treatment of the purpose and history of deaf clubs, see Baker and Cokely, *American Sign Language*, 331; Lane, Hoffmeister, and Bahan, *DEAF-WORLD*, 13, 1–38, 438–39. Also see Stephanie A. Hall, "Door into Deaf Culture: Folklore in an American Deaf Social Club," *Sign Language Studies* 73 (1991): 421–29, which offers an insightful ethnographic description of a Philadelphia deaf club in the 1980s. Brief mention is made of Chicago's Pas-a-Pas Deaf Club in Jack R. Gannon, *Deaf Heritage: A Narrative History of Deaf Americans* (Silver Spring, Md.: National Association of the Deaf, 1981), 214.

34. Hasenstab, Personal Journals, October 18, 1890.

35. Cited in Berg, *A Missionary Chronicle*, 47, emphasis added.

36. One reference comes from Hasenstab's letter to Elliott, November 20, 1892. In another letter to Elliott, December 25, 1892, Hasenstab described attending a Christmas social at Chicago's deaf club. For further examples of Hasenstab's early participation in Pas-a-Pas Club events, see Hasenstab, Personal Journals, July 1 and July 13, 1891, wherein plans for a club picnic were discussed.

37. Cited in Berg, *A Missionary Chronicle*, 47; emphasis added.

38. Hasenstab's final "report of standing" is dated June 25, 1879, and is found in the Hasenstab Family Scrapbook, 13.

39. Philip J. Hasenstab, High School Compositions, 1887–1879, (Hasenstab Collection), 25–29; also Hasenstab's original handwritten "Valedictory Address," Hasenstab Family Scrapbook, 23.

40. In a journal entry dated June 27, 1891, Hasenstab claimed to weigh 137 pounds; several months later, in a letter to Georgia Elliott, October 27, 1892, the thirty-year-old Hasenstab claimed to weigh "136 pounds, a gain of four since the opening of school." Hasenstab Personal Journals. Further, his passport for travel to Europe, issued June 27, 1889, from the U.S. Department of State, described Hasenstab as five-feet-and-eight-and-one-half-inches tall, with a high forehead, a nose that was "quite long," a medium-sized mouth, a long face, a fair complexion, and light hair (see Hasenstab Family Scrapbook, 29).

41. Phillip J. Hasenstab, "Valedictory Address," Hasenstab Family Scrapbook, 23.

42. The World Congress of the Deaf was held in Chicago in 1893. Hasenstab, along with many other prominent deaf and hearing leaders, was on the program to address the participants on the assigned topic. He also led a Sunday worship service on July 16, 1893, at the same congress; the service was international in that it consisted of deaf visitors from various countries (see Crawford Elliott to Anna Elliott, his mother, July 17, 1893, Hasenstab Family Scrapbook, 37.

43. The first eight ordinations of deaf men all took place in either the Episcopal Church or the Congregational Church.

44. Hasenstab's local preacher's licenses and ordination credentials are all found in the Hasenstab Family Scrapbook, 53–55. For additional information on local preachers and ordination classifications, see the *Membership Manual of the Methodist Episcopal Church* (New York: The Methodist Book Concern, 1916).

45. Hasenstab, Personal Journals, September 2, 1890.

46. The degree is preserved with a number of other Hasenstab family items and bears the date June 12, 1914. Details of how Hasenstab received word of this honor and his response of surprise and humility are recorded in his Personal Journals, May 9, 1914.

47. A seventy-fifth anniversary celebration program, some personal notes by Hasenstab with respect to the occasion, and other written documents from the event are included in the Hasenstab Family Scrapbook, 69.

48. The birthday card is preserved in a file with a number of other Hasenstab family items and documents (private collection).

49. Krafft, *A Goodly Heritage.*

50. *Cited in Krafft, A Goodly Heritage,* 45.

51. Cited in Krafft, *A Goodly Heritage*, 45.

52. For example, see letters from two grateful mothers, Mrs. Mary Hicklin (November 6, 1889) and Mrs. Bibb (October 2, 1891); both letters can be found in Elliott, Collection of Personal Letters, and both are cited in Krafft, *A Goodly Heritage*, 70–71. Also see the letter of James Tate, Superintendent of MSD to Philip and Georgia Hasenstab, April 9, 1920, Hasenstab Family Scrapbook, 12.

53. For examples of Elliott's letters of encouragement and support to Hasenstab with respect to the Chicago work, see those dated March 16, 1890; June 25, 1890; May 5, 1891; August 24, 1891; February 19, 1892; and March 16, 1892, Hasenstab, Collection of Personal Letters.

54. Elliott to Hasenstab, July 2, 1890, 3–4, Elliott, Collection of Personal Letters.

55. See monthly issues of Hasenstab's *The Silent Herald,* where various church officers were regularly listed. The February 1926 issue of *The Silent Herald* (p. 3) reports that Georgia Hasenstab served terms as the vice president of both the Susannah Wesley Circle and the Ladies' Aid Society.

56. A letter of April 25, 1898, from Georgia to her husband discussing a sermon she delivered is found in the Hasenstab Family Scrapbook, 48. Also see Hasenstab, *The Silent Herald,* July 1926, 3, for a further reference to Georgia filling the pulpit for her husband.

57. Philip Hasenstab was employed at the Illinois school for eight years and was there during the revival of the 1880s. Both Georgia Elliott Hasenstab (1876–1887) and Henry Rutherford (1884–1896) attended the Illinois School for the Deaf during that time.

58. Northern Illinois Conference of the United Methodist Church, "Memoirs: Henry S. Rutherford," in *Journal and Yearbook, Official Proceedings of the One Hundred and*

Thirtieth Annual Session at De Kalb, Ill., (Chicago: Northern Illinois Conference of the United Methodist Church, 1969), 236.

59. Sheridan, "Tenth Anniversary," 6.

60. Daniel Moylan, a deaf man from Maryland, was ordained by the Methodists in 1900. Peggy A. Johnson, "The History of Christ United Methodist Church of the Deaf" (unpublished manuscript, Christ United Methodist Church of the Deaf, Baltimore, Md., 1995) provides a historical description of Moylan's life and work.

61. Rutherford's Chicago residence varied from time to time but was always listed in each edition of *The Silent Herald*. Rutherford's assistance in Chicago is verified by entries in Hasenstab's Personal Journals. For example, on December 28, 1913, Hasenstab noted that Rutherford provided a devotional for the deaf Epworth League in Chicago, and on December 29, 1913, Rutherford helped Hasenstab prepare *The Silent Herald* for circulation.

62. Northern Illinois Conference of the United Methodist Church, "Memoirs: Henry S. Rutherford."

63. Sheridan, "Tenth Anniversary," 5.

64. Alexander M. Manson, "The Work of the Protestant Churches for the Deaf in North America, 1815–1949, Part III," *American Annals of the Deaf* 95 (5): 474.

65. Northern Illinois Conference, "Memoirs: Henry S. Rutherford," 236.

66. Frederick A. Norwood, *The Story of American Methodism* (Nashville, Tenn.: Abingdon, 1974), 334, 352.

67. Sheridan, "Tenth Anniversary."

68. See Hasenstab's "Mission Notes," *The Silent Herald*, April, 1906, 4. This note mentions that "the deaf have contributed a little over fifty dollars toward furnishing her room."

69. See Krafft, *A Goodly Heritage,* 96–97. Also see Hasenstab's "Mission Notes" in the following issues of *The Silent Herald*: July 1907, 5; August 1909, 4; January 1910, 4.

70. For news of Smith's resignation, see Hasenstab's "Mission Notes" in *The Silent Herald,* October 1910, 4.

71. Krafft, *A Goodly Heritage,* 78; Sheridan, "Tenth Anniversary," 2.

72. Douglas C. Baynton notes that Sheridan delivered her own paper at the convention in 1882, "being the first woman to do so." Douglas C. Baynton, *Forbidden Signs: American Culture and the Campaign against Sign Language* (Chicago: University of Chicago Press, 1996), 74. He comments further that four years before, in 1878, she actually prepared another paper for an earlier convention, though it was read by "a male colleague" (73–74). Sheridan became a prolific writer. For examples, see *The Silent Herald,* December 1913; *The Silent Herald,* December 1923. Her most ambitious work was an eighteen-month series of articles on the topic of revival that appeared in *The Silent Herald* between October 1909 and March 1911.

73. Baynton, *Forbidden Signs,* 74.

74. In a journal entry dated June 24–July 4, 1890, Hasenstab wrote of "visiting with the dear ones [i.e., his family] and attending the camp meeting for the promotion of holiness." Later in the same entry, Hasenstab noted that "Miss Sheridan and her brother Wilbur were there," but the crowd was smaller than usual because the "weather was exceedingly warm nearly all the time." On July 2nd, Hasenstab reported testifying at the camp meeting about his own conversion and having claimed "the blessing of entire sanctification;" he noted that "Miss Sheridan [was] interpreting" for him. For other references to Sheridan attending and interpreting the camp meeting, see Hasenstab, Personal Journals, July 24–August 2, 1891; July 27–29, 1892.

75. For references to Sheridan leading Bible classes and prayer meetings, see *The Silent Herald*, May 1906, August 1906, October 1906, March 1907, December 1908, and February 1914. For references to her preaching in Chicago for Hasenstab, see *The Silent Herald*, October 1910, July 1911, and August 1912; also see Hasenstab, Personal Journals, May 31, 1914. For references to her evangelistic meetings in Baltimore, see *The Silent Herald*, March 1907, April 1907, and July 1914.

76. For examples of references to Sheridan's visits, see Hasenstab, "Mission Notes," *The Silent Herald* for the following dates: June 1926, 5; January 1927, 3; March 1927, 3; August 1928, 3; and February 1931, 2.

77. *The Silent Herald*, January 1926, 3.

78. For more details of Sheridan's death and funeral and for others' thoughts on her life, see Hasenstab, "Mission Notes," *The Silent Herald*, June 1933, 2.

79. In recent years, the term *coda* has often been used to describe those who have grown up with deaf parents. *Coda* is an acronym that stands for a hearing "child of deaf adults"; members of this particular social group are typically afforded special privileges by deaf community members who recognize that codas possess insider information and unique experiences that make them bilingual and bicultural. See Lane, Hoffmeister, and Bahan, DEAF-WORLD; Thomas H. Bull, ed., *On the Edge of Deaf Culture: Hearing Children/Deaf Parents Annotated Bibliography* (Alexandria, Va.: Deaf Family Research Press, 1998).

80. For further references to her interpreting, see Hasenstab's "Mission Notes" in the following issues of *The Silent Herald*: January 1917, 4; December 1917, 4; May 1918, 2; and December 1919, 2.

81. Hasenstab, *The Silent Herald*, May 1922, 2.

82. Hasenstab, *The Silent Herald*, August 1924, 2; Hasenstab, *The Silent Herald*, December 1930, 4.

83. Northern Illinois Conference of the United Methodist Church, "Memoirs: Constance Hasenstab Elmes," in *Journal and Yearbook, Official Proceedings of the One Hundred and Thirty First Annual Session at De Kalb, Ill.* (Chicago: Northern Illinois Conference of the United Methodist Church, 1970), 299.

84. For more information on the development of professional sign language interpreting, see Nancy Frishberg, *Interpreting: An Introduction* (Silver Spring, Md.: Registry of Interpreters for the Deaf, 1986); quotation from Northern Illinois Conference, "Memoirs: Constance Hasenstab Elmes."

85. The 1890 census distinguished between those who were designated "deaf and dumb" (population of 450) and those who were "deaf; but not dumb" (population of 504); the latter were those who had intelligible speech. The 1930 census changed its designation altogether to "deaf-mutes" and gave several conditions that had to be met to satisfy the definition (e.g., age at onset of deafness, how much one can hear when directly addressed, etc.). The change in labels, definitions, and manner of collecting data all point out the inconsistency used in counting deaf people over the years. Therefore, caution should be exercised when using these data. The 1890 reference to 400 deaf people actually comes from a letter written by Crawford Elliott to his mother (undated), after Crawford had dinner with Hasenstab. Crawford's letter is included in Georgia Elliott's Collection of Personal Letters, August 4, 1890. The 1930 figure of 2,000 comes from several sources. For example, see Hasenstab, *The Silent Herald*, May 1927, 4, and May 1928, 2; also see *The Story of the Methodist Episcopal Mission for the Deaf* (Chicago, Ill.: Chicago Mission for the Deaf, n.d.), likely written around 1930, included in the Hasenstab Family Scrapbook, 67.

86. Sunday service attendance records apparently were not kept consistently beyond the early years; or, if they were kept, the records were not preserved. Attendance

data therefore are derived from several sources. See, for example, Hasenstab, Personal Journals, November 16, 1913; Hasenstab, "Mission Notes," *The Silent Herald*, May 1927, 3.

87. The Chicago Mission's regular schedule of services and events was published on the back page of each issue of Hasenstab's church newsletter, *The Silent Herald* (1903–1941). The information with respect to services and times has been gleaned from that source.

88. The Epworth League Devotional Meeting actually first appeared on the Sunday schedule of *The Silent Herald* in May 1918 and remained on the schedule through 1941.

89. See Hasenstab, "Sabbath Services," *The Silent Herald*, January 1927–December 1932. Also see Hasenstab, "Mission Notes," *The Silent Herald*, January 1927, 2.

90. Hasenstab, *The Silent Herald*, December 1929, 4; the first mention of the latter groups is found in Hasenstab, "Mission Notes," *The Silent Herald*, December 1925, 3–4; also see "December Announcements" in the same issue, p. 6.

91. Hasenstab, *The Silent Herald*, April 1903, 14.

92. A combination of family photographs, article clippings in the Hasenstab Family Scrapbook, and references in Hasenstab's *The Silent Herald* (1903–1941) support these claims.

93. *The Silent Herald*, July 1914, 4.

94. Hasenstab, "Mission Notes," *The Silent Herald*, May 1915, 4. In Hasenstab's Personal Journals (April 14–21, 1915), he identifies the schools as Georgia, Florida, and Tennessee.

95. *The Silent Herald* June, 1920, 2.

96. *The Silent Herald*, January 1927, 2.

97. Hasenstab, *The Silent Herald*, August 1926, 3.

98. Hasenstab, Personal Journals, September 2 and 3, 1890.

99. Hasenstab, *The Silent Herald*, September 1904, 36.

100. Hasenstab, *The Silent Herald*, June 1923, 2.

101. For Chicago Mission support, see Hasenstab, *The Silent Herald*, July 1927, 3.

102. Although *The Story of the Methodist Episcopal Mission for the Deaf* is undated, references within the eight-page booklet place it either in the late 1920s or in the early 1930s. The booklet provides a concise historical description of the Chicago Mission for the Deaf; a copy can be found in the Hasenstab Family Scrapbook, 67.

103. All of the totals and averages that appear in this paragraph come from tabulating data that are included under "Appointments" in Hasenstab's monthly issues of *The Silent Herald* (1903–1941).

104. The first indication of slowing down is recorded by Hasenstab in his "Mission Notes," *The Silent Herald*, December 1937, 3. He notes being hospitalized and having to take pills "after . . . ha[ving] not taken any medicine for twenty-four years."

105. See Baynton, *Forbidden Signs*.

106. Tom Anderson, "Religious Education in the Schools for the Deaf," *American Annals of the Deaf* 82 (1937): 433–39.

107. The Chefoo School for the Deaf was reportedly the first deaf school opened in China. Mills was honored for her efforts on behalf of deaf people in China by both Edward M. Gallaudet, president of Gallaudet College, and Theodore Roosevelt, president of the United States. Mills died in 1929. For a detailed description of Mills' life and the Chefoo School, see Anita D. Carter, *Sketch of the Life of Annetta Thompson Mills, Founder of the Chefoo School for the Deaf* (Chefoo, China: James McMullan, 1938).

108. Hasenstab, *The Silent Herald*, January 1906.

109. Quoted in Hasenstab, *The Silent Herald*, January 1925, 3.

110. The first mention of providing scholarship support for students is found in Hasenstab, "Mission Notes," *The Silent Herald*, November 1907, 4. For examples of publishing the names and amounts of annual donors, see *The Silent Herald*, January 1911, 5; January 1914, 7; February 1917, 5; January 1918, 5; February 1919, 3; and January 1920, 5. Pictures of deaf Chinese students being supported are included in the following issues: January 1910, 5, and June 1914, 3.

111. The student's letter, from Sen Gwei Hsiang, is printed in *The Silent Herald*, March 1931, 3.

112. *The Silent Herald*, September 1904.

113. A letter from Rev. David Spencer of the Japan Mission of the Methodist Episcopal Church to Philip Hasenstab, February 11, 1905, addressed the spiritual needs of deaf Japanese people. In Hasenstab, Personal Letters. The following year, the topic was discussed by Hasenstab in his "Mission Notes," *The Silent Herald*, April 1906, 4.

114. Hasenstab, *The Silent Herald*, September 1911, 3.

115. Hasenstab mentioned a deaf ministry in India in *The Silent Herald*, December 1914, 3; a deaf ministry in Turkey is noted in *The Silent Herald*, May 1915, 6.

CONTRIBUTORS

Reginald Boyd attended the Pennsylvania School for the Deaf and the Model Secondary School for the Deaf in Washington, DC. He graduated from the latter in 1974 and from Gallaudet University in 1981. An instructional technology specialist at the Texas School for the Deaf, his avocation is reading and researching deaf history.

Barry A. Crouch, widely published in the journal *Reconstruction History* and the co-author of *A Place of Their Own: Creating the Deaf Community in America*, was a professor of history at Gallaudet University at the time of his death.

Mary French is a technical writer at Vanu, Inc., in Cambridge, Massachusetts.

Brian H. Greenwald, an associate professor of history at Gallaudet University, received a B.A. in history from Gallaudet in 1996 and a Ph.D. in American History from George Washington University in 2006. His dissertation examined Alexander Graham Bell's involvement in the American eugenics movement.

Harlan Lane is the author of numerous books about the history and culture of deaf people, including *When the Mind Hears: A History of the Deaf* and *A Deaf Artist in Early America: The Worlds of John Brewster, Jr.* He is Matthews University Distinguished Professor in the Department of Psychology, Northeastern University.

Harry G. Lang has published several books in the areas of deaf studies and deaf biography, including *Edmund Booth: Deaf Pioneer* and *A Phone of*

Our Own: The Deaf Insurrection Against Ma Bell. He is a professor in the Department of Research and Teacher Education at the National Technical Institute for the Deaf, a college within the Rochester Institute of Technology.

Kent R. Olney is Chair of the Department of Behavioral Sciences and Professor of Sociology at Olivet Nazarene University in Bourbonnais, Illinois. He received an M.A. from Gallaudet University in 1985. His Ph.D. dissertation (University of Oregon, 1999) is entitled *Religion and the American Deaf Community: A Sociological Analysis of the Chicago Mission for the Deaf, 1890–1941.*

Richard Pillard is a professor of psychiatry at Boston University School of Medicine.

Jill Hendricks Porco graduated from Gallaudet University in 1993 with a degree in history. She currently serves as the production coordinator for Gallaudet University Press.

Michael Reis is a 1970 graduate of the Indiana School for the Deaf and a 1975 graduate of the University of Tennessee. Since 1991 he has been developing a statewide history of deaf people in Indiana. He disseminates his findings through published articles, a historical yearbook, exhibits, short stories, and local newsletters. His writing has previously appeared in the anthology *Deaf History Unveiled: Interpretations from the New Scholarship.*

John Vickrey Van Cleve is a former professor of history at Gallaudet University. He is the co-author of *A Place of Their Own: Creating the Deaf Community in America* and editor of several books, including *Deaf History Unveiled: Interpretations from the New Scholarship,* and *Genetics, Disability, and Deafness.*

INDEX